AROUND THE WORLD WITH LBJ

AROUND THE WORLD WITH LBJ

MY WILD RIDE AS
AIR FORCE ONE PILOT,
WHITE HOUSE AIDE,
AND PERSONAL CONFIDANT

Brigadier General James U. Cross,
UNITED STATES AIR FORCE (RETIRED)

With Denise Gamino and Gary Rice

UNIVERSITY OF TEXAS PRESS
AUSTIN

First paperback edition, 2012
First edition, 2008
Requests for permission to reproduce
material from this work should be sent to:

    Permissions
    University of Texas Press
    P.O. Box 7819
    Austin, TX 78713-7819
    www.utexas.edu/utpress/about/bpermission.html

∞ The paper used in this book meets the minimum requirements
of ANSI/NISO Z39.48-1992 (R1997) (Permanence of Paper).

Library of Congress Cataloging-in-Publication Data

Cross, James U. (James Underwood), 1925–
  Around the world with LBJ : my wild ride as Air Force One pilot, White
House aide, and personal confidant / James U. Cross, with Denise Gamino
and Gary Rice. — 1st ed.
     p.   cm.
  Includes bibliographical references and index.
  ISBN 978-0-292-74777-7
  1. Cross, James U. (James Underwood), 1925– 2. Johnson, Lyndon B.
(Lyndon Baines), 1908–1973—Friends and associates. 3. Presidents—
United States—Staff—Biography. 4. Air pilots—United States—Biography.
5. Air Force One (Presidential aircraft)—History—20th century. 6. Air
travel—History—20th century. 7. Johnson, Lyndon B. (Lyndon Baines),
1908–1973. 8. Presidents—United States—Biography. I. Gamino, Denise.
II. Rice, Gary. III. Title.
E847.2.C76   2008
973.923092—dc22

                                      2007043296

THIS BOOK IS DEDICATED TO MARIE, MY BELOVED WIFE OF sixty-two years; the memory of our firstborn daughter June; and our three living children, Jeanie, Joanie, and John. Their love and encouragement have been the foundation for anything I would ever accomplish in my life's work as a military aviator. Often absent from our home hearth for months at a time, I was sustained by their love always.

My eternal thanks, as well, to my great White House staff and the outstanding flight crew of Air Force One. Although there are too many to acknowledge here, each was the best ever to come down the pike, and they know who they are. And lastly, my heartfelt thanks to Denise Gamino and Gary Rice, whose contributions made this book possible.

CONTENTS

AROUND THE WORLD WITH LBJ

CHAPTER ONE

THE LONGEST DAY

LYNDON JOHNSON RODE AIR FORCE ONE WITH TOTAL confidence. He was the ultimate back-seat pilot, ordering last-minute trips to sometimes secret destinations, including a circumnavigation of the globe that allowed the flight crew mere catnaps. No president before or since has given Air Force One quite the same impetuous workouts.

And I was his enabler.

My Secret Service code name was Sawdust. I figure I got that name because I was a country boy from the sawmill and piney woods country of southern Alabama who never lost his backwoods drawl. But it just as easily could have applied to what was left of me after some of those uncomfortable times when Mr. Johnson took me to the woodshed with his legendary temper fully loaded and cocked. Lyndon Johnson only chewed on those he respected. If he didn't like you, he ignored you or gave you the silent treatment. He must have liked me a lot. In fact, he became a father figure to me after my own father died when I was thirty-seven.

I was President Johnson's Air Force One pilot. I bucked the inviolate military chain of command to fly where and when he wanted. Protocol, rules, and red tape couldn't stop us. We did it his way, obstacles be damned. He wasn't always the most pleasant personality to be around, but he was the best co-pilot in adventure anyone could ever have had.

Flying was just the half of it. I was the only Air Force One pilot in history to have one foot in the cockpit and the other in the White House inner circle. I flew the plane and joined the political ground crew, too, as the full-time Armed Forces aide to the president with an office in the East Wing. Double the duty, double the fun. And I juggled those two full-time jobs on one military salary, of course. No free lunch, either. I had to pay for my meals aboard Air Force One.

As Armed Forces aide and Director of the White House Military Office, I had to provide liaison with the Pentagon; supervise Camp David, the presidential mountain retreat outside Washington; corral the presidential yachts, helicopters, planes, and cars; run the White House Mess; line up military officers to be social escorts at White House functions (Chuck Robb fell in love with and married the president's daughter Lynda, after I brought him into the White House as a social aide); supervise and provision the secret underground bomb shelters for the president, his key staff, and his cabinet; write the presidential condolence letters to families of U.S. soldiers killed in Vietnam; maintain plans for the funerals of all living former presidents; and more.

Day after day, I handled my high-level duties along with any personal requests that came in from the president or his family. When Lynda and Chuck decided to marry, they told me first and asked for advice on how to break the news to the president and Lady Bird. I flew to Dallas on the president's privately owned King Air with a handful of Johnson jewels so that Stanley Marcus, the CEO and president of Neiman Marcus, could appraise them and craft them into rings, brooches, and necklaces as presents for Lady Bird and the Johnson daughters. I ran interference with the pesky San Antonio tailor who made the president's famous khaki ranch clothes and often phoned the White House hoping to win government contracts in return. I flew to Mexico to look at property for the president. I even had to keep Johnson's cattle from using his Texas ranch runway as an outhouse. I never knew what task might be thrown my way. So I made it a point to be available at all times, even if it meant lurking just out of sight in case the president called my name. I lived in a constant state of readiness.

I've often been asked what a typical or routine day at the White House was like. There was just no such thing. But people can't stop wondering what the military pilot of Air Force One did all day in a business suit at the White House. Perhaps if I replay the highlights of one random day, it will become clear why my job description wasn't worth the paper it was printed on. Take February 29, 1968. It was Leap Day, and that pretty much describes what I did all day. I thought it would never end.

8:45 A.M.   No sooner did I arrive at my East Wing office than the president summoned me to the family quarters on the third floor. His bedroom had three televisions and a full view of the Washington Monument—behind bullet-proof glass. A couple of chairs were arranged near his big, canopied bed, but he had long since finished with any bedside conferences with other aides that morning. He was already in the middle of his morning shave, but he was still conducting meetings. I was relieved that this was not going to be one of those days when I had to towel off his backside. "You don't need to flight train today," he said. "There's too much going on!" The president knew I had scheduled my twice-weekly air time with the crew of Air Force One, because I had sent him a memo the day before describing my plans. I always called or sent him a memo anytime I expected to be away from my White House office.

The memo, on a 3 × 5 card, had three boxes the president could check: "Yes," "No," and "See me." He had checked "Yes," so before I left home that morning I had called one of my co-pilots, Colonel Paul Thornhill, at Andrews Air Force Base to set up a four-hour flight after lunch. Now we were grounded.

The president was worried about his son-in-law, Pat Nugent. Even before Pat married Luci Baines Johnson on August 6, 1966, letters had poured into the White House from Americans who thought he ought to be in Vietnam with the tens of thousands of other young Americans in uniform. Pat had been in the Wisconsin Air National Guard and had been roundly criticized for transferring to a Washington unit when he became engaged to Luci. After the wedding, the Nugents had moved to Austin and Pat had transferred once again, this time to the Texas Air National Guard. Every move brought criticism from those who thought he had received special treatment as a weekend warrior. The most vicious letters came from family members with loved ones fighting in Vietnam. I remember one that quoted the Declaration of Independence: "We hold these truths to be self-evident, that all men are created equal." The letter writer accused the president of pulling strings for his son-in-law even though he once had said if he had a son he would be proud to have him serve in Vietnam.

The president, always mindful of bad publicity, could have been twisting Pat's arm and trying to persuade him to go overseas, but I doubt it. Chuck Robb, a Marine captain who had married Lynda Johnson on December 9, 1967, already had orders to go to Vietnam in March. Eventually Pat decided he didn't want to be left behind. His own brother had gone twice to Southeast Asia. The president wanted me to quietly arrange to have Pat transferred back to his former Guard unit at Andrews, the 113th Tactical Fighter Wing. According to rumors, that unit was to be activated for duty in Vietnam. The president wanted me to "make it look right and be discreet." He instructed me to "be very close with this." I had no problems with arranging a special transfer for Pat, whom I considered a friend and an upstanding young man. I wouldn't go through normal military channels. In my opinion, too many young American men were refusing to fight and engaging in all kinds of fraudulent schemes to get out of the draft, so I didn't see anything wrong with pulling a few strings to get someone into Vietnam.

Earlier in the war, Lynda had sought my help in getting her then-boyfriend, Hollywood actor George Hamilton, assigned for helicopter training. But the man with the perpetual tan never made it to Vietnam. He won a deferment based on his mother's need for his economic support. The public outcry had been relentless. Now Pat was ready to go to war, and if transferring him to Andrews helped him get there, I had no qualms about working with the Pentagon to make it happen. The potential for accusations of favoritism and special treatment didn't bother me. I told the president I would get it done.

Then the president told me why I couldn't be airborne after lunch. He had finally decided to take a vacation. "Do we have any military resorts or beach areas secure enough for me to stay for a few days?" he asked. "I want to soak up some sun and maybe play a little golf." There was no doubt that the president needed to get away. I had been thinking he ought to go stay at his ranch for a month or so. The Vietnam War and the drumbeat of protest against it were taking a toll on him. He not only looked tired, he sounded tired. Everyone close to him—family, friends, and staff—had been urging him to take a vacation. He'd finally given in. Looking back, that could have been a sign that the president had already made up his mind not to seek reelection. The country was becoming more divided every day, and nothing he said or did seemed to help. In private, he looked like a defeated man. I know he was an anguished man. Just one month later, he would announce his decision not to run.

"I believe the State Department has a facility in the Virgin Islands," I told him. "I'll have to check it out. There's also a beach club at Eglin Air Force Base in Florida. And Ramey Air Force Base in Puerto Rico could probably accommodate your visit. I know that base, and I've been there before. It can be secured."

He wanted to leave the next morning for Houston, then go to Beaumont, Texas, for a dinner in honor of Democratic Representative Jack Brooks. From there, he wanted to go to Marietta, Georgia, for the rollout of the new Lockheed c-5a Galaxy transport plane, the largest airplane in the world at the time and only eighteen yards shorter than a football field. "Find a spot to vacation for a few days," he said. "And by the way, you call General J. P. McConnell and tell him the president wants him to come along with us." McConnell was chief of the Air Force.

I made some calls to confirm Ramey as our destination and walked with the president to the White House theater, where he was meeting with the nation's governors, and then on to the Oval Office.

10:35 A.M. Just as I returned to my office, George Christian, the presidential press secretary, was calling. Word was getting out about tomorrow's possible trip. Rumors had been rampant the last couple of days about a trip with several possible destinations. The president liked to keep his trips under wraps until the last possible moment—even from me sometimes. And I was the pilot! There had been times when I had such short notice I barely had time to call my crew, order them to "Fire up the big bird!" and then dash to the Marine helicopter on the South Lawn to ride with the president to Andrews Air Force Base. Fortunately my crew always had the engines running, and I was two steps ahead of the president in jumping into my cockpit seat. On the night of his election in 1964, however, I received such short notice we were leaving town that I couldn't find my socks in the hotel and had no time to search. I don't think the president ever found out he had the only barefoot Air Force One pilot in history.

I told George everything I knew. Those of us in the inner circle tried to keep one another informed. We could never rely on the president to be forthright with all of us all of the time, so we had to pass the word among ourselves. "Now, George, I surely wouldn't want you to broadcast this around," I said.

George had the tough job of trying to keep the press from finding out too much while giving away just enough information that they would be packed and ready for takeoff. I heard later that the press never got the word to pack summer clothes for the trip to Puerto Rico, and they were fuming. "What kind of crap is this?" one of them growled. Johnson always told us he didn't want advance word of travels getting out because he might change his plans on a whim, and a public cancellation would raise all kinds of rumors about the state of the presidency. I didn't care what the press did or didn't know. I just needed to know whether a press plane was going or whether a press pool would be riding on Air Force One.

10:55 A.M. I called Colonel Ray Cole, an Air Force friend of mine in the Pentagon, about getting Pat to Vietnam. Cole worked for General McConnell, who was someone willing to help whenever I called. In fact, when I was named White House military aide in 1965, McConnell told me, "There are going to be a lot of folks here with long knives out for your ass, Cross.

And I'm the only guy who can save you. If you need help, you call me." And I always did. I had called McConnell the day before and advised him that Pat Nugent wanted to go to Vietnam. He told me to work it out with Colonel Cole. Cole said the best way to proceed was to have Pat write a letter to the commander of his old Guard unit at the 113th Tactical Fighter Wing and request a transfer to the unit and orders for active duty. This sort of thing would cause some head wagging, but not much.

11:04 A.M. I returned a call from a contractor at our Air Force One maintenance facility in New York about eliminating the arm of the couch in the stateroom on the plane. The president never seemed to stop tinkering with all of his assets. If it wasn't modifications on his plane, it was the shower at his ranch—he wanted a high-pressure stream of water, and he wanted it yesterday. I always had a handful of renovations to worry about.

11:35 A.M. I called Major Donald Short, another of my Air Force One copilots, and gave him the itinerary for the trip to Texas, Georgia, and Puerto Rico. He needed to get started on checking runway lengths because the Boeing 707 used as Air Force One ordinarily needed 6,000 feet to land. We had to make sure we would have the landing strip we needed, or find alternate airports. He had to look at weather forecasts and plane weights and start calculating. We didn't have a moment to lose.

11:45 A.M. The president was expecting me in the Oval Office so we could leave together for the farewell ceremony for Secretary of Defense Robert McNamara, who after seven years at the Pentagon was taking a job as president of the World Bank. The public ceremony was scheduled to begin at noon at the Pentagon. Unfortunately for all of us, the festivities were going to be outdoors, and it was rainy and cold enough to make your teeth chatter. I didn't pull on my long johns that morning because I thought I was going to be flying all afternoon in the cozy cockpit of Air Force One, where a month earlier I had had my flight engineer, Chief Master Sergeant Joe Chappell, install a special little heater for my feet. I knew the McNamara ceremony was going to be fairly short, but I hadn't expected a cold rain to be falling. My uniform suddenly felt mighty thin.

The day before, I had prepared a nearly minute-by-minute script for the president to follow during the ceremony. Little did I know how badly we would be thrown off schedule, or that our mishap would be front-page news the next day. The *New York Times* would later refer to it as "a decidedly untidy last day at the Pentagon." We were supposed to arrive at the

Pentagon at straight-up noon. My playbook was specific and orderly and, I thought, left no room for surprises. It would allow Johnson to make his obligatory appearance, review the troops, offer some short remarks, and be on his way—all in just twenty-one minutes. In and out. Short and sweet. Just the way the president liked to handle these ceremonial duties. Every move was choreographed: "12:01 P.M. The president proceeds through cordon to reviewing stand (Note: During walk, four ruffles and flourishes, 'Hail to the Chief,' and a flyover of Air Force and Navy aircraft will take place). 12:03 P.M. nineteen-gun salute for Secretary McNamara, followed by review of the troops. The president will walk with Honor Guard Commander and Secretary McNamara—president is on the right." And so on. I worried about what would happen to the flyover of twenty planes if the president did not arrive on time. The planes, including the new F-111 fighter bomber that had not yet seen combat, required seventeen minutes to rendezvous for the flyover because of air traffic in the Washington area. If they were turned away from the Pentagon at the last minute because the ceremony was off schedule, it would take another seventeen minutes to re-form for the flyover pattern. And I knew I'd catch unshirted hell from Johnson if he had to wait anywhere near that long just to be saluted by air.

Fortunately we left the White House right on time, even though the rain was hammering down. Also riding with me in the presidential car were several of the president's closest aides, special counselor Harry McPherson, domestic adviser Joe Califano, and speechwriter Will Sparks. The president talked a little about his meeting that morning in the White House with the nation's governors. When Califano asked Johnson whether he had accepted questions from the governors, he said no and recalled how the late House Speaker Sam Rayburn had taught him to deal with people. Rayburn told him there are two basic ways to treat people: butter them up and hug and squeeze them or, to get even better results, give them a "kiss my ass" approach. I had seen enough of the governors' meeting to know the state leaders had received Rayburn's second treatment.

Within minutes we were pulling into the Pentagon's first-floor garage, and McNamara was there to meet us. We learned that the flyover had been scrubbed because of the worsening skies. But the outdoor farewell ceremony was still planned for the raised lawn overlooking the Potomac River. I boarded McNamara's private elevator with the president, the defense secretary, and ten others, including White House aides and a military elevator operator, Army Master Sgt. Clifford Potter. The elevator would be a speedy shortcut to Secretary McNamara's office on the fourth floor. Or so we thought. Up we went, but before we realized what was happening, the elevator just stopped. There was no sound of gears grinding or cables snapping, no jolt or bounce. McNamara immediately reached in front of the sergeant to push some buttons. "Let me see if I can't get this to work," he said. Nothing happened. "Turn the switch to automatic, and let's see if the elevator won't operate as it normally does," he said to the sergeant. Again, nothing.

"Isn't there an emergency switch?" someone asked.

"You'd better use the phone," McNamara said.

The sergeant picked up the wall phone and was able to reach a maintenance man. "We're stuck between the second and third floor," he said. We had no idea how he knew exactly where we were, because the floor indicator lights showed nothing.

"Do you have a full load there?" the maintenance man asked.

"We sure do," said the sergeant.

I could tell the president was ticked off just by looking at his stony face. "What's wrong with this thing?" he barked.

"Don't ask me," McNamara said. "I don't work here anymore."

I didn't blame the president for being impatient. We hardly had time to spare. He was due at the State Department after the Pentagon ceremony, and I needed to take care of a jillion things for our multi-leg Air Force One trip the next morning. The president maintained his cool pretty well, although he needled McNamara for not being able to keep the elevators running in his own building. He said he was going to leave out of his speech the line praising McNamara for bringing efficiency to the Defense establishment. Then he teased him by noting that the Defense Department thought so highly of him that the staff was trying to keep him until the last possible moment. Will Sparks busied himself with reading the small print on the elevator card and found out we were riding Elevator Number Thirteen. "That's probably the cause of our trouble," he told McNamara.

But McNamara said, "No, that's the trouble with having 29 days in February." The president asked what the elevator capacity was supposed to be. The sign said fifteen. He counted heads and found there were thirteen. Someone mumbled something about people being overweight.

It was getting stuffy by this time. Someone pried the inside doors open a crack so that air could come in from the elevator shaft, and Harry McPherson unscrewed the ceiling plate and pushed it up about half an inch. Later we found out that pushing that trapdoor ceiling automatically cut off electricity to the elevator and delayed us even longer. It still felt like we were breathing stale air, so the president told Will to try to get some more fresh air by wedging the notebook containing his speech in between the outer doors. We could see only the bottom half of the outer doors, so it was obvious we were stuck between floors. From inside, we could hear someone—it turned out to be an Air Force colonel—running up and down a stairway shouting, "They're stuck! They're stuck!" But no one was visible on the landing outside the doors, and someone began grumbling about the lack of help.

Secret Service Agent Clint Hill got on his walkie-talkie and ordered other agents to go to every floor until they found us. "Open the damn doors," he snapped. Within a few minutes, we saw several people show up on the floor. Finally, a maintenance man in a green General Services Administration uniform got the outer doors open.

By that time, we had been trapped for almost fifteen minutes. We were about three feet below the floor line of the fourth floor. I was probably the youngest and most agile one aboard, so I scrambled out first. Several others followed. Someone found a leather chair with wooden handles, and we lowered it into the elevator so the president could step on it and climb out. I grabbed his hands, and several of us pulled him out first, followed by McNamara and the others. Things like that are not supposed to happen to the president of the United States, but you never knew what might jump up and bite you on a day in the White House.

We walked down the stairs to the River Entrance, where General Earle Wheeler, Chairman of the Joint Chiefs of Staff, and Paul Nitze, Deputy Secretary of Defense, greeted the president. Outside it was bitterly cold and still raining hard. I accompanied the president to the outdoor reviewing stand for the official troop review and nineteen-gun salute. As if being stuck in an elevator for twelve minutes with hardly any room to turn had not been enough of an insult to the president, the public address system failed miserably. The president spoke for only a few minutes, but the sound of the driving rain and lack of a microphone prevented almost everyone from hearing a word he said.

The president called McNamara "the textbook example of the modern public servant." I couldn't help but think that McNamara was deserting the president at one of the lowest moments in the Vietnam War, even though his departure had been in the works for months. With America still reeling from the Tet Offensive, and Marines still under siege at Khe Sanh, the president needed his supporters more than ever. But McNamara, the architect of the war for both Presidents Kennedy and Johnson, the slick-talking academic who was so good with the charts and graphs, and the man who had been so optimistic for so long—he was crawling away and leaving the whole mess on the president. So much for loyalty and sense of honor. I thought he was an arrogant egghead, and I was glad to see him go.

Everyone was soaked—me, the president, McNamara, and the entire crowd gathered for the ceremony. I held an umbrella over the president, who at the last minute had donned a topcoat and hat. McNamara was bareheaded and wore only a blue suit and no overcoat. For twenty minutes, the three of us huddled under the umbrella to try to keep dry, but it didn't work. The umbrella malfunctioned, and water dripped on the president's head. He was prone to catching colds and the flu, and all I could think about was how cold I was without my long johns and how this weather would surely make the president sick. I found out later that Johnson told the other White House aides that he was wet because of the umbrella holder—me. "There was some kid holding an umbrella over my head which had a hole in it, and the water was running down the shoulder of my coat," Johnson related. "He was holding it so that all the water, which was running off the top of the umbrella, fell on McNamara's glasses, who was standing at attention going blind. I told the kid to move the umbrella to the right, and he moved it to the left, so that the only person who was protected then was him." Not a flattering portrait of my best attempt to keep the president dry, but he just liked to exaggerate. He was a lot drier than anyone else, especially me.

12:47 P.M.   Having missed lunch, I was back in my White House office trying to sketch out possible flight plans to various destinations.

1:20 P.M.   I got a visit from Sam Houston Johnson, the president's younger brother who lived, off and on, in the family quarters of the White House. Sam liked to chase women and drink during the day as a warm-up for his nocturnal liquid intake. He showed up in my office in his usual state—tipsy. "Well, maybe we ought to have a little nip," he teased. He knew I wouldn't drink while I was working, but he couldn't help needling me.

Sam was to Lyndon Johnson what Billy Carter was to President Jimmy Carter—a loose cannon who drank too much and often wasn't taken seriously. He was an embarrassment to the president, who had asked me to try to keep watch over Sam. I considered Sam a good friend, albeit an unconventional one. He was a free spirit and always full of colorful stories about his carousing. But I tried to avoid Sam most of the time because I didn't want the president to think I was too cozy with him.

Sam wandered into my office on this day because he'd heard some rumblings about the possible presidential trip. "Well, are we going to Texas tomorrow?" he asked. I had to be very careful. Obviously the president wasn't telling Sam about the trip, so I couldn't either. I just gave him some vague responses until he left.

2:40 P.M.   A man from Chrysler called looking for me. I was in charge of the White House auto fleet, which consisted of Fords, Mercurys, and a few Cadillacs. The auto companies rented the cars to us for only one dollar a year, and each year we got new ones. The president had been pushing me to obtain a Chrysler station wagon for Lynda, but I had no time to meet with the Chrysler man on this day, so it would have to wait.

5:40 P.M.   Pat Nugent called to check on the letter I had drafted for him. He needed to mail the letter with his signature to Brigadier General Willard Milliken, commander of the 113th Air National Guard unit in Washington, his former unit. The letter from Nugent requested extended active duty with assignment in Southeast Asia.

5:45 P.M.   The president placed the first of what would be four calls to me in the next fifty minutes. He had a copy of Pat's proposed letter to General Milliken and wanted to read it to me even though I was the one who had written it. The president was double-checking every line of the letter. He thought the letter referred to the wrong Guard unit, and he noted that Milliken was not the officer who had offered Pat a promotion. We went over the letter, word for word, in phone calls that he placed at 5:52 P.M., 6:17 P.M., and 6:36 P.M.

The president did not want the public to know that Pat's way to Vietnam had been arranged by me and the Chief of Staff of the Air Force.

Then I went back to making all the phone calls to prepare for our Air Force One trip, on March 1, including getting the plane moved from Andrews Air Force Base to Dulles International Airport in Northern Virginia instead of Washington's National Airport because of all the snow and ice.

9:30 P.M.   Heavy snow fell as I left the White House to drive home to suburban Maryland. I had to take it slow and steady just to keep from sliding off the road. I could hardly see the pavement. Just my luck to have to maneuver through a snowstorm at the end of a long day of charging through the unpredictable obstacle course that was the Johnson White House. A short night's sleep in my own bed would be my reward. I couldn't wait to collect.

CHAPTER TWO

THE EARLY YEARS

WE WERE SUPPOSED TO BE PICKING COTTON, BUT WHEN you're ten years old, it's easy to get distracted. My friends and a couple of cousins were lying around in the shade on that hot Alabama summer day in 1935, talking and joshing one another, trying to figure out how we could sneak away from the cotton patch and find a swimming hole. The Pleasant Home farm community where I grew up was far off the beaten path, sixty-five miles north of Pensacola, Florida, and eighty-five miles south of Montgomery, Alabama. It wasn't that the rest of the world passed us by; the rest of the world didn't even know we existed.

We rarely saw an automobile, with the exception of the rural mail carrier and the "rolling store"—a big covered truck that churned small clouds of dust when it came down the sandy dirt road once a week with staples like sugar, flour, and seasonings. Airplanes? We had seen photographs, but none of us had ever seen a real one.

With no warning, a loud noise interrupted our daydreams. It sounded like a big engine of some sort. One of my buddies, trying to show off the worldliness that he didn't have, bet it was one of those big airships from the Navy base at Pensacola. We all looked skyward, and suddenly it was overhead—not a blimp but an airplane, a noisy, aluminum-looking crate. It was probably 500 feet high. It seemed huge and incredibly fast. We all waved and hollered until it went out of sight.

At that very moment in my young life, my fate was sealed. I told my pals, "When I grow up, I'm going to be a pilot." As I think back on that day, what we thought was a monstrous airplane probably had a wingspan of about seventy-five feet or so, and engines in the dinky 350- to 400-horsepower range. It couldn't have gone faster than ninety to one hundred miles per hour. The plane had to have been a Ford Tri-Motor, a workhorse of a plane that was one of the first commercial airliners to go into service. Of course, I knew none of that then. But that first brush with aviation planted a seed that would grow into a full-blown career that would reach its pinnacle when I flew Air Force One. You catch the flying bug and it never lets you go. All pilots know what I mean.

I WAS BORN ON APRIL 25, 1925, IN RURAL COVINGTON County, Alabama, and spent the Great Depression growing up with hard-working but dirt-poor relatives trying to squeeze a living from the land. My parents, James Kension Cross and Susie Jesse Wells Cross, lived in a place called headquarters camp, in a company-owned dwelling made from a converted wooden railroad boxcar. A small gathering of rough wooden buildings and converted railroad boxcars served as local headquarters for a large wood-products firm named the Horseshoe Lumber Company. My father was employed by the company to run a pump station supplying water from a nearby creek to the small, narrow-gauge steam locomotives used to haul harvested timber to sawmills and lumber markets.

When the stock market failed in 1929, followed soon by the Great Depression, the Horseshoe Lumber Company went bankrupt and disappeared from the scene. With my father now unemployed and with no means of support, my family had to move back a few miles to my grandparents' farm in Pleasant Home, though my mom and dad soon began to migrate from place to place throughout the South for Dad to do construction work. I was the oldest of seven children, so there was always work to be done to provide enough food. During the summer months, when garden crops were maturing, the entire family would spend days harvesting, peeling, canning, and preserving fruits and vegetables to get us through the coming year. Around Christmastime, we would take a full day to slaughter and dress a dozen hogs. Sausage-making, using intestines as casings, was a part of the ritual that fewer and fewer Americans ever experience. And all the meat that wasn't canned was put in the smokehouse for preservation. We had no refrigerators or freezers; in fact, we had no electricity in most rural communities of our county until after World War II.

After I was ten, I stayed with my grandmother on the farm while my parents and younger siblings continued to travel to find work. My regular daily chores included milking two or three cows, then feeding the hogs, chickens, and mules, all before breakfast. Next came bringing in wood for the cook stove and fireplaces before preparing for school. A school bus came down the dirt road in front of our farm, but because we lived less than one-and-a-half miles from school, we were not allowed to ride it. I never could understand why that rule existed, especially on many cold and rainy mornings when the driver sounded his horn as he passed those of us walking to school. I remember complaining to a favorite uncle about the practice, and all he said was, "Boy, that builds character. And if you run instead of walk, it builds muscle and will improve your lungs."

For those educated in the local twelve-grade country school, there was little or no social activity. Mr. and Mrs. James Catoe's tiny country store, the Pleasant Home School, and the Pleasant Home Baptist Church served as the only gathering places for what little socializing occurred, since the nearest town, Andalusia, was thirteen miles away. Once every two or three months, when it became absolutely necessary to make the grueling journey to town for essential clothing, shoes, animal feed, and so on, we would hitch a trusty but blind family mule named Swimjenny to what locals called a one-horse wagon, and the tortuous journey would begin at daybreak, usually on a Saturday. We would return well after nightfall. Because the road was not paved until 1933, its surface of sticky Alabama red clay was nearly impassable after heavy rains for all except mule- or horse-drawn conveyances.

Our lifestyle was primitive by today's standards. It was a time of taking cool summer showers beneath a fifty-gallon barrel on a seven-foot platform, and visiting a two-hole outhouse, equipped with a back issue of a Sears and Roebuck catalog to use or peruse as necessary. I still have, and proudly display in my garage, the five-foot by two-foot single-piece cypress two-hole seat board from that bygone privy.

They say ignorance is bliss, and I certainly fit the bill. Although the times were likely trying for my parents, I still fondly recall swimming in the creeks, hunting, fishing, and roaming the piney woods. What kind of life could be better for an active boy?

But Army recruiters showed up in 1943 when I was a senior at Pleasant Home School, and I was more than ready to leave the nest. They found a willing and eager recruit, especially when they talked about pilot training. I filled out the paperwork, took a battery of tests, and passed a rigorous physical examination. The paperwork was then forwarded to the local draft board, and I waited for my induction notice, confident that I soon would be zipping through the air in my fighter plane, blasting enemy planes out of the sky over Europe or the Pacific. Three days after I graduated from high school, my induction notice came in the mail, and I reported for duty on June 24, 1943.

The recruiters had promised me a fighter assignment if I successfully completed pilot training. They also promised that the flight training would occur in Mississippi, Northern Florida, and Alabama, places so close to home I could visit my family and girlfriend every weekend. The promises turned out to be empty.

Instead, I was put on a Trailways bus to Dothan, Alabama, and then transferred to a smoky old steam troop train full of young draftees. No one told us where we were headed. The train stopped in Jacksonville, Florida, near the Atlantic Ocean. I was blackened from head to foot by the loco-motive's smoke pouring through the open windows of the train. Everyone was a mess. Word came that we would be in Jacksonville for five hours, so I headed to the local YMCA with Joseph Moye Eddins, a young man from Troy, Alabama, with whom I had just become acquainted. We took a hot shower, but had to wear the same sooty clothes for the next leg of the mystery trip. We rode all night, but it was impossible to sleep. Just before daylight, the train stopped and a tough-looking little man in a khaki uni-form and flat-brimmed felt cavalry hat came aboard. With a voice like a foghorn, he yelled, "All right, you morons, fall off this train. Your asses now belong to me. My name is Corporal Moose. You will remember me because I am the meanest little son of a bitch you will come to know here in Miami." That's how we learned where we were. "I will tell you when to eat, when to sleep, when to talk, when to piss, and where to go. I own your sorry asses for the next eight weeks; get used to it." So much for being close to home with weekends off!

After basic training, I boarded another troop train of converted box cars and rode for five grueling days and nights. Again, no one told us where we were going. When the train finally stopped, we looked out the window and saw a sign: Reno, Nevada. The Aviation Cadet Program had brought us to the University of Nevada for three months of college classroom work in geography, history, English, civics, math, public speaking, and physical fitness. Most of us were just young high school graduates who hadn't yet had an opportunity to attend college, so we nicknamed our assignment "charm school." The best part was the food. The university's kitchen cooked five-star meals, much better than the Army chow in Florida. There were a lot of pretty young girls in college there too, but we weren't allowed to fraternize with them.

In November, we marched to the train depot for another overnight trip to who-knew-where. We landed in Santa Ana, California, where we were assigned to begin the ground phase of training as either pilots, navigators, or bombardiers. I was closer to my dream of piloting a plane. But I was just as excited to get my first off-post pass since being drafted. It came on Christmas Eve, when I was homesick beyond despair. I took a train through what was then farm country on a 90-minute rattletrap ride to Union Station in downtown Los Angeles. The United Service Organizations (USO) had advertised on the radio that local families would pick up lonely servicemen at the Brown Derby, known as the Restaurant of the Stars, and take them home for Christmas. I envisioned being chosen by a beautiful Hollywood movie star to be wined and dined at famous bistros. No such luck. A married couple old enough to be my parents picked me up and drove me to their modest home in Glendale. I was shown to a bedroom and given no supper. They woke me at 7 A.M. on Christmas and drove me back to the Brown Derby. I would have had more fun with a lump of coal in a Christmas stocking.

I finally got to fly an airplane on March 21, 1944. I was at a civilian contract primary flight-training school in Dos Palos, California, which was overseen by half a dozen military officers. The plane was an open cockpit bi-wing PT-13 Stearman trainer. I was so excited my heart was pounding. It was just what I'd dreamed of—fur-lined leather jacket, leather helmet with goggles, white scarf, fur-lined boots, and an open cockpit. The roar of that powerful engine—probably 200 horsepower—was lifting me into the heavens, just where I wanted to be. And then I got airsick. I threw up my guts and tried to get my helmet off to catch the mess, but lost my helmet and goggles in the slipstream. It was revolting. Nothing could be worse. Or so I thought, until my instructor, Mr. Ralph Greene, later ordered me to clean up the airplane.

Greene and I didn't get along too well after that first flight, so it wasn't long before he told my flight commander, Mr. Henry M. Klett, that I should be given a washout ride and sent to the infantry or the cavalry. I was beyond crushed. I was only eighteen and already a failure. I thought I'd been doing well in the air, especially when I heard stories in the barracks from the other guys about their ground loop crashes, short landings, near-collisions, and other mishaps. If I didn't make it through pilot training, it would devastate my family and friends back home. But within a day or so, Klett took me up and had me run through spins, stalls, landings, and the other maneuvers cadets were supposed to know after about ten hours of flying time. After the third landing at an auxiliary field, we taxied to the other end of the runway, and I figured he wanted me to make my last takeoff. But Mr. Klett said, "Cross, I don't see a thing wrong with your flying skills or your attitude. So I'm going to let you go. I'm getting out right now and going over to the phone shack and rest. You go ahead and make two solo landings and take-offs, then come back for me and we'll head back to the main base."

I was overjoyed. "I'm going to be a hotshot fighter pilot after all," I thought.

From then on, Klett, the most experienced instructor pilot at Dos Palos, took me under his wing as his only student. He taught me more about flying than any of the other students were learning. Later, my classmates would ask me how to do outside loops, hammer head and whip stalls, falling leaf maneuvers, and eight-point slow rolls—maneuvers none of them were being taught.

By the time I finished the next phase of flight training in single engine BT-13s (Vultee Vibrators) at Gardner Field near Taft, California, I was at the top of my class. Upon graduation, my instructor, First Lieutenant Dan Fischer, recommended me as the most qualified potential fighter pilot he'd seen in his teaching career. I was sure I was on my way to combat. "Look out, you Japanese zero pilots," I said to myself. "I'm going to be on your six o'clock with 50-caliber guns blazing."

I couldn't have been more wrong. The military had other plans for me. I was sent instead to the remote Marfa Army Air Field in far West Texas. What a sorrowful outrage! The only thing that took the sting out of my new assignment was that it was nearer to my home in Alabama. I would get twenty days of leave after this training class in twin-engine planes, and I could visit home as a new second lieutenant.

I finally got my pilot wings and commission in Marfa, and headed home for the first time since being drafted. I then reported for temporary duty at Malden Army Air Field in Missouri, but within a few weeks was reassigned to Bergstrom Field in Austin, Texas, where I would be taught to fly a C-46 heavy transport plane. I arrived at Bergstrom still incensed that I hadn't been assigned to the sleek fighter planes I knew I was meant to fly. Brash and bursting with youthful ignorance, I wrote a polite but indignant letter to U.S. Senator John Bankhead Jr. of Alabama, uncle to the beautiful, husky-voiced actress Tallulah Bankhead. I told him I had been promised the opportunity to fly fighters, and thought I should be in a P-38 fighter plane. Needless to say, I got no help from him. Typical politician. When you need 'em, they're not there, particularly if you have no political clout. To be fair to the good and honorable senator, I suspect he realized I was just a scatterbrained kid of nineteen who wasn't even eligible to vote at that time. I did, however, get a nice form letter from him.

Bergstrom was a base where I knew my way around. My family had moved around the country because my father was a field superintendent for a large contractor out of Atlanta, Georgia. He had supervised the building of Bergstrom during World War II. He'd even hired me as a water boy on the project in the summer of 1942. So, being assigned to Austin in 1945 was a homecoming of sorts. I liked it even better after I bought a motorcycle and met a beautiful blonde teenage girl in town named Marie Campbell. She was only sixteen, but she stole my heart. She wasn't afraid to jump on the back of my Harley and hang on while we rode the streets and highways of central Texas. I was almost four years older than Marie and was set on a path that would take her away from her family, but she said yes when I proposed, and we've been together ever since. We married in July 1945, and my best man was Joe Eddins, the Alabama friend I'd met on the filthy train to basic training in Florida. We had pulled the same assignments since our induction, including Bergstrom. In fact, I was best man at Joe's wedding when he married a young woman, Susie Hudnall, from nearby Johnson City, Texas, in April 1945.

After we completed our flight training at Bergstrom in the twin-engine Curtis-built C-46 transport planes, Joe and I were lucky enough to be assigned to the same flight crew. We were going to fly the famous "Hump" over the Himalayas in the China/Burma/India theater. It was a highly dangerous air route over the tallest mountains in the world, with deadly weather conditions. I had Joe as my co-pilot; Corporal Lawrence Coyle, nineteen, of Brooklyn, New York, as radio operator; and Sergeant John Leber, twenty-four, of Wrightsville, Pennsylvania, as flight engineer. We flew the Hump for eight months, and it was the most valuable flying experience one could have ever endured.

The enemy wasn't fighter planes or anti-aircraft fire. It was the treacherous weather conditions, coupled with the highest mountains in the world and terrain that was only partially mapped and surveyed. Ground-based navigational aids were practically non-existent, and on-board navigational equipment often did not work or gave erroneous readings. Winds often blew in excess of 100 knots. A crew thus could be hundreds of miles off-course without a clue where they were. So many planes disappeared on those icy peaks that the air routes were dubbed "the aluminum trail." We flew gasoline supplies, and constantly worried about a fire. It was a youthful adventure and one I am deeply grateful to have survived.

After I came back to the United States in February 1946, I was discharged from active duty and assigned to the Army Air Corps Reserves. I enrolled at what is now called Auburn University, but I was far from a happy-go-lucky college kid. I supported a new wife with a baby on the way, went to school full-time on the GI Bill, flew every weekend in the Reserves, and held a part-time job as a carpenter (not a very good one). As I scrambled to make ends meet and ran myself ragged every day, I often asked myself why in the world I had ever left a good-paying job flying airplanes for Uncle Sam.

I was recalled to active duty in October 1948 as Cold War tensions heated up in Berlin. By this time, the Army Air Corps had been redesignated the new United States Air Force. While I expected to be sent to Europe for the aptly named Berlin Airlift, I was sent instead to a transport unit at Clark Air Force Base in the Philippines. We flew C-46 transport planes like the ones I had flown over the Hump. I was a little anxious at first because the planes had been in storage for a couple of years before they were restored to flying status. The planes flew well, however, during our missions to New Guinea, Guadalcanal, Borneo, and Indonesia. Our job was to provide airlift support to a reconnaissance unit that was photo-mapping the Southwest Pacific region, and an Army graves registration task force trying to find the missing remains of American soldiers and Marines killed in the Pacific war. More assignments in troop carrier and military airlift commands around the world occupied me and kept me away from home 80 percent of the time until 1958.

Then I got my big break. I applied to the 1254th Air Transport Group—the Special Air Missions unit whose job was to provide air transportation for the president, vice president, and other high-ranking government officials. I figured you had to know someone important to get into that unit, but I put my application in anyway. I was tired of flying C-124s, which we called Big Shakies, out of Dover Air Force Base, Delaware. I had 6,000 hours of flying time and good character ratings, so I got the assignment.

Being selected for this elite unit was the highlight of my military career to that point. Only the best pilots and support personnel were selected. The motto of that special unit, which today is known as the 89th military airlift wing at Andrews Air Force Base in Maryland, is "Experto Crede," a Latin phrase for "Trust one who has had experience." It was hard to believe I now was part of this elite outfit. I was ecstatic, and even told the owner of a little all-purpose country store near our house adjacent to Dover Air Force Base that I would soon be leaving for Washington, D.C. He always wore overalls and liked to sit by a potbellied stove. "Oh well," he said, "I'm retiring pretty quick and going to Florida. One of these days, I'll see the president's airplane go over and I'll know you're flying it."

I said, "Whoa, whoa," and had a good laugh. Later, as I arrived in Washington, it dawned on me that I actually might be fortunate enough someday to shake the hand of a real U.S. president. Little did I realize how prophetic that country storekeeper had been.

A day or two after I reported for duty, a veteran pilot became my sponsor and mentor, teaching me the Special Air Missions (SAM) rules and regulations and helping me begin training on the various types of airplanes I would fly. It was a welcome initiation into what was casually referred to as the VIP, or "hotdog," unit. Crewmen in the Special Air Missions unit always wore dress uniforms, and the planes were spotless. We ate five-star meals. This was quite a switch from the dirty, shopworn transport planes I had flown for years. Flight suits had been our uniforms, and cold box lunches, C rations, and stale coffee had been our on-board meals.

Before long I was piloting planes for people like Secretary of State John Foster Dulles, Vice President Richard Nixon, the occasional senator or congressman, and every once in a while an ambassador, prime minister, and perhaps a king or queen of a foreign country. Then came the opportunity I had hoped for: a chance to fly, and perhaps even shake the hand of, a U.S. president.

President Eisenhower normally traveled aboard a four-engine VC-121 Lockheed Super Constellation, piloted by Colonel William G. Draper, his pilot and Air Force aide. But this time, in late October 1960, the destination was a small private airport in Shenandoah, Virginia. The president's big plane, nicknamed the Columbine, was too large and heavy for the runway. Colonel Clifford O. Korbol, my squadron commanding officer, assigned me to fly the president in a twin-engine VC-131 Convair that would not overtax the little runway. I thought, "Boy, this is heady stuff—getting to fly President Eisenhower." Draper came along to provide help and guidance, and I'm sure he checked me out as well.

I was determined to give the president a perfect flight. I never dreamed some jerk in a small plane would sabotage me. But that's exactly what happened.

About two miles out from the Shenandoah airport, as I was on my final approach with the wing flaps and landing gear down, some nut in a small airplane pulled onto the runway without looking and started his takeoff roll. The tiny airport was not FAA-controlled, which meant someone taking off had to check to make sure the skies were clear. This clown was heading straight for our plane. It wasn't a close call. I was traveling at 130–140 knots and had plenty of time to reapply power to the engines, pull up the flaps and gear, and make an unscheduled circle to come back in for a second try. I was thoroughly ticked off, big time. "Oh, shit," I thought. "Now who in the hell is that dumb SOB? Here I am on my first trip with a president of the United States, and I certainly don't want to screw it up."

I had an intercom on the plane, but I didn't use it to explain why we had to circle around again. Draper came up front and asked me what happened. "Well," I said, "some dumb guy pulled out on the runway in front of us and, simply for safety reasons, I decided to take the airplane around."

He didn't seem concerned. "Oh, well," he said. "No problem."

As I turned the plane, I made sure I kept the little plane in sight. I was going much faster than he was; top speed in that small plane was probably only 90 miles per hour, and he wasn't there yet. He was below me, and I passed over him as I brought the plane around to line up for a second try at landing.

I never found out the name of that pilot who could have ruined a perfect flight. I never filed a complaint, because he didn't violate a rule, just a safety practice. It was as if he'd pulled up to a stop sign and gone through the intersection without looking. Our plane carried no presidential seal, and our tail number was so small at that distance that I'm sure he never knew he had delayed the president of the United States. For all I know, he was a student pilot on his first solo.

We landed about four minutes late, and Ike never said a word. He rewarded me with warm thanks, a handshake, and a broad smile as he disembarked. A few days later, I got a personal letter of thanks from Eisenhower.

Not long after President Kennedy was inaugurated in 1961, we got word that the Special Air Mission's twin-engine Convairs would be replaced by a sleek, fast, and efficient four-engine plane, the VC-140 Lockheed JetStar. I was selected along with three other pilots to head the training program, and was sent to Lockheed's manufacturing plant in Marietta, Georgia, in June to learn everything I could about the new plane. After five months, I became the first pilot qualified to fly the plane, and flew the first one off the production line back to its new home at Andrews Air Force Base in October. I then became immersed in training other crews at Andrews to fly the JetStars, which were being delivered to the Air Force at the rate of two or three a month. We would eventually get twelve of them.

The Jet Age had arrived! And once word got out that the new VC-140 jets were assigned to Andrews, all the Washington big shots began to insist they travel by jet aircraft only. Cabinet members and other VIPs, who had been happy to fly in our two-engine Convairs, four-engine Lockheed Constellations, and Douglas DC-6s, called for the jets to be made available immediately even though Air Force authorities hadn't planned on putting them officially into service until early 1962. The planes carried a crew of four and up to eight passengers (though later two of the planes were reconfigured to fit thirteen). Senator Barry Goldwater, R-Arizona, himself a pilot and a major general in the U.S. Air Force Reserves, even wanted to take a JetStar up for a test flight. In early November 1961, I was assigned to accompany him. He arrived in his flight suit, and I saluted him. But he stuck out his hand to shake mine, looked at my name tag, and said, "Cross, I'm Barry Goldwater." He had no airs about him; he was just a regular guy and easy to like. I invited him to climb into the pilot's left-hand seat, and I got into the right cockpit seat. "How do we get this thing started?" he asked. Hearing that, I figured he wasn't particularly interested in learning all about the new plane, so I started the four engines, called the control tower for taxi and takeoff information, and told the senator to release the brakes. As we taxied, I briefed him on takeoff and flying speeds, and off we went. Goldwater was like a kid with a new toy. We climbed to 25,000 feet and ran through some stalls and recoveries and several touch-and-go landings, and I had him accelerate to Mach .86, 86 percent of the speed of sound, or the maximum "red line," the speed which we were not to exceed. After more than two hours of flying, we called it a day. When we came to the terminal and stopped the engines, Goldwater sat silent in the pilot's seat for a few minutes, rubbing his hands over the switches and knobs, throttles and instruments. Then, in a wistful tone, he said, "You know, Cross, flying a great airplane like this one is like having sex. You get too old for it, but you never want to give it up."

Early in December 1961, I received word that I was to pilot a trip for Vice President Lyndon Johnson. I had never met the man, and I was nervous. Now, I had nothing against Johnson, but his reputation for having a white-hot temper and a tendency to dress down pilots and crewmembers was well-known to everyone in the unit. That reputation began to build while he was Senate majority leader and the unit occasionally had to fly him somewhere. Word was out that Johnson could destroy the career of anyone who got crosswise with him. Or at least that was the fear. I counted myself lucky that I had managed to avoid a Johnson trip until now.

The vice president wanted to use the new jets, and he didn't want to wait until they were in full service. Johnson had to attend an event in Chicago, and then wanted to go on to his Texas ranch. The Air Force brass went into orbit. The runway at Johnson's Texas ranch wasn't the best in the world, and Air Force authorities were concerned about safety. Only 5,000 feet long, with a four-foot fence at the south end, and a ten-foot embankment at the north end, the runway was narrow, and sometimes cattle roamed freely on and around it. Worst of all, it had a 136-foot hump in the middle, which required some special piloting techniques.

My commander, Colonel Orlo Harkness, called me into his office and said, "Cross, you are the most experienced pilot we have for the JetStars, so you take this trip with LBJ."

"Yes, sir," I said. I didn't want to let him know I was about half scared to death.

"Be extremely careful," Harkness said. "Vice President Johnson is the kind of man who can ruin your career if you don't watch out. He's really tough. He's really eaten up several of our pilots in the past."

The last thing I wanted to do was screw something up, so I was nervous as hell. I didn't want any of that infamous Johnson wrath coming my way. I vowed to make it a perfect trip. All the talk about the landing strip's unusual configuration convinced me I needed to see it, needed to feel it under my wheels. I wanted to practice landing the JetStar at Mr. Johnson's ranch. So I phoned the vice president's office.

Johnson's personal Air Force aide, Colonel Howard Burris, gave me the Texas go-ahead. A few days before the Chicago trip, I flew the JetStar to LBJ's ranch in the Texas Hill Country. I landed from south to north a few times, and then practiced landing from the north. The runway steadily rose when landing from south to north. But the bigger problem was landing north to south. The runway appeared to drop at just about the point of touchdown. I had to find just the right balance between flying it a little longer and making sure we didn't run out of runway length. It was a bit of a hassle, but nothing too serious for a Hump pilot who'd survived the Himalayas with not much more than a prayer to guide me.

"We can do it," I told my colonel when I returned to Washington. "It won't be like landing at Dulles airport, but we can do it. And do it safely."

"Well, you'd better tell them we can't do it," he said.

"All right, sir," I said. "I will."

I phoned Colonel Burris and told him it was a "no go." It seemed that no sooner had I hung up, I got a call from Johnson himself. I decided to come clean.

"Well, sir, my group doesn't want us to do it, but it can be done," I said.

"Do you think it's safe?" he asked.

"Yes, sir," I said. "I wouldn't go if I didn't."

"Well, let's just do it," he said. "We'll call [Air Force Chief of Staff] General LeMay, or call whomever we have to."

I wasn't about to call four-star General Curtis LeMay, whose legendary bombing raids over Europe and Japan in World War II had made him big-ger than life and nearly untouchable. I never knew what happened next, but someone must have called LeMay, because I got word that the trip was on again.

I was as ready as I could be to meet Lyndon Johnson. I just wish it hadn't been storming in Chicago.

LBJ didn't like to make the drive to Andrews on Suitland Parkway, the main thoroughfare from Washington to Andrews in 1961. So I flew the plane the short ten-mile hop to Washington's National Airport, just a few miles from the White House. Johnson arrived and wanted a quick tour of the new JetStar. He looked it over and liked what he saw. He asked me a couple of questions about its capabilities, then seemed ready to go.

"Can we make it to Chicago, Major?" he asked.

"Yes, sir," I said. "The weather's a little bad."

"Well, don't take any chances," he said. "Now you remember when I had my own plane down there at the ranch about a year ago. Those boys came in there one night, and they got down too low and they crashed and killed themselves.

"I could have been on that plane," he said.

Earlier that year, on February 19, the pilot and co-pilot of Johnson's private, two-engine Convair 240 crashed in a nighttime thunderstorm seven miles from the ranch. Johnson had been at the ranch, and the two men were trying to ferry the plane the seventy miles from Austin. When they found rain sweeping the ranch runway, they turned around and were heading back to Austin when they slammed into a hill.

I didn't anticipate any such trouble en route to Chicago. Takeoff was smooth, and our first stop was Chicago, where the vice president was to be met by city officials and taken to speak at a luncheon. We ran into cloudy weather with turbulence and icing, and as we arrived over the Chicago area, air traffic control required us to circle and hold for about fifteen min-utes. Of course the greeting party had to cool their heels a bit.

When we finally landed, the vice president was in the mood to growl. "I don't like or expect to be late for appointments, especially causing discom-fort for these Chicago political folks waiting for us here in the cold," he told me as he got off the plane. I'd always thought of myself as apolitical up to that point. I had just gotten my first lesson in politics. If you're going to fly the vice president, then you should know a little about politics.

The weather hadn't improved when Johnson returned to the airport and we took off for his ranch in Stonewall, Texas. Icing, turbulence, and unex-pected headwinds ensured we would arrive late at the ranch. My mood was as gloomy as the weather. I figured a Texas-size ass-chewing would await me when we got to Texas. We were late getting to Texas, but I was pleasantly surprised—hell, I was shocked—when Johnson said, "Nice trip, Major. That's a nice little airplane. Hope to see you again soon."

My second encounter with Johnson came on January 2, 1962, and was an experience I'll never forget. Johnson's aide, Colonel Burris, sent word that LBJ was to be picked up in Texas and flown to Palm Beach, Florida, to meet with President Kennedy about a major reorganization of the U.S. Army. Burris made it clear that Johnson wanted to arrive in Palm Beach exactly at 3:55 P.M., not a second later. He would rendezvous with President Kennedy, who was already in Palm Beach, and they would meet a plane from Washington arriving at 4 P.M. with members of the president's cabinet and Pentagon leaders. Talk about a tight schedule.

The mission instruction file included a phone number for calling the vice president when I arrived at Bergstrom Air Force Base in Austin. My co-pilot, Captain Paul Thornhill, had already calculated we would need to leave Austin at 12:30 P.M. Central Time to make it to Florida on time. The nonstop flight would take two and a half hours "block to block"—that is, from the time the plane's door closed in Austin to when the door opened in Florida.

I arrived at Bergstrom at 9:30 A.M. and dialed the Austin number to contact Johnson. I was a little surprised when he answered the phone himself. I stammered a moment before saying, "Sir, this is Major Cross, and we are here to fly you to Palm Beach."

I knew the situation had gone awry when the vice president said, "Where are you? I didn't hear you come in, and I don't see you out on my ramp." I suddenly realized that the Austin number I had been given rang at the vice president's ranch—seventy miles from Austin—and he expected us to fly to the ranch and pick him up there.

I explained that we were at Bergstrom, but the vice president said, "I don't want to leave from Bergstrom. Come on out here. I want to leave from my ranch." I explained that there was no jet fuel at the ranch, and we would need to take on fuel if we were going to fly nonstop to Florida to make the appointment.

Johnson wasn't fazed. "Well, Major, you just send one of those big fuel trucks from Bergstrom and get on out here."

The problem was that if we took on enough fuel to get to Florida, the plane would be too heavy to take off from the 5,000-foot runway at the ranch. If we were to leave from his ranch airstrip, we'd have to stop somewhere en route to take on fuel, and we'd be late to Florida.

The vice president wasn't happy to hear this. "Well, Major, I don't know why it is that you Air Force people can always find some way to screw up my plans. Damn it, that being the case, I'll just have to make do. What time will I have to leave from Bergstrom to make Palm Beach before four o'clock?" I told him we would have to be gone from Bergstrom by 12:30 P.M. I thought the situation was now straight, and that the vice president would arrive at Bergstrom in plenty of time.

As the morning wore on, I started to get worried. Then twelve-thirty came and went. Then twelve-forty-five, and still no vice president. About that time, an operations officer ran from the terminal and told me that Johnson was on his car radio, patched into the telephone network, and wanted to talk with me. "Major, this is Lyndon Johnson. What time do I have to leave Bergstrom to reach Palm Beach a little before four o'clock?" It was as if we had never had the conversation a few hours ago. I reiterated as diplomatically as I could that we should have been airborne at twelve-thirty.

"Oh, Lord, Major," Johnson said. "You've got me in a hell of a dither. I have to be there to meet President Kennedy a minute or so before four o'clock."

I bit my tongue. "Although it likely will be impossible to make it by four, Mr. Vice President," I said, "we will certainly do our best for you. Where are you right now, sir?"

"I'm in Oak Hill right now, doing 90 miles an hour on Highway 290," he said.

I told him we were ready to go and the weather was fine, but my stomach churned even more. Oak Hill, an Austin bedroom community, was a good 20-minute drive from Bergstrom, even at breakneck speed. "Oh my God," I thought, "he won't be here before two o'clock."

His tardiness would eliminate what little chance remained of getting to Florida on time. Dejected, I walked toward the plane, trying not to think of the dire consequences. But before I reached the airplane, a big Lincoln convertible came roaring up with Johnson, alone, at the wheel. He jumped out almost before the car stopped rolling. "Let's go!" he yelled, and started running toward the plane. I was right behind him. It was clear that Johnson had told a little fib about being in Oak Hill going 90 miles per hour. Obviously, he was just outside the Bergstrom main gate when he called. He just wanted to get everyone in the hell-bent-for-leather mode.

Thornhill, seeing the car drive up, began to start the two right-side engines. By the time Johnson sat down, I had my seatbelt fastened and my radio headset on, and Thornhill had the other two engines running. We had clearance to taxi away from the terminal at 12:52 P.M., twenty-two minutes behind schedule. Bergstrom tower told us the surface winds were blowing from the north, requiring the use of Runway 35 North. The parallel taxiway to the runway was nearly three miles long. Here again I could see another seven- or eight-minute delay, since we were required to taxi from the terminal at the north all the way to the south end of the runway. I was desperate, so the moment we turned onto that long taxiway, I jammed the throttles to the stops and our taxi speed increased to 120 knots. Bergstrom tower, puzzled by our actions, called and said, "Air Force Two, you are not cleared for takeoff on the taxiway."

Thornhill told them, "We're not taking off. We're just in a big hurry to get where we can."

I threw it into reverse thrust so we could slow down enough to make the turn onto the runway and said, "Let's make this thing go!" The tower then cleared us for takeoff, and we roared into the blue.

Our original flight plan called for us to fly direct to Baton Rouge, direct to Pensacola, direct to Orlando, then to Palm Beach. Air Force regulations prohibited the JetStar from flying over large bodies of water, but I figured if we didn't make Palm Beach before four o'clock, my goose was cooked anyway. Turning southeastward, I informed the FAA we were changing our flight plan to go directly across the Gulf of Mexico to Tampa and then direct to Palm Beach. We flew at maximum, red-line speed, not worried about fuel efficiency, and it worked. The somewhat shorter route and our speed meant we arrived at Palm Beach a moment or so before President Kennedy drove up behind the wheel of his own Lincoln convertible. As Johnson disembarked, he said, "Major, I knew you could make it."

I never heard another word about violating the Air Force over-water restriction. Air Force regulations might be sacred, but not when a vice president of the United States is involved.

Johnson exchanged pleasantries with the president, then invited him aboard to tour the plane. The president took a quick look around and said, "This is a nice little airplane, Lyndon." Then he looked at me, winked, and added, "But it's not nearly as nice as mine." The plane carrying the dignitaries from Washington arrived shortly, and Johnson and Kennedy were gone. The day that I worried would end in a major-league, career-ending ass-chewing for me instead ended in a warm glow, with a wink from the president of the United States and the realization that I had been in the midst of the small talk of the leaders of the United States of America. I was a long way from that Alabama cotton patch.

I was standing by the JetStar the following afternoon when the vice president returned to the airport to be flown back to his Texas ranch. As his limousine approached, he lowered the window and waved for me to follow. He stopped at the nose of President Kennedy's Air Force One plane to use the White House telephone. I trotted the fifty or so yards to where he was and waited a respectful distance away. Defense Secretary Robert McNamara was driven up moments later. After Johnson finished his phone conversation, he and McNamara exchanged a few words. Then Johnson said, "Bob, this is the Air Force man I talked to you about last night."

The secretary shook my hand, mumbled a few words of greeting, then picked up and used the White House phone himself. I couldn't hear what he was saying because I was distracted—by the vice president. Johnson took me by the lapels of my coat, and came within a few inches of my face as I thought, "Oh boy, what now?"

Then he said, "Major, I don't know whether you will appreciate this or not, but I've decided you are a can-do man. I told Secretary McNamara last night that the vice president of the United States ought to have his own personal pilot and plane. All the presidents since Roosevelt's time have enjoyed that privilege, and I think it's high time the vice president of the United States should have that same recognition. I told McNamara that I wanted you to be my pilot, and the JetStar in which you brought me here yesterday is to be reserved for my exclusive use. I'll let you know later what changes I want you to make on the plane, Major. And by the way, I particularly don't like the interior configuration of the passenger cabin."

Just moments before, I had been wondering whether I had a future in the Air Force. Now I was suddenly to be personal pilot to a vice president. Could I survive in such a high-powered environment? How could something like this happen to an unremarkable junior Air Force officer, especially since this mission was only my second encounter with this powerful man?

Most of all, I wondered what I was in for. I would soon find out.

CHAPTER THREE

BRINGING HOME A HERO

LYNDON JOHNSON COULDN'T FLY AN AIRPLANE, BUT THAT didn't stop him from acting like he was my co-pilot. He liked to pick out the plane, the route, and the flight times. And once he made up his mind, he didn't want the plans to change. Even if we had to break the rules. In fact, Johnson didn't care about anyone else's rules when it came time for him to fly somewhere. He wanted to go, and he wanted to go immediately, and he wasn't interested in hearing why he couldn't go. He didn't care about flight procedures or Air Force rules or protocol. When he wanted to go somewhere, the only things he wanted to know were when we were leaving, when we would get there, and how the weather was. He was not going to let Air Force regulations stand in his way.

I learned that lesson on just my third encounter with Mr. Johnson. It was one of the most celebrated trips Johnson ever took. President Kennedy assigned Vice President Johnson to fly to the Caribbean and pick up John Glenn after he had successfully orbited the earth three times on February 20, 1962.

The Glenn flight was the first big triumph of the U.S. effort to get back in the space race. We had been getting our butts soundly kicked by the Soviets ever since October 5, 1957, when they launched the first Sputnik into Earth's orbit. We were all shocked by that launch because we in the United States felt that space technology was our field to dominate. Our national pride was bruised. Edward Teller, one of the creators of the hydrogen bomb, said that the United States had lost "a battle more important and greater than

Pearl Harbor." Our setback in the space program was a national humilia-
tion, and caused the nation to question our education system. In the 1950s,
the European press had derisively called our aborted launches "flopniks,"
as our unmanned rockets, boosters, and launching pads sometimes exploded and melted into flames. No one knew those dismal early days of
the space race better than Johnson. When he was Senate majority leader,
he had chaired a series of hearings to investigate the impact of Sputnik.
A parade of scientists and military leaders had declared that the Soviet
Union was winning the space race. Then Johnson sponsored the bill that
created NASA, the National Aeronautics and Space Administration, which
was designed to get the United States back in the chase.

Things didn't look much better in April 1961 when the Soviet Union's
Yuri Gagarin became the first human being in space. And then the Soviets
sent another man into space—Gherman Titov, who orbited the earth seventeen times in August 1961. It was just flat-out mortifying for the United
States to get beaten in the space race. By 1962, the country was primed
for some success, and John Glenn's four-hour-and-fifty-six-minute flight
gave America reason to holler. *Time* magazine said Glenn was the biggest
American hero since Charles Lindbergh. The largest television audience
in history at that time—135 million—looked on as Glenn's space capsule,
Friendship 7, made its fiery re-entry and splashed down in the South Atlantic Ocean.

The plan called for Glenn to be brought back to the Caribbean, where he
would spend a couple of days on Grand Turk Island in the Bahamas being
debriefed and undergoing tests and medical exams. Then Johnson was to
fly down to greet Glenn and bring him back to Cape Canaveral, and President Kennedy would pick up the ceremonial duties from there. Kennedy
had signed legislation in 1961 that made the vice president the presiding
officer of the National Aeronautics and Space Council. This event would
be the biggest and most glorious since Johnson had assumed the post.

I first learned about Johnson's trip a few days before Glenn's orbital
flight. The vice president's aide, Colonel Burris, called me at Andrews Air
Force Base outside Washington to give me a heads-up. Then Johnson followed up with his own call. I was thrilled. Pilots in the Special Air Missions
unit at Andrews don't often get phone calls from someone as important as
a vice president of the United States.

"The president wants me to go down to Grand Turk Island, where John
Glenn will be," Johnson said on the phone. "We'll bring him back to Cape
Canaveral for a big ceremony, and then we'll come back to Washington.
I'm going in my JetStar, and I want you to get it arranged."

I said the only thing I could say: "Yes, sir, Mr. Vice President."

But I wasn't at all sure we could land on Grand Turk Island. The airstrip there was only 5,000 feet. Ordinarily, we would have preferred to have 6,000 feet to land or take off. But we could safely use a 5,000-foot strip—if the runway was in good condition. On Grand Turk, the runway was made of crushed coral that had been packed, graded, and stabilized. It was hardly the ideal landing surface.

But that was only one of the problems. We also would need to refuel the JetStar on the island because our flight from Washington would be about 1,600 miles, almost draining our supply. We'd never make it back to Florida without more fuel. I had my doubts about whether there was any fuel on Grand Turk Island.

As soon as I hung up with the vice president, I made a round of phone calls. The news wasn't good. Just as I thought, there was no aviation fuel on Grand Turk. Even if there had been, there were no trucks to bring it to the JetStar. I didn't want to imagine the sight of the vice president's plane out of fuel and stranded on a dusty coral runway in the middle of nowhere with me sitting in the cockpit twiddling my thumbs.

I called Colonel Burris to tell him the trip was in trouble. "Well, figure out some way to do it because the vice president insists that we do it," Burris said. "It's a national event, a world event, and President Kennedy wants him to do it."

What could I say? "Okay," I replied. "We'll toy around with what we can do."

I called my contacts at the Pentagon and ran through all of my options: Could we fly a C-130 Hercules cargo plane to the island with an air bag full of fuel for the JetStar?

No. Too dangerous.

How about loading trucks full of jet fuel and flying them in on a C-130?

No. The tank trucks would expand at high altitude, and fuel would leak out.

I threw out one last, desperate idea: What if we brought in a KC-97, the big plane normally used for airborne refueling? But instead of fueling in mid-air, we'd just land it and use it as a fuel station for the JetStar. We'd jerry-rig some hose to the long nozzle that usually gives airborne Air Force jets a drink of fuel and run it over to the JetStar.

That idea also was rejected by Pentagon brass. They said all the airborne tankers were reserved for the Strategic Air Command, which kept nuclear bombers aloft around the clock.

I called Colonel Burris again and said I'd hit a wall. It wasn't long before my phone rang. It was the vice president. He wasn't happy or interested in hearing reasons why we could not make the trip. "Now we've got to do this," Johnson said. "The president wants me to do it. I want to do it. It's one of the greatest national events in our country's history, sending a man into orbit and bringing him back alive. And it's going to be a big celebration. You call Curtis LeMay."

Even after getting an order from the vice president of the United States of America, a major in the Air Force does not pick up the phone and casually call General LeMay, chief of staff of the U.S. Air Force. LeMay had a reputation as a mean, tough hombre. This was the tough old bird who had led the bombing runs on Europe and Japan, including a raid on Tokyo that killed more Japanese in one night than the atomic bomb dropped on Hiroshima. He looked like he could chew up nails and spit out rivets one by one through his teeth, which usually were clamped down on a cigar.

I had seen for myself that LeMay didn't let anyone tell him what to do. When I was an operations officer stationed at Goose Bay, Labrador, after World War II, I saw LeMay land in a KC-97 tanker and get off the plane smoking a cigar. Smoking was banned on those planes, and within fifty feet of them. The idea was to prevent a spark from blowing plane and crew sky-high. But LeMay was so tough he intimidated aviation fuel into not exploding.

I wasn't the only man in the Air Force scared of LeMay. My wing commander at Andrews, Colonel Tim Ireland, told me not to call LeMay. But the vice president and his staff told me I had to. I didn't like getting caught in the middle, but that was the way the mop flopped. I knew I could be court-martialed for insubordination if I disobeyed Colonel Ireland, but I gutted it up and called LeMay anyway. In the ultimate chain of command, I knew the vice president trumped my colonel.

I got through to LeMay with little difficulty. He surprised me with his willingness to help. He even bought into my idea to send a KC-97 down to the island ahead of time and to have it stand by on the ground to refuel the JetStar. "Well, I think that will work," he said. "What we'd have to do is put some long hoses on the refueling boom." That was exactly the idea I had in mind. I don't think this technique was ever used before or since. After all, those planes are designed for mid-air refueling. But you can jerry-rig anything, provided you have the guts to do it.

LeMay, of all people, knew the Air Force didn't ordinarily allow those tankers to refuel anything but Strategic Air Command planes. He wrote the damn policies. SAC was his baby. LeMay's greatest accomplishment in the Air Force was transforming SAC into a powerful war machine against the Soviets after World War II. He got the tankers assigned to SAC in the first place. And I was asking LeMay not only to refuel a non-SAC airplane, but to turn one of his prized tankers into a service station.

But he winked at the rules and cleared our way. He was a bright man and was used to doing whatever had to be done to get the job accomplished. Maybe LeMay knew that a vice president also trumped a general, or maybe LeMay just got a kick out of bending the rules too.

Pretty soon, everything was set for Johnson's trip. Before our flight, we sent down the KC-97 tanker, along with a C-130 with ground-based power units to help us start the airplanes and a backup JetStar so we'd be covered if our plane failed. Johnson wanted to leave Washington on February 23 at 4 A.M., which would put us on Grand Turk at about 8 A.M. By then, John Glenn's post-orbit testing and debriefings would be over and he would be ready to leave for the afternoon ceremony in Florida, where he would meet President Kennedy.

With all the pre-trip planning and finagling out of the way, I left my office at Andrews Air Force Base for home, planning to have an early dinner with Marie and the kids. I wanted to catch some sleep before heading back to base to get the JetStar ready for departure. We lived just a few miles from Andrews, and as I drove home the weather was clear and the winds were in our favor.

After dinner, I tried to unwind and enjoy time with my family. I was glad all the unnerving preparations were over. But the phone rang about 8 P.M. Major Joseph Lentine, my squadron operations officer, was on the line.

"Jim, have you checked the weather lately?" he asked.

I told him I had checked three or four hours ago, and the weather forecasters said it was going to be good.

"Look out the window," he said.

It had now been dark for several hours, and the blinds were closed over our sliding glass door in the dining room. I ran to the door and shoved aside the blinds. I couldn't see fifty feet, the fog was so thick. Lentine said the fog was going to last all night. He told me I should call Johnson and cancel the flight. Here we go again. The ride was getting bumpy, and we hadn't even taken off yet.

I called the weather office at Andrews. Things were worse than I thought. The officer said we were, indeed, stuck with this weather all night, and that the same clouds extended all the way past Atlanta, almost to Cape Canaveral. It was clear above 3,000 feet, but it didn't matter. In Air Force terms, it was zero-zero. Zero visibility and zero ceiling. Weather unfit for flying, the regulations said. The trip was off.

The only thing I could do was call Colonel Burris, the vice president's aide. He insisted that I be the one to phone Johnson at home and give him the news. Oh, shit. Burris had been on the receiving end of the infamous "Johnson treatment" plenty of times when the vice president didn't get his way. This time, Burris figured it was my turn.

I was sure I was going to get my "six o'clock position" chewed out by Johnson. When fighter pilots get on the tail of an enemy plane, they say they're locked on its "six o'clock." I wanted to save my six o'clock. But I was stuck in a trap between aviation rules and Johnson's temper.

Johnson lived at the Elms, the mansion he had bought from Perle Mesta, the well-known hostess to the capital city elite. Even though Johnson was vice president, his home phone number was listed in the Washington phone book, as was his daughters' separate number. I looked up the number—WO6-4030—and called, chewing my nails and hoping he wouldn't bite my head off. Johnson answered the phone himself with that drawn-out Texas "heh-lo" that I later came to know so well.

"Mr. Vice President, I have some bad news," I told him, bracing for an explosion. "The weather just stalled on us. It wasn't forecast. It was supposed to have been good all night, but here it is. If you look out the window, it's just awful."

"Yes, I can see it," he said. "What're our options?"

"Sir, I don't know. We could go, but the Air Force prohibits us from taking off in anything under a half-mile visibility."

"Well, what've you got out there?"

I tried to explain calmly. "It's absolutely zero-zero now. Zero ceiling. Zero visibility."

I could feel the rumblings of a coming explosion. Johnson reminded me I had told him earlier that good weather was predicted.

"Why the hell aren't you and these weather people better attuned to changing conditions?" Johnson asked, his voice rising. "You mean to tell me that you can't fly in this kind of weather?"

"I could make it," I told him honestly. "I've actually flown completely blind a lot of times, in practice and for real during World War II. But the Air Force won't let me go. Zero-zero conditions, no go."

The problem was not taking off in the pea soup. The problem would be if there were some sort of emergency necessitating an immediate landing. Getting down safely in the fog would be the tricky part. It was doable, but tricky and dangerous enough that Air Force regulations prohibited zero-zero takeoffs in non-wartime situations.

Johnson exploded. "Dammit, Major! LeMay told me that I could have anything I wanted! I don't know why in the hell it is, that every time I want to do something, you and all them damn colonels and generals over there won't let me have what I need and want. By God, you just pick up the phone and call General LeMay and call his hand. Tell him that I said I have to go and that he should let you take off."

I'd already pushed my luck once with LeMay, and it had cost me plenty of heat with my commander at Andrews. Now I had to do it all over again. To cover myself, I called Colonel Ireland, my wing commander who had forbidden me to call LeMay earlier. Ireland wasn't happy to hear from me. You can't go in this weather, he told me. And hell no, you can't call General LeMay. I hated to argue, but I had to.

"Now, look," I said, "the vice president told me to call General LeMay personally. I called you first, but I want you to know that I don't have any choice. I mean, after all, he's the vice president of the United States, and I don't want to defy the man. I'm kind of between a rock and a hard spot."

Ireland wasn't pleased. "Well, by God, you can't go and you won't go," he said. "We've got rules." Ireland might have been thinking that he would be the one who would have to face the heat if the plane went down and killed the vice president while taking off in prohibited weather conditions.

I hung up the phone in anguish. I knew I was going to catch unshirted hell no matter what I did. I had heard Johnson's fury was lethal enough to be in a category all its own, so I knew I'd have to disobey my colonel.

LeMay was at home, but his Pentagon aide patched me into the general's personal phone. I quickly explained my dilemma. "Well, I don't see any problem," LeMay said. "Can you make it?"

I told him I could do it. "I don't have any qualms about taking off. We've got good instruments, and I'm a good instrument pilot. I've got lots of experience, and I can do it. And the vice president insists that we do it."

LeMay didn't hesitate. "Well, just do it," he said.

I told the general I had just one concern. If I was to pilot this mission on this foggy occasion, I needed the absolute and unqualified moral support of the Air Force and its commanders. LeMay assured me I had his blessing and his full confidence.

By the time I called Colonel Ireland to inform him the trip was still on, he'd already heard. He was really sore about it. In fact, the whole unit was up in arms about the trip, and I was the focus of their anger.

By now, it was close to 11 P.M. I called the vice president back to fill him in. I shared the fact that a lot of people were still upset and did not want me to go. "Well, we're going to go if you think you can make it," he said. "What time should we leave?"

I told him we should leave quickly. If the fog worsened so I could not even see the runway lights, then I might change my mind about whether the flight could take off.

"Hell, no!" Johnson said. "Let's just get ready and go right now. You can just loiter along once we get up, and I can get a good nap on the way down."

A nap was the furthest thing from my mind. I was wide awake after all the hellish uproar. And I had to get to the base to get ready for the flight. I couldn't afford to have anything go wrong with this one.

The fog was the worst I'd ever seen. I couldn't even make out the runway from the hangar. But I knew I could get the eight-passenger JetStar into the clear after we were airborne. I had 300 hours of flying experience in the new Lockheed JetStars, and had logged 8,000 total flying hours in all types of airplanes. The Special Air Missions planes were so well maintained that I felt absolutely certain nothing would malfunction and require an emergency landing in the fog. If we encountered a truly grave emergency and had to come down in a hurry, I would not hesitate a moment to land back at Andrews or Dulles International Airport. We had the very latest all-weather flight instrumentation and the very best radio and radar equipment for navigation.

It took more than an hour for a Secret Service agent to drive Johnson from his home to Andrews through the foggy night. The agent drove right out to the airplane, and Johnson got out and tried to peer through the fog. As he walked up the ladder steps to the JetStar, he turned and looked at the fog again.

"Boy, it's pretty bad, isn't it?" he said. "You think we can make it?"

I assured him I could fly through the fog. But I couldn't even see through the fog to taxi to the runway. Fortunately, I had help. Colonel Ireland, who had calmed down by now, had been waiting at Andrews since LeMay cleared us for departure and had rigged up a solution to the fog. Ireland had commandeered one of the base's Ford station wagons that carried the big, illuminated "Follow Me" signs, and as soon as we started the JetStar's engines, he jumped into the station wagon and inched along in the fog just ahead of the plane, leading us down the taxiway. My co-pilot was Major Lentine, the squadron operations officer who first alerted me to the weather so many hours ago.

When we got to the runway, we had clearance to take off, of course. I doubt if any other plane on the Eastern Seaboard was even near a runway in this fog. We could just barely see two white runway lights on either side of the strip. We braced for takeoff by lining up our gyroscope compass and watching those two runway lights a few feet in front of us.

As I put the throttles to it, the two runway lights blurred into the next two runway lights fifty feet ahead. We gathered speed and saw two more lights, then two more. We just stayed between the lights and lifted off. We climbed with no problem, and within seconds the fog was out of sight. We were on top and in the clear.

Johnson was nowhere to be seen either. The minute he boarded the plane, he tossed off his overcoat, unbuttoned his shirt, and took off his pants. He pulled his pajamas from his bag and put them on. He seemed to have forgotten all about the fog. He headed straight for the tan couch in the passenger cabin. He put a pillow under his head, covered up with a blue regulation Air Force blanket, and slept through the entire flight.

I flew at 41,000 feet to keep the ride smooth for Johnson. I stayed above the clouds, avoiding turbulence and conserving fuel. Our hurried departure had put us ahead of schedule, so to avoid a night landing I held the JetStar at about 350 miles per hour instead of the usual 500-miles-per-hour cruising speed.

As we approached Grand Turk, dawn was just breaking. I could already see a crowd gathered at the little airport on the seven-mile-long island. We came in nice and easy, and I put the wheels down on the coral strip. Not as many bumps as I had figured. We arrived well ahead of our regular schedule. Johnson thanked me for the good flight, but didn't have much else to say as he went to eat breakfast in the mess hall at NASA's tracking station. He was the kind of fellow that, once he got what he wanted, well, that's what you were supposed to have done. No looking back.

When I taxied the JetStar into a parking space on the crowded strip, I realized that my best-laid plans to have a backup JetStar on hand were for naught. The pilot who had brought it in had mangled a wing tip against a parked car or plane when he was trying to taxi in a tight space among the other aircraft. The plane was worthless, and it was a good thing we didn't need it. My refueling plan, however, went off perfectly, and I got the JetStar fueled up and ready to head to Florida with Glenn and the vice president.

A crowd of about 200 islanders and some British dignitaries gathered at the airport to see the takeoff. Johnson did his usual professional job of working the crowd. For a few minutes, Glenn seemed to have been forgotten. But as they boarded the JetStar, the crowd let out a big "Hip, hip, hooray!" for the spaceman. Also along for the trip were NASA director Robert R. Gilruth and some other officials from the agency, who visited with Johnson and Glenn in the back of the plane as we flew to Florida, reliving the anxious moments of the orbital flight and the splashdown.

After a while, Glenn came up to the cockpit and sat in the jump seat for about thirty minutes. He talked about how much he loved flying airplanes. I was thrilled to be flying America's number-one hero. It was hard to imagine that he had just circled the earth three times and now sat in my cockpit like any other ordinary pilot. I couldn't stop asking him questions about the spaceflight, weightlessness, food, equipment, sights, and sounds. I wanted him to tell me everything. And he did. He told me he loved weightlessness, said he was hooked on it like a heroin addict was hooked on mainlining.

I asked him what the best part of the whole adventure had been.

"Well," Glenn said, "I'd just like to tell you that before the spaceflight we were puckered up. And worried. I'd not had a bowel movement for four or five days. But I just had a wonderful experience in the lavatory in the back of your airplane. I've left you a rather pungent souvenir."

Landing at Patrick Air Force Base and rolling up to the passenger terminal a few minutes later was an exhilarating experience I'll never forget. I was on top of the world. Not too many jobs are better than being able to bring home America's biggest space hero. A huge crowd was waiting for Glenn and roared its approval when he stepped onto the tarmac. Our job was done.

CHAPTER FOUR

JOINING THE INNER CIRCLE

THE MORE TIME I SPENT WITH THE MERCURIAL LYNDON Johnson, the more he revealed of himself. It wasn't long before I became a go-to guy. I guess he liked the way I parted what was left of my hair.

My new, more intimate role in his life became crystal clear when the extraordinary Eleanor Roosevelt died. The former First Lady's funeral was scheduled for November 10, 1962, in Hyde Park, New York, with burial at the Roosevelt estate. Of course, President and Mrs. Kennedy were going. They would fly on Air Force One to Stewart Air Force Base near the military academy at West Point. Former Presidents Harry Truman and Dwight Eisenhower also would attend the funeral. Johnson called to let me know he was going too.

"Now dammit, Cross," he said. "I don't want to get up there and get delayed by the president's plane. The president always gets air traffic control priority, and if we go to Stewart or anywhere around there, hell, air traffic controllers will let the president get off first. I've got to be back at the Elms at 5:30 tonight. Why don't you figure out someplace we can land so we won't be affected by Kennedy's airplane?"

It so happened that all the JetStars in our fleet had been temporarily grounded. A deficiency in the structural integrity of the tail section had to be repaired. Johnson would have to fly up in an older prop plane—a C-131 Convair. He wasn't happy about the slower airplane. He didn't like it any better when I told him I couldn't be his pilot. I hadn't flown the Convair in more than a year, so I was no longer qualified.

"Come along anyway," he said, "as liaison between me and the flight crew."

I thought we could land the vice president's plane, Air Force Two, in Poughkeepsie, New York. That airport was only about six miles south of Hyde Park, while Stewart Air Force Base was more than 20 miles down the Hudson River from the Roosevelt compound. I figured Johnson would have no trouble taking off first. I figured wrong.

I called my friend Air Force General William McKee, who had been head of the Air Force Logistics Command before his recent promotion to vice chief of staff under General LeMay. I told him of LBJ's concerns and asked whether Poughkeepsie would work. He agreed and promised to brief the air traffic controllers.

The vice president's Convair carried about eight of us to New York with him. One of the passengers was Johnson's Army aide, Colonel Bill Jackson, a good man. I stayed with the plane's crew when Johnson and his small entourage left for Mrs. Roosevelt's service. It had been raining, and the skies were bleak.

The rain fell again in earnest during the final minutes of Mrs. Roosevelt's interment in the family's garden cemetery. The presidents, the vice president, and other male guests were bareheaded, and it must have been miserable.

Johnson was supposed to return to the Poughkeepsie airport by helicopter, but driving rain turned the chopper back. A motorcade drove up to retrieve him, but it was still coming down hard. The crew and I were glued to the Secret Service radio. "He's five miles out," they told us, and we got everything ready to go. The crew started the engines as soon as Johnson drove up.

"Let's go!" he said in an irritated voice.

"Yes, sir," was all I could say.

We got to the runway but no farther. The air traffic controllers wouldn't let us go. Apparently someone didn't get things right. All planes in the area were grounded, but somehow Air Force One managed to slip out from Stewart Air Force Base. Johnson was steaming in the back of the plane.

I was still in the cockpit trying my best to find a way up and out of the mess when Colonel Jackson appeared. He was almost in tears. He'd been on the painful receiving end of the infamous "Johnson treatment" and was near the breaking point. He was even biting his nails.

"You've just got to go back there and talk to him," Jackson told me.

I walked to the rear cabin stateroom thinking, "It's my turn to face the music." Johnson was flat-out furious. He needed to be back home at the Elms to host a party celebrating the engagement of one of his secretaries, Geraldine Williams, who was going to marry newspaper journalist Robert Novak.

"Well, dammit," he said. "I thought you told me that we'd land over here at Poughkeepsie and Kennedy would land over there at Stewart Field and we'd be able to get out. Why is it that the vice president of the United States can't get a little priority once in a while?

"Why in the hell couldn't the air traffic control system let the president's plane take off in a westerly direction, my own plane to the east, then guide us both back to Washington at different altitudes?"

It was a question I could not have answered, so I didn't even try. Johnson didn't just spew his anger. He held me down while he did it. He sat in a big swivel chair in the VIP stateroom as I squatted next to him. His strong left hand held my right wrist. I couldn't get away; my knees were locked. I only managed a few "Yes, sirs" when there was a seconds-long break in the tirade. I guess he wanted me to feel as trapped as he felt. It worked. I felt like a roped calf.

As his temper finally cooled, he lapsed into a melancholy soliloquy as I remained frozen in a deep squat.

He told me Bobby Kennedy hated him. That he'd accepted the vice presidency only after JFK and then-House Speaker Sam Rayburn had insisted that Richard Nixon would win the White House if Johnson wasn't on the Democratic ticket. That the vice presidency was a nothing job; that he was tired of having to kiss everybody's ass, and that no one appreciated him. He said he was dreaming of life after the vice presidency. He reminded me that Mrs. Johnson owned television and radio stations and that they had sufficient funds to provide for their family so he needn't worry about a job.

"I should never have taken this damn job," he said. "Hell, when I get out of being vice president, I'm just going home to Texas. By God, they don't love me, and I'm just going home to my ranch."

It was the first of many times that Johnson unburdened himself to me. I realized I'd earned his trust with my discretion and loyalty.

My legs were numb by the time the weather cleared a little. Thankfully, I was rescued when a crewman came back to let me know we'd been cleared for takeoff. I was never so happy to get back to a cockpit.

IN MID-NOVEMBER 1963, I FLEW LBJ TO A NUMBER OF political appearances in the western United States. At 1 A.M. on November 20, we landed at his Texas ranch. Johnson told me to fly his JetStar back to

Washington and take a few days off. He planned to campaign with President Kennedy in San Antonio, Houston, Dallas, and Fort Worth, and then return to Washington on Kennedy's backup plane. He wouldn't be needing me in Texas. I made a quick hop to Bergstrom Air Force Base on the outskirts of Austin, and the crew and I rested until about noon the next day. Before flying off to Washington, I called the vice president to see if he had any new instructions. "No," he said, and his last words were, "I'll see you Monday, Major. God bless you."

I was in my office at Andrews AFB on Friday, November 22, catching up on paperwork. My wife, Marie, called about noon with news that my cousin, John C. Cross, and his family had dropped by. I had not seen those folks in more than fifteen years, so I headed home for a brief visit. My cousin, an Army master sergeant, was en route to Fort Dix, New Jersey, to be processed for duty in West Germany. We were enjoying a light lunch when the ringing of the telephone interrupted us. Special Air Missions Operations Sergeant Ken Johnson delivered the news: "Red Alert, Major. President Kennedy has been shot in Dallas, Texas. Everyone is to report to their place of duty immediately."

I rushed from the house, and by the time I got to my office, Walter Cronkite was reporting that President Kennedy was dead. We stayed on Red Alert for the next six hours or so. All of our airplanes were immediately fueled up and were ready to go. I was on standby in case I needed to pick up a dignitary or, God forbid, rush to a crisis scene. A Red Alert puts everyone in the military into immediate readiness. Bomber crews around the country were ready to go, foot soldiers were ready to get hauled off, everybody was ready to be deployed to a trouble spot. I remembered the Red Alert during the Cuban Missile Crisis a year earlier. But this was the first Red Alert with no visible enemy. We were operating under an imagined threat to the United States, possibly even World War III, and it was nerve-wracking. I just bit my nails and waited. Just waited.

"Oh, my God! What now?" I thought.

They released us while Air Force One was flying back to Washington with the new president. I figured he'd be glad to see a familiar face when he landed, so I decided to head to the flight line and meet the poor man. I was anguishing with him, and for him. But when he landed, I realized everything had changed. Hell, I couldn't get within 500 yards of the airplane because of tight security. He never even saw me. And I wasn't sure I'd ever see him again.

The assassination of John F. Kennedy changed Lyndon Johnson's life dramatically and forever. It changed mine, too.

I had been close to the vice president for a couple of years, and he was always accessible by phone. He often telephoned me personally to ask a question or send me on an errand. I didn't make a habit of calling him all the time, but I always knew I could phone him directly if I had an answer to one of his questions or wanted to ask him something. I figured all that access was a thing of the past. Now he was president and surrounded by a palace guard of advisers and bureaucrats. I doubted that I, a junior-ranking Air Force major, would ever again be as close to him. He was probably thinking, "I've got all these generals and admirals over here now, and that little major out there, what can he do for me?"

I'll admit I had visions of being the new Air Force One pilot. But as the days passed, I worried about being transferred to some obscure assignment. Maybe Thule Airbase in Greenland. Or, even worse, Diyarbakir Airbase in Turkey. I'd been there a time or two and sweated at the thought of returning to that hellhole. The officers above me had always been irritated about my relationship with Lyndon Johnson, so I figured they might gladly reassign me into oblivion.

I was pleasantly surprised, however, when the president called me at home in mid-December 1963. "Now, I want you to continue flying my Jet-Star," he said. "I also want you to get qualified in that big jet."

He told me he had asked the Defense Department to send me to school to get qualified in the Boeing 707 that was used most often as Air Force One. In reality, any plane carrying the president is considered to be Air Force One. Johnson told me I would be the understudy and co-pilot to Colonel James B. Swindal, who had been President Kennedy's pilot, until I was fully qualified to take command. That made my day.

But even during my term as understudy presidential pilot, Johnson expected me to troubleshoot any military matters that annoyed him, despite my having no authority to do so. He didn't care about procedure, protocol, or the chain of command when he wanted something done. He just wanted results, and he wanted them yesterday.

One day he ordered me to fire a general—and I was only a major.

The incident happened in late 1963, just weeks after the Kennedy assassination, when life was busy around the LBJ Ranch in Texas. The White House military office was making major improvements in communications, security, fire protection, ground transportation, and other areas to make the ranch more secure and comfortable for the new president. All the activity brought a lot of air and ground traffic in and out of the ranch.

Brigadier General Godfrey T. McHugh had been Air Force aide to President Kennedy and continued in that role for a short time with President Johnson. Johnson had had trouble with McHugh from the get-go. On the day Kennedy was shot, McHugh refused to take orders from Johnson aboard Air Force One when it was still parked at Love Field in Dallas. McHugh told Johnson that he answered to only one president. That was the beginning of the end for him.

One day just before Christmas, the general decided to fly to the LBJ Ranch to see how the improvements were going. He piloted an Air Force T-39 Sabreliner, a plane he was only marginally qualified to fly. His landing at the ranch runway was okay, but he promptly taxied off the parking ramp and buried the main landing gear in the mud. He was stuck. Eventually a crew had to be trucked 70 miles from Bergstrom to dig the plane out. And once they arrived, they had a solid eight hours of work ahead of them.

I was unfortunate enough to be close by when the president happened to drive by the airstrip. He blew his top when he saw the plane up to its belly in the mud. He asked me what the hell was going on. I think he thought I had something to do with the plane burying itself in his mud. I explained that General McHugh was the culprit. The president really exploded then. "Who the hell is he, and what's he doing on my ranch, anyway? Get him the hell off my ranch, and don't ever let him come back! You fire him!"

Well, obviously an Air Force major couldn't fire an Air Force general, and I really wasn't in a position to throw him off the ranch, either. But as luck would have it, there was a VC-140B JetStar loaded with brass and bureaucrats about to depart the ranch for Washington. I went to the general and explained that it would take hours for a team to get to the ranch from Bergstrom to dig his plane out, so perhaps he could save time by riding back to Washington on the JetStar. Another crew could fly his plane back to Washington when it was flyable. He took me up on the offer, and was probably happy to leave the embarrassment behind. It wasn't long before General McHugh left his position and retired from the Air Force. I never found out if he was pressured out, but I know I didn't have anything to do with his exit.

In early 1964, I attended the Trans World Airlines training school in Kansas City, a month of classroom instruction and two weeks flying the aircraft simulator. I came back to Andrews Air Force Base for actual flight training. By May, I was the president's primary co-pilot.

My transition to presidential co-pilot also caused problems for me with my pilot, Colonel Swindal. President Johnson felt a whole lot closer to me than he did to Swindal. He often wouldn't deal with Swindal. The president would come up to the cockpit, ignore Swindal, and say, "Now, Cross, I want you to do this." Swindal was a full-bird colonel, and I was a lowly major, so you can imagine how this went over.

A similar tense situation developed in the White House military office. The president sometimes went around the director and military aide, Major General Chester V. "Ted" Clifton, a holdover from the Kennedy administration. The president would call me at home in the middle of the night, and say, "Cross, I want you to call General Clifton and tell him I said this and I said that." That really put me on the spot. A major isn't supposed to call a general and tell him, "The president wants you to do this."

My wing commander at Andrews, Colonel Ireland, also resented my passing along orders from the president to reconfigure the inside of the JetStar, change the paint scheme on the presidential aircraft, and things like that. "Well, who do you think you are?" he would ask. "If the president wants that done, he ought to tell the Secretary of Defense." Of course, that wasn't the way Johnson operated. The president just told me something and expected the situation would be taken care of. At one point, Ireland tried to have me transferred out of the Special Air Missions wing, but the orders got canceled after Johnson intervened.

Co-piloting Air Force One during the 1964 presidential campaign was hectic and exhausting. We sometimes made as many as six stops in a single day. Johnson's hands looked like hamburger meat from the greetings and handshakes of so many well-wishers. The logistics were daunting: arranging for communications and parking accommodations for Air Force One, stairs to enter and exit the plane, ground power units, and motorcades for ground transportation, as well as making arrangements for the chartered press plane. It was all a blur, but the campaign rolled on without a hitch.

The day before the election in November 1964, we made our last stop— Bergstrom Air Force Base in Austin, Texas. General Clifton, the president's military assistant, told the flight crew to get plenty of rest because the president would not be going anywhere on Election Day, and would await the voting results in Austin.

"When the president gets the election results tonight, he's going to want to go back to the ranch," Clifton said. "Nine or ten o'clock, whenever the results are in. He'll go by helicopter, but you all stay loose. Everybody stay loose. We never know what he might do."

Colonel Swindal and I played golf at the Bergstrom course on Election Day morning, then spent the afternoon and early evening with friends at a cookout on Lake Austin. Thunderstorms cut the party short, but we didn't mind. It meant a second good night's sleep at the Hotel Gondolier on Town Lake in Austin. I was snoring before Goldwater even had conceded. The phone woke me at 11 P.M. It was Air Force Chief Master Sergeant Paul Glynn, the president's valet.

"The weather went sour," he said. "We're on our way to the airport right now. He wants you to fly him in his JetStar to the ranch."

I jumped out of bed and grabbed all the clothes I could find in the darkness. It was barely enough to make a uniform. I couldn't find one of my socks, my hat, or my necktie, and I didn't bother to tie my shoelaces. But I figured the president wouldn't notice. Technically, I was in violation of Air Force regulations and could have been reprimanded under Article Fifteen, but I knew that no one would report me. I raced to my rental car and made it to Bergstrom Air Force Base in minutes. I had already told Glynn to call the base and have them get the plane ready. At the base, I realized that Glynn had exaggerated. I had to wait for the president to arrive, but that was better than the other way around.

We launched into darkness and, with our superior weather radar, avoided the storms for an uneventful short hop to the ranch. When we landed, the president said, "Now, Major, from now on I want you to stay right here with this JetStar on this airstrip. You and your boys can stay up there at the Jordan place."

From that night on, whenever we flew to Bergstrom on the big Boeing 707 and he helicoptered to the ranch, I would always have the JetStar flown out to the ranch. It was always at the ready for him. I was too. I got to know the LBJ Ranch runway as well as I knew my own driveway at home.

FROM THE AIR, THE PRESIDENT'S TEXAS RANCH LOOKS sort of like a T-bone steak. The Pedernales River glistens along the southern boundary, and the paved airstrip slices the property at a right angle to the river, stopping just 300 yards or so from the water's edge. The two routes, one liquid and one asphalt, form an almost perfect T-head where the two worlds of Lyndon Johnson merged. The Pedernales nurtured his deep Hill Country roots; the runway brought the outside world to his doorstep.

The president's big plane, the customized Boeing 707 (VC-137-C) that most people know as Air Force One, never landed at the Texas ranch. The caliche soil under the runway was not stable enough to support the big plane.

That runway brought almost as much controversy and conjecture to the ranch as it did passengers. Everyone seemed to have an opinion about that sliver of asphalt. Some people griped that the government was providing Johnson with a private airport at taxpayer expense. Others saw a conspiracy in the navigational and radio equipment we added.

But as the man who flew the planes in and out of Johnson's ranch, I can tell you that the landing strip was absolutely necessary for allowing the president to carry out his official duties while in Texas. And I can assure you the runway was nothing fancy. Far from it. Landing a plane there was no picnic. It wasn't for beginners. It was a psychological challenge to land a jet airplane on that narrow airstrip.

The Johnson family home, known as the Texas White House, is only about 75 yards west of the southern end of the runway, near the Pedernales River. If we had ever tried to land a large plane coming from the north, it would have wreaked havoc on the garden, the swimming pool, and the pool house. I tried as often as possible to land to the north, away from the river and the family compound.

"Why do we always land uphill?" the president asked.

"Mr. President," I said, "if our brakes and reverse engine thrust ever malfunctioned, we might end up in the river."

My biggest headache with the landing strip was its peculiar hump in the center. The terrain rose 136 feet in the first two-thirds of the runway when landing from south to north, as we most often did. This climb also meant that when we landed in the opposite direction, from north to south, the runway seemed to sink at just about the point when a pilot expects to touch down. I had to be extremely careful. If I came over the crest and the plane was still floating and hadn't touched down, the runway seemed to fall out from under us. I had to keep going longer and longer, and keep floating and descending. I had to ease the pressure on the nose to allow it to set down a little quicker and cut the throttles a little more so I didn't run out of runway before touching down. If a pilot didn't time everything just right, he'd have to get on out of there, just lift back up and come around and try all over again.

The runway didn't always allow me to make a smooth-as-glass landing. People who have little knowledge about flying (and that included Lyndon Johnson) think a smooth landing is what counts. But what really counts is whether the pilot knows what to do in thunderstorms and when multiple planes are in the area. To hell with the landing. Any landing you can walk away from is a good landing.

I made sure I briefed every pilot coming into the ranch about the peculiarities of the runway. I required every plane to call in advance so I knew when it was due. Landing wasn't a piece of cake, I told them, but an experienced pilot could handle it. We had a good operation out there. Never had a mishap on my watch.

Another runway feature every pilot had to pay attention to was the narrow width and crown effect. The runway was only seventy-five feet wide. It sloped away to each side, which required pilots to keep a plane precisely on the center line while rolling to a stop. Deviation to either side of center would rapidly push a plane's momentum to one side or the other with possibly disastrous results.

The landing strip was a little short, too. The runway originally had been built in 1953 as a grassy strip. In the late 1950s, it was paved with asphalt and lengthened to 5,000 feet. When I began flying Vice President Johnson, the strip was just barely suitable for a plane the size of the JetStar.

A four-foot-high fence marked the south end of the landing strip, and a ten-foot embankment confined the north end, where numerous trees just added to the danger. There were no overruns at either end. That left little room for error in the JetStar. And Johnson didn't like me to turn the plane in the middle of the runway. He always insisted that I taxi to one end of the runway, turn around, and taxi back.

Soon after I became Johnson's pilot, I told him the runway needed improvement.

"We really ought to do something about that runway," I said.

"What do you want?" he asked.

He and I went to inspect the runway with my JetStar co-pilot, Paul Thornhill.

"We want the fences moved back," I said, "the trees cut down at the north and south ends, a 1,300-foot extension at the north end, and turn-arounds at both ends."

He agreed and ordered his ranch crew to make the improvements.

In 1963, the work was complete. We had a 6,300-foot-long airstrip that had been resurfaced and retrofitted with a turnaround pad at both ends. A helicopter pad was added near the north end, as well. It also had good lighting and minimal facilities for glide slope identification at night and in bad weather. It wasn't up to the standards of an international airport, but we could make instrument landings in rainy or overcast weather.

I finagled a mobile control tower out of the Air Force. Most Tactical Air Command bases had small, mobile towers for use in training pilots. They sat on the ends of the runways even though the bases had regular control towers to manage all the major traffic. The mobile tower on base had a pilot in it, and he monitored all air traffic. If he saw something unsafe, he could override the major tower.

I didn't want to spend any money to build a control tower at the Johnson ranch, so I got the military to donate a mobile tower. The tower was fully equipped with radios, weather vanes, rain gauges, and all the other

gadgets you need to run a small airport. All we had to do was plug everything in, and the radio channels came alive. As long as we weren't trying
to land day and night and in all kinds of weather like at Chicago O'Hare
or Dulles International Airport, the tower was perfect for our needs. We
didn't have radar, but we had a radio facility that a pilot could home in on
to make an instrument approach. Our minimums were 800 feet and two
miles. So, if pilots couldn't see 800 feet down to the ground and two miles
ahead, they'd have to land somewhere else.

We trained some controllers from the regular air traffic control force at
Bergstrom Air Force Base in Austin. And any time the president was at his
ranch, I would activate the tower so it could communicate with incoming or departing airplanes. The mobile tower was connected by telephone
"hot lines" to the Federal Aviation Agency control system. It also had lines
to the FAA weather station and the weather office at Bergstrom. We had
instant communication. Whenever Mr. Johnson or his family were flying
to the ranch, I would ask the Secret Service to inspect the runway before
we arrived and clear any debris. Ranch cattle that roamed the pastures
were the worst offenders. They often plopped their calling cards wherever
and whenever they pleased. The manure had to be removed quickly, or the
acids and salts would weaken the asphalt and cause it to crumble.

Johnson nearly shocked me out of my underwear one evening by men-
tioning the cow manure problem at a party. I had been part of a group
that spent the day with the then-vice president boating on Lake Granite
Shoals in the Texas Hill Country and later enjoying a barbecue dinner at
his lake house. With no warning, the president turned to Jesse Kellam, a
close confidant and the general manager of the Johnson family's television
and radio holdings in Austin.

"Jesse, Major Cross tells me your cows [emphasis on 'your'] have been
shittin' on his [emphasis on 'his'] runway," he said.

He told Kellam they were causing holes in the runway pavement.

"So forevermore, keep your cows off Major Cross's runway," he said.

I never considered it my runway, but Johnson did. He gave me control
over all decisions about maintaining that runway, and I called the shots
on whether it should be open or closed based on weather, nightfall, and
other factors.

The president had plenty of friends and visitors who flew private planes
directly to the ranch. But, in typical LBJ fashion, he always wanted them
to arrive on his timetable. Of course, he never wanted to show his control-
ling hand.

That's where I came in. I was the maestro of the air space.

My job was to cajole incoming guests into arriving at a specific time that was convenient to the president, but perhaps not for them. I guess you could say I was conducting a symphony of airplanes according to the tempo set by the president. If a Beechcraft or small jet was due to land at, say, 1 P.M., but the president had decided to go for a swim at that hour, I would stall the flight. I would get on the radio and try to be as polite and diplomatic as I could.

"Sir," I would ask the pilot, "I wonder if it would be convenient for you to come at 2 P.M., because we're going to have the runway closed." I would throw out a plausible excuse—cattle on runway, Secret Service inspection, and so forth. Quite naturally, the pilot would demur and agree to delay arrival. As far as I know, my hoodwinking was never discovered.

Of course, the runway may or may not actually have been closed. Sometimes, the president was just driving up and down the runway in his Lincoln convertible. He'd put on a favorite beret, get behind the wheel, and take off like he was on a scenic highway.

Every plane that landed at the ranch had to receive advance permission from me. I controlled use of the airfield by publishing what was called a NOTAM, a Notice to Airmen, in all the major flight publications. Pilots had to call the ranch switchboard, which forwarded the calls to the military aide's office. I worked out of a trailer next to the Johnson home that served as an office, command post, and my sleeping quarters.

Transient planes flying over the area were prohibited from coming within a two-mile radius of the ranch. The president didn't want any Sunday afternoon fliers coming over to look or land uninvited. A time or two, a plane landed because the pilot claimed he was out of fuel or in mechanical difficulty. Of course, we never closed the runway to an airplane in trouble.

We never had a security breach at the landing strip. Every plane that landed was met personally by me or by someone on my staff. If the plane carried a VIP, I made sure I was there to meet it. A lot of times, the president didn't show up to meet guests until I had already welcomed them to the ranch. I didn't want any VIP guest to get off an airplane without someone standing there to say, "Good morning." I also watched the luggage to make sure that all visitors' bags were handled properly and delivered to the residences without getting lost.

The Secret Service always showed up for each landing, too. The only way someone in a plane could have caused mayhem was if he had been willing to sacrifice his own life by crashing directly into the LBJ Ranch house. And chances were, a suicide pilot wouldn't find the president at home. Of course, in the middle of the night, the president would be in his bed. But at night, we shut the runway lights off so the ranch was more difficult to see from the air. We kept the lights on only when we were expecting a plane. Johnson didn't like the runway lights for many reasons. He thought they were wasteful, and he didn't want them serving as a beacon for any pilot who happened to fly over. I never worried about a plane doing bodily harm to the president. I never even considered the possibility. It was a different world back then.

CHAPTER FIVE

ANGEL IS AIRBORNE

"CROWN, THIS IS ANGEL, OVER."

"Roger, Angel, this is Crown, go ahead, over."

"Roger, Crown, Angel is airborne. Over."

Whenever that momentous call crackled across the airways from Air Force One, the flying White House had just lifted into the sky from some airport in the world and was on its way to a place where the president of the United States had urgent diplomatic or political business to conduct. "Angel" was the code name identifying the presidential aircraft. "Crown" was the code name for the White House.

None of the Air Force One trips I flew or arranged for Lyndon Johnson was routine. His pace and personality made each flight indelible, and last-minute changes were never unexpected. The human commotion was worse than any atmospheric turbulence.

Many of our air trips have a special place in my memory. Johnson wasn't aboard the aircraft on some of them, but he choreographed each and every one.

In June 1965, Ed White and James McDivitt were the two biggest heroes in the United States. The two Air Force lieutenant colonels orbited the earth 62 times in their *Gemini 4* capsule, and White captivated a live TV audience in the millions when he became the first American to walk in space. His twenty-two-minute adventure was broadcast around the world. After the four-day mission ended with a successful splashdown, the astronauts went on a week-long, parade-filled nationwide tour. At the end, the astronauts and their wives flew to Andrews Air Force Base and helicoptered to the White House lawn. They lunched with Vice President Hubert Humphrey and congressional leaders, rode in another parade, and were scheduled for a gala reception at the State Department that would climax with a movie of their flight. Then, at the invitation of Lady Bird Johnson, they were to spend the night at the White House, winding down and relaxing.

At least that was the way the night was supposed to end. But the president rewrote the script.

The president had been watching the Soviets steal the spotlight all week at the Paris Air Show, and he wasn't happy. Executives from the American aerospace industry had been calling and telling him the lackluster American pavilion was ignored by the crowds that instead thronged to see Soviet cosmonaut Yuri Gagarin, the first man in space. Gagarin even brought his spacecraft and stood beside it shaking hands with anyone who wanted to meet him. In addition, the Soviets displayed what was the world's largest transport plane. We were getting a major-league shellacking in the Cold War propaganda front.

The president did a slow burn for a few days, then decided he had to do something spectacular if he wanted to upstage the Soviets. He came up with the idea of flying the astronauts and their wives to Paris and making a grand entrance. They'd steal the Soviets' thunder and capitalize on all the hoopla surrounding the spacewalk. NASA administrator James Webb was lukewarm to the idea. He feared French president De Gaulle wouldn't take kindly to the uninvited visit. He thought the trip might be criticized as a cheap publicity stunt and take away from all the positive vibes already generated worldwide by the spacewalk.

But Webb didn't have a chance once the president got him on the phone. The first words out of the president's mouth were "Jim, why can't these astronauts go to the Paris Air Show?" When Webb tried to explain that the Paris Air Show represented "something really big" for De Gaulle, Johnson interrupted. "Well, we don't give a damn. I just want to make something big for the United States. I don't care if they [the astronauts] go to the German Air Show, too. We are in such damn bad shape in the world that we ought to take anything we can." The president noted the negativity surrounding the Vietnam War and its casualties. "I'm getting them killed in Vietnam by the dozens," he said. The air show trip would bring a welcome blast of good publicity.

Webb still thought a razzle-dazzle assault on Paris would be "moving too fast." And besides, he gently argued, the astronauts were needed in the United States for debriefing, and were awfully tired.

Johnson would have none of that. "What's wrong with the astronauts going to the goddamn air show?" he asked, losing patience. He said he wanted to impress "two or three fat congressmen" visiting in Paris, "get their goddamn minds off the air show and see what America is doing in the world." The president said he would supply Air Force One for the trip, and Webb could even sleep in his bed. He told Webb to tell his wife to "get your gown, put on some perfume, and let's go get in the president's bed." And there would be room in the back of the plane for the astronauts to stretch out, too. "This is Thursday, you can be back on Sunday." He told Webb to make plans to go, "unless you've got something more important or you're dead and don't want to go."

Webb, folding as he got the "Johnson treatment" full-blast, told the president he loved him. "You know I'll do anything for you," he said. "Goddamn it, then quit debating with me," Johnson said, "and get ready and let's go."

Everything was at warp-speed now. The president got me on the phone and told me to fire up Air Force One. I mustered up a flight crew and prepared a flight plan for Paris. The president headed to the State Department. Before a packed house of foreign diplomats and high-ranking U.S. officials, the astronauts were showing a twenty-minute movie of their flight. Suddenly, there was a flurry in the back as Secret Service agents entered and stationed themselves along the sides of the auditorium. The president, wearing a brown tuxedo, entered through the rear doors, walked to the front row, and squeezed into a space that was made for him between Webb and Vice President Humphrey.

When the presentation was over, Johnson stood up and drawled that he might have promoted the astronauts to full colonel had he known how good the movie was. When the applause and laughter died down, he shocked everyone in the room except Webb when he told White and McDivitt, "Gentlemen, I want y'all to go to Paris as quickly as possible and take your lovely wives with you." The astronauts looked at each other like they couldn't believe what they heard. Then the president looked at Humphrey and Webb and said, "Hubert, you go along with them, and you go too, Jimmy. Take your wives. You can use my airplane."

Things really moved fast. State Department photographers snapped passport photos while the astronauts and their wives were greeting the diplomats in a receiving line. Passports were hastily prepared for everyone who needed one. The astronauts and their wives were rushed to the White House for a pre-flight nightcap. Patricia McDivitt and Patricia White both pleaded that they had nothing to wear because they hadn't planned on flying to Paris. No problem, the president said, they could borrow clothes from Lady Bird, Luci, and Lynda Bird. And Luci and Lynda even volunteered to babysit the astronauts' children at the White House. The two Patricias headed for White House bedrooms where they were hastily fitted with traveling clothes. Meanwhile, Humphrey, Webb, and other dignitaries making the trip assembled at the White House. Helicopters carried the party in the middle of the night to Andrews, where I waited with Air Force One. As the helicopters lifted off, Lynda and Luci stood on the White House lawn in their nightclothes with the astronauts' children waving good-bye.

We finally left Andrews about 4 A.M. Upon touching down that afternoon in Paris, I deliberately taxied and parked Air Force One near the gigantic Antov AN225 Soviet transport that had been getting all the attention. It was sort of my own attempt at Cold War one-upmanship, and I think our arrival took the shine off that big red bird.

De Gaulle reportedly was miffed that he had received so little warning that the vice president and the astronauts were on the way. But the visit was a huge success anyway. White and McDivitt were real troupers; both had bad colds, and neither had slept much during the flight over. But you wouldn't have known it. They worked the crowds, gave lectures, appeared on French TV, and posed for pictures with Yuri Gagarin. They got so many phone calls on a radio talk show that the Paris telephone exchange was shut down. By the end of the visit, De Gaulle, who at first had refused to meet with Humphrey and the astronauts, invited them to the presidential palace for an audience.

Humphrey bubbled even more than usual when he later briefed the president. "We had a wonderful trip. It was just fine. My goodness. We had an excellent reception, and I think the two astronauts did themselves up nobly." As for me, the trip was one of the most enjoyable I ever flew while working for the president. I consider autographed portraits of Ed and Jim and Vice President Humphrey to be among my most prized mementos.

In a sad postscript, Ed White died on January 27, 1967, when a fire erupted during a routine test of the *Apollo 1* spacecraft at Cape Kennedy. Astronauts Gus Grissom and Roger Chaffee also perished. Ed was only thirty-six. He would have been among the first three astronauts to launch the *Apollo* moon mission. I was the one who had to tell the president the sad news after the National Military Command Center in the Pentagon found me. "Oh, my God!" the president said. We'd lost friends as well as national treasures. A few days later I accompanied Lady Bird Johnson to White's funeral and burial at West Point, his alma mater.

A FEW WEEKS LATER, ON JULY 19, 1965, MY GLUTEUS MAXIMUS received the worst fire and flack I would ever get from the president. The occasion was a trip to take him and his official entourage to the funeral of Adlai Stevenson, the 65-year-old U.N. ambassador who had dropped dead of a heart attack on the streets of London on July 14.

Colonel Swindal was still serving as Air Force One pilot, so I made the trip as co-pilot. I was also in charge of all planning and logistics for the flight to Central Illinois, where Stevenson would be buried in his hometown of Bloomington.

The Bloomington Airport runway couldn't accommodate the Boeing 707 (Air Force One) or the JetStar, so I had to come up with an alternate solution. I spent almost all weekend making arrangements and writing proposals. We could land the big presidential jet at Chanute Air Force Base in Rantoul, Illinois, 50 miles southeast of Bloomington, or at the airport in Springfield, 65 miles to the southwest. Or we could put down at the airport in Peoria, 40 miles northwest of Bloomington. The president would decide. Once we landed the presidential plane, we could get to Bloomington either by helicopter or in a C-47, which seats about fifteen passengers. Chanute AFB had two C-47s that could make the 25-minute flight to Bloomington. Helicopters would make a faster trip, but we would have to bring them in advance from Washington.

The president had an entirely different idea. He wanted me to send a VC-131 Convair to Chanute. He thought the helicopters were uncomfortable and expensive to operate, and he wanted to bring about 40 people, far more than one C-47 could hold. In the end, though, the helicopters were chosen for the short hop to save time.

The president and Mrs. Johnson had spent the weekend before the funeral at Camp David with more than a dozen guests, including the author John Steinbeck and his wife. The Steinbecks would be accompanying the entourage to Bloomington. I joined the guests at the presidential retreat on Sunday, but was so busy coordinating all the loose ends that I hardly considered it a "retreat." We left Camp David on three of the presidential helicopters early Monday morning for the funeral. The helicopter carrying Lady Bird, Luci, and the Steinbecks left first in order to stop at the White House to pick up Supreme Court Justice Arthur Goldberg and his wife. Goldberg, who had been on the high court for just three years after serving as President Kennedy's Secretary of Labor, would be Johnson's choice to replace Stevenson as ambassador to the United Nations. And Goldberg would be in for some big-time LBJ arm-twisting on this ride.

We left Andrews Air Force Base on Air Force One at 9:21 A.M. and landed an hour and a half later at Chanute Air Force Base. It took just minutes for us to divide up among three helicopters for the quick hop to Bloomington. There, the president was met and greeted by Stevenson's eldest son, Adlai Stevenson III, and Vice President Hubert Humphrey. Humphrey had gone to London to accompany Stevenson's body back home. Several hundred mourners and onlookers had gathered as well.

The president's motorcade stopped first at Stevenson's three-story boyhood home, where his sister, Elizabeth "Buffie" Ives, lived. The streets were lined with crowds, and the police had trouble keeping the camera-toting onlookers roped off. The president and Mrs. Johnson paid their respects for about thirty minutes while the rest of us waited in the cars outside.

There were thousands of people everywhere trying to catch a glimpse of the president and coming out to show their devotion to Stevenson, their former governor and two-time Democratic presidential nominee. By the time the motorcade started to head for the Unitarian Church on the edge of town, the traffic was horrible. We got caught in the damnedest traffic jam I've ever seen. The president and a few of the lead cars made it through, but the car I was riding in with White House Chief of Staff Marvin Watson couldn't keep up with the motorcade. We got trapped in the back, and the presidential cars got away. We figured we'd never make it to the church on time and worried even more about getting through the traffic back to the Bloomington airport. We had to be there when the president came back or we would be left behind. We decided to ditch our plans to attend the funeral and the interment and hightail it back to the tarmac. As things turned out, we had plenty of time because the president and Mrs. Johnson went back to Mrs. Ives's home for lunch after the service at the cemetery.

The helicopters took us back to Chanute, and we lifted off in Air Force One at 2:30 P.M. That's when my real work began.

The president, as usual, had offered several folks a ride back to Washington aboard Air Force One. Our new passengers included Governor Edmund "Pat" Brown of California, Secretary of Labor Willard Wirtz, U.S. Court of Appeals Judge Carl McGowan, Senator Paul Douglas of Illinois, and several House members: Representative James Roosevelt of California and Representatives Roman Pucinski and Sidney Yates of Illinois. The Steinbecks and the Goldbergs rounded out the VIP list.

We had forty-one passengers. With that many high-powered guests on board, I knew transportation could be a problem when we landed at Andrews in ninety minutes. I called ahead to make sure we had plenty of helicopters and limousines lined up. The Marine One helicopter would be at the back of the plane for the president, who usually deplaned from the rear door, and two other helicopters would be waiting at the front door. A fleet of cars was parked between the choppers. Some passengers needed to return to the White House; others were headed to Capitol Hill and beyond.

The president always expected everything to run flawlessly, and I was determined to make sure it did. I thought I had the perfect plan, so I pulled a stack of 3 × 5 index cards out of my briefcase and handed them to my assistant, Major Hugh Robinson. "Go back there and make out a card for every single passenger on this airplane," I told him. "Then check with the president as to who should ride on what helicopter or in what car. Give each passenger a card with their assignment and instructions as to where their ride will be sitting on the tarmac parking ramp at Andrews Air Force Base."

Robinson and the president put their heads together. "This fellow and this fellow and this fellow are going with me," the president said. "And this one is going to the Capitol." They ran through the entire passenger manifest, and Robinson wrote on each little white card a passenger's name along with instructions on which staff car or helicopter to enter. The index cards were passed out before we landed. The card system may seem like excessive direction, but we had to do it that way. Otherwise, some of those passengers would have been totally mixed up. No matter how high people rise in life's political echelons, some can't even find the door of the plane. I'd seen it happen over and over.

When we touched down at Andrews, I was ready to spring into action. I jumped from my pilot seat and scrambled down the steps to the tarmac, and I do mean fast. I was going to personally direct passengers to the appropriate helicopter. I didn't want anyone wandering around with no sense of where to go. But as the passengers left the plane, the index cards they handed me didn't match my master list of which guest was to go where. Nothing added up. It was as if all the cards had been thrown up in the air and reshuffled. The passengers kept coming so fast I couldn't make sense of the mess. I was the one confused and in need of direction.

Then it hit me. The president had changed his mind at the last minute. As he left the plane, he evidently told some of his friends, "Well, you come on and go with me back to the White House." The unforeseen changes screwed things up beyond imagination, and there I was rushing around like a house on fire trying to direct people—and I lost the battle. The domino effect took over: There were just sixteen seats on each of the helicopters, so when you change one seat assignment, you just screwed up two or three others on the other chopper. You change two seat assignments, then everything goes to hell in a bucket. It was like a Manhattan intersection with the traffic lights malfunctioning and a tourist trying to direct traffic.

And then—God forbid—I looked up and saw the president. He had left Air Force One through the rear door and was on board Marine One. He was sitting in the swivel chair by the helicopter's big window and mouthing the words, "Come here!" He was madder than a hornet. "Damn it, Cross. I don't know why in the hell it is that you Air Force colonels can screw things up like this. Why can't you learn to do things right? Now, if you can't get this mess straightened out—by God—I'll find somebody who can."

He stayed in my face for what seemed like a full minute. In all of my eleven years serving Lyndon Johnson, it was the worst butt-chewing I ever endured. And it all happened in front of Justice Goldberg, Senator Douglas, Judge McCowan, Governor Brown, and Secretary Wirtz, no less! No one said a word. It was perfectly quiet after the president finished with my "six o'clock." Of course, I was thoroughly humiliated and suspect that was just what the president wanted. Some of the guests felt sympathy for me—I could see it in their eyes and facial expressions.

The helicopter flight crew closed the exit doors, so I had nowhere to go. I was a prisoner to the president's temper. I couldn't get off the bird, much as I would have liked, so I went to the back of the chopper and sat down on the floor. There wasn't a seat back there, but that made no difference to me. As we flew back to the South Lawn of the White House, all I could think of was that my career was likely finished. I just sat there on the floor with no seatbelt and suffered my disappointment. Happily, the president never mentioned that instance of my dereliction again, and within a few days I received a nicely autographed presidential photo from him.

JOHNSON WAS AS SURPRISED AS ANYONE WHEN ONE OF HIS planes brought the most famous comedian in Mexico to his Texas ranch in early 1966. But he didn't seem to mind. It was a mission of mercy.

The president and those of us in his large entourage were spending the New Year holiday at the ranch that year. Romance was in the air—and in the newspapers. The engagement of Luci and Pat was still big news, and

Lynda Bird had just returned from a four-day trip to see a boyfriend in Wyoming. She had been back at the ranch less than a day when actor George Hamilton flew in from Paris to accompany her to a New Year's Eve party. On New Year's Day, Lynda and Hamilton flew to New Orleans for the Sugar Bowl football game. The president loved seeing his daughters so happy.

Politics, though, was uppermost in Johnson's mind. He was troubled that Senator Paul Douglas, an Illinois Democrat, wanted to retire. Liberal Republican Charles Percy was gunning for that Senate seat, and the president was determined that it would remain in Democratic hands. The professorial Douglas had been relaxing in Oaxaca, Mexico, for more than a month, using the vacation to work on his book, *In Our Time*. Johnson knew the senator had been trying to see him about several issues, including the location of a new atomic accelerator. But Johnson was more worried about the recent price hike by Bethlehem Steel Corporation, the nation's second largest steel producer. The president feared the price hike could lead to inflation and affect the war effort in Vietnam. Douglas was an Ivy League–educated economist, and Johnson needed his advice.

Johnson phoned Douglas in Oaxaca at about 6:30 P.M. on New Year's Day and invited him to the ranch. "If you'd like to," Johnson said, "I could send my plane down to pick you up tonight or early in the morning, early in the morning probably, and you might come up and have lunch with me.

"You know Bethlehem has raised this damn steel price on me . . . I wish, though, I could talk to you about this steel thing now."

Douglas agreed and the president told me to send his JetStar. Lady Bird's older brother, Tony Taylor, was spending the holiday at the ranch with his wife, and Johnson volunteered him to go to Mexico to pick up Douglas. Taylor ran an import trading business in Santa Fe, spoke fluent Spanish, and was a frequent traveler to Mexico. He agreed to go. He liked the president and had campaigned for him in 1964 in Texas towns along the Mexican border, where large numbers of Spanish-speaking voters lived.

I would not be making the trip. As usual, the president wanted me nearby. I was stuck at the ranch, even though my family was celebrating the holiday with my wife's parents in Austin, seventy miles away. I assigned Major Donald Short, one of my co-pilots. The JetStar at the ranch was what I liked to call the Air Force One of the JetStar fleet. It was painted just like the big 707 and even had the presidential seal on it.

The JetStar left the ranch early on January 2. It must have been a beautiful flight, because Taylor later described it as a once-in-a-lifetime experience. "I've never seen such a sight in my life," he said.

"I remember very well we left before dawn, and just as we got over Vera

Cruz, at a terrific altitude [we saw] all the great peaks of Mexico standing up and the rays of the sun hitting the mountains. I felt a bit like an
astronaut.

"There was Citlaltépetl in the foreground, Iztaccíhuatl and Popocatépetl
in the background, which must have been more than 250 miles from Vera
Cruz."

Lady Bird had admonished her brother not to pick up any "stray Mexi-
cans" on the trip because she knew he always bumped into friends and
acquaintances on his business trips south of the border. "Okay, I won't,"
Taylor told her.

He did end up running into a lot of friends in the Oaxaca airport, where
he picked up Senator Douglas and his wife, Emily. And a couple who was in
some kind of trouble noticed that Taylor spoke Spanish and begged him to
give them a lift to Mexico City, where the JetStar had to refuel. "Well, Senator Douglas is in charge. You ask the senator about that," Taylor told them.

"Yes, you may go to Mexico City," Senator Douglas said, obviously unafraid of any repercussions from Johnson for the spontaneous gesture.

A bigger surprise awaited them in Mexico City. In the airport, Taylor
was approached by one of Mexico's most famous citizens: Cantinflas, the
beloved comic actor famous for playing the loyal valet to Phileas Fogg in
Around the World in 80 Days. Cantinflas's real name was Mario Moreno
Reyes. He was a small man with big ears who was beloved for his slap-
stick comedy and rapid-fire gibberish. He was known as the "Mexican
Charlie Chaplin" because of his trademark mustache and disheveled cos-
tume—baggy pants that always fell down and a little cap cocked atop his
wayward hair.

Taylor knew his brother-in-law liked and admired Cantinflas because
he had heard the president mimic the actor's trademark broken English. I
had met Cantinflas several times when he and the president attended the
same events. I always figured that Johnson identified with Cantinflas, a
man who had been born in a slum and had risen to worldwide fame and
fortune through the sheer force of his personality and talent. Both men
could light up a room, but each sought comfort away from the limelight in
working a cattle ranch. Cantinflas had a 1,000-acre spread in Mexico.

Cantinflas was in a panic because his wife of twenty-nine years, Valentina, was gravely ill. Valentina was a pretty, blonde Russian dancer
who had met Cantinflas in the variety tent shows that traveled through
Mexico in the 1930s; it was she who had pushed him into films. Sadly, she
was in the last stages of cancer. They were traveling with a doctor to get
top-notch medical treatment at the renowned Scott & White Memorial

Hospital in Temple, Texas, about sixty miles north of Austin. Cantinflas, a multi-millionaire, owned and piloted his own plane, but it had just been grounded by engine trouble. He pleaded with Taylor to allow his wife and their small party to fly to Texas. This time, Taylor didn't ask permission from Senator Douglas. Lady Bird's warning against picking up passengers echoed in his mind, but he ignored it. "Come aboard," he said. Major Short knew there could be questions about using a U.S. Air Force plane to bring in foreign nationals on an unauthorized mission, but his compassion overruled his reservations. "Doggone it, this is something that's for a human being," he thought. "Damn the regulations." I was proud of him for pushing through the red tape and would have been disappointed if he had not.

Once airborne, Cantinflas realized that in his haste to find emergency transport for his wife, he had forgotten the necessary papers for travel into the United States. "Oh, let's go get our papers," he told Taylor. But Taylor, knowing the president would be more than able to smooth over any international travel violations, waved him off.

"Your papers won't be necessary," he told Cantinflas. "The president would like to have you for lunch, and I see that your wife isn't well. I'm sure we can arrange those papers."

Once Major Short became airborne in Mexico City, he called me and I alerted customs and immigration authorities. They sent agents by car to the LBJ Ranch, where we had no problems clearing the Cantinflas party into the United States. The president and Mrs. Johnson urged them to come in and rest a while and have lunch. Cantinflas politely declined, opting instead to leave immediately aboard President Johnson's personal Beech Queen Aire for the clinic in Temple. The president phoned Scott & White on behalf of the comedian's wife, saying, "Mrs. Moreno will be arriving shortly, and I hope you will do everything in your power for her."

It was wonderful to see everyone jump into action with such compassion. Here was a woman who was dying of cancer, and why shouldn't the president of the United States, and the U.S. Air Force, extend a hand of friendship to someone as beloved as Cantinflas? After all, it was the president who would have to take the heat, and it certainly didn't seem to bother him. Unfortunately, despite our interventions, Mrs. Moreno died in the Temple hospital just three days later.

I WISH I COULD HAVE TAMED THE WEATHER FOR ALL OF our trips on Air Force One. Our skies were mostly smooth, but once in a while we tangled with weather so bad even the songbirds were grounded. President Johnson didn't flinch at such moments, but Mrs. Johnson and her press secretary, Liz Carpenter, were white-knuckle fliers.

Liz always sent word to the cockpit when she was frightened. During one storm, my assistant, Major Haywood Smith, came up front and said, "Jim, ole Liz is worried to death back there. What are you going to do?"

I said, "We're doing everything we can."

He returned to the cabin, and Liz asked, "What's going on up there?"

Smith told her, "I don't know. There wasn't anybody up there."

A real stomach tosser hit us on a night flight on February 16, 1966. I was a passenger, because the president was flying to Atlantic City in one of the four new $1 million VC-131 Convair prop-jets the Air Force had overhauled at his insistence for the Special Air Mission fleet at Andrews. I wasn't qualified to fly it, but the president wanted me aboard. He was speaking to the American Association of School Administrators. Our VIP guests included most of the New Jersey congressional delegation and the Reverend Billy Graham, who was staying over at the White House.

We left Andrews AFB outside Washington at 5:12 P.M. for the thirty-one-minute flight. The weather was marginal in Atlantic City, but we made the trip anyway, with the hope and assumption that it would clear and allow us to land. The sky was shrouded in clouds. I was up front with the pilot, Major Fred Hemm, but we weren't sure we could land. Clouds and fog enveloped us. We needed to be able to see the ground from 200 feet above and a half-mile ahead in order to safely land. Those were the authorized cloud ceiling and visibility minimums for landing.

I headed back to the president's compartment to tell him we might have to pull up and go around and perhaps return to Washington. But as I walked by Reverend Graham, he reached out and grabbed my arm.

"Jim, I'm worried about this weather," he said.

"Well, don't be alarmed," I said. "You don't see me being frightened, do you, Reverend?"

"Well, would you sit with me?" he asked.

"Of course I will, Billy," I said, "but first I have to go back and speak with the president for a moment."

Johnson was in his cabin visiting with the twelve New Jersey congressmen and Senator Harrison Williams. "We might make it; we might not," I said. The president wasn't concerned; his speech was not scheduled until 8 P.M.

I hurried back to Reverend Graham and took the spot next to him.

"Would you hold my hand?" he asked.

"Sure," I said.

He began to pray, and I bowed my head. I'd been raised in the Pleasant Home Baptist Church in rural Alabama, so his prayers were familiar. I kept to myself my wonderment that a man of God would be concerned about mortality on this bumpy night. I was humbled beyond words that such a world-renowned disciple of God felt more secure and safe with the president's regular pilot sitting confidently by his side.

We circled once over the socked-in airport, and the air traffic controller approved our attempt to land using the Instrument Landing System. Hemm broke into the clear, saw the runway center line lights straight ahead, and touched down so smoothly that I don't think the president or his VIP guests even realized we'd landed.

The chartered civilian plane carrying the White House press corps made one pass at landing but didn't make it in. Weather can change in a split second. The press didn't like spending a couple of hours bumping around in a murky sky without getting a story to write. So several reporters wrote news articles that suggested Air Force One had made an unsafe landing.

"Ceiling Is Low for Johnson Landing," read the *New York Times* headline two days later.

"As far as persons on the ground could tell, the plane came in 'on little cat feet' like the fog in Sandburg's poem and was not seen or heard until it had started taxiing toward the administration building," said the February 18 article by Joe Loftus.

The article reported that the Atlantic City tower said Air Force One had landed with a cloud ceiling of only 100 feet and visibility of one-quarter of a mile. "The White House today quoted the president's military aide, Lt. Colonel James U. Cross, as saying that the ceiling was 300 feet and visibility was one-half to three-quarters of a mile."

It went on to say, "Reminded that the field had been closed to commercial aircraft, Colonel Cross said 'weather is a very perishable commodity.'"

The article was garbage. I never did anything to endanger the life of Lyndon Johnson, his family, his friends, or any other passenger aboard Air Force One. And every other pilot in our special unit, including Major Hemm, was eminently qualified and adhered to the highest possible safety standards. Our safety record was spotless, and it remains so today. There has never been an accident or a fatality in that elite Special Air Mission (SAM) unit in more than sixty years of operation. What would a world-class commercial airline give to have such a spotless record?

ANGEL WAS SOMEWHERE OVER THE NORTH ATLANTIC flying toward West Germany for the funeral of former German Chancellor Konrad Adenauer when President Johnson got the idea that we had forgotten someone.

It was April 23, 1967, and Adenauer had died three days earlier at the age of ninety-one. He was the first chancellor of postwar West Germany and the man most responsible for getting that country up and running after its almost complete destruction during World War II. Not only was he one of the most important world leaders of the twentieth century, but he was also an old acquaintance of the president. We had a full complement of dignitaries on board for the flight to Germany: Secretary of State Dean Rusk; General Lucius Clay, the former governor of the U.S. zone in West Germany and the mover behind the Berlin Airlift; labor leader George Meany; and former CIA director Allen Dulles, who had major expertise on Germany. The West German ambassador to the United States, Heinrich Knappstein, was also on board.

But in the midst of all those big guns, the president's thoughts turned to an old friend from the Hill Country. Father Wunibald W. Schneider, born in Bavaria in 1907, had realized his boyhood dream of becoming a Catholic priest after years of working as a gardener in England, Germany, and Switzerland. He was caught in Ireland by the outbreak of World War II in Europe in 1939. He spent eleven years there before finally going to Rome and becoming ordained as a priest at age forty-seven. His German background led to an assignment in the United States, where he was sent to the Hill Country of Texas. In 1954, he arrived in Fredericksburg, a historic town near the LBJ Ranch that was settled by German immigrants. As part of his Fredericksburg ministry, he also was the priest at St. Francis Xavier Catholic Church in Stonewall, just a stone's throw from the Johnson ranch. And that's where he was to cross paths with Johnson. Johnson wasn't Catholic, but he attended the church occasionally when he had Catholic friends staying at the ranch. He met the priest in the mid-1950s, when Johnson was in the Senate. They formed a lasting friendship that continued after Johnson became vice president and president. Father Schneider routinely got dinner and barbecue invitations to the ranch, some on short notice. So he became accustomed to the president's way of doing business—often last-minute, but always with a flair.

In 1961, Adenauer visited the United States when he was still chancellor of West Germany, and he included a trip to the LBJ Ranch as part of the itinerary. Johnson asked Father Schneider to perform a special Mass for his visitor and his entourage of about twenty people. As Johnson put it, "Father Schneider, we are getting company Sunday, and German Chancellor Adenauer is coming. As you know, he's a very strict Catholic, and he wouldn't miss Mass for anybody." Father Schneider went all out, pulling out a sermon in German and rounding up some area Germans to sing a few songs in their native tongue. Later, at a barbecue on the LBJ Ranch, Johnson pulled aside his friend and said, "Father Schneider, we need to say grace before we eat. We have to pray when Adenauer is here. Do it in German. I don't understand German, but the old man [Adenauer], it makes him happy." All went well, and Adenauer wrote a letter of thanks to Father Schneider when he was back home. The president also was delighted with how smoothly things had gone.

During that flight to Germany for Adenauer's funeral, the president took time to visit with Ambassador Knappstein. The president told the ambassador of his long affection for the German people, and related how he had grown up among the German community in Fredericksburg and Stonewall, attending a school where he spoke German for the first three years. "But all I know now," he said, "are the dirty words." Johnson also shared a story about Father Schneider and the little Catholic church in Stonewall. The president, sitting close enough to the ambassador to finger his tie clasp at one point, said he had thought of bringing Father Schneider along on the trip to Germany for the funeral, but was afraid that he would be so overwhelmed with his own responsibilities that he would not have time to "look after" his old friend. Clearly, the president felt he had sadly erred by not bringing Father Schneider. It stayed on his mind.

I landed Air Force One at Cologne/Bonn Airport, and a motorcade took the president to the residence in the American Embassy compound. The next evening, the president invited me to a dinner party at the Embassy to celebrate my forty-second birthday. He gave me a gold presidential watch and a promotion. "The Air Force is making you a colonel for your birthday," he said. I then traded my lieutenant colonel's silver leaves for a "full bird" colonel's eagles.

I could tell the president was still thinking of Father Schneider. During dinner, he asked me to find out if there were any government planes coming over from the United States and to see if Father Schneider could be put on one.

Thus began my own version of a West German airlift.

I immediately phoned Washington and learned that Army General Lyman L. Lemnitzer, the Supreme Allied Commander in Europe, was due to return to his post in Germany. I also found that the president's JetStar was still at his ranch and due to depart for Washington. General Lemnitzer's pilot, Colonel Elmer Dunn, was a close friend of mine, so I called and asked him to pass along the president's wishes to his boss.

Father Schneider was playing bingo in Stonewall when my executive secretary, Ann Webb, tracked him down and told him the president wanted to fly him to Germany for Konrad Adenauer's funeral. The priest didn't believe it. Webb instructed him to go to the ranch, and we would fly him to Washington and then on to Germany. He said he would have to get permission from his bishop to leave the country. I imagine the president would have interceded with the bishop or even the Vatican if he had needed to, but that wasn't necessary. The next day, Father Schneider called my White House office and said he could go. He boarded the presidential JetStar and immediately ran into one more thing he couldn't believe: he was the only passenger, and he had his own attendant to bring him drinks and look after his every need on the way to Washington. Not many non-presidents get service like that. Talk about once-in-a-lifetime experiences.

Once we got him to Washington, we put him on General Lemnitzer's plane. The general personally looked after the priest, keeping him fed and entertained during the long trip to Europe. Father Schneider said they spent most of the trip talking, even when they were supposed to be catching some sleep.

I met the plane in Bonn about 8 A.M. and took Father Schneider to meet the president at the Villa Hillenbrand, where he and his party were staying. I rang the doorbell. Marvin Watson met us at the door and went upstairs to announce the priest's arrival. The president, still lying in bed, yelled, "Bring him up!" After Father Schneider made his way to the bedroom, the president beamed with happiness and gave him a big embrace. You could tell the president was delighted to have his old friend close at hand. Tickled, as a matter of fact.

Later, during the memorial services at Bundeshaus, Father Schneider sat nine rows behind the president. But Johnson never let him get out of his sight, turning his head several times to glance at him. Father Schneider recalled that one German newspaper wrote that Johnson was irreverent and constantly looked around during the service. Of course, he wasn't being irreverent. He was just making sure that his old friend was all right.

After the services, Johnson introduced Father Schneider to Charles De Gaulle, British Prime Minister Harold Wilson and, as the priest put it, "all the big shots." Father Schneider felt that Johnson had directed the Secret Service to keep a watchful eye on him so he wouldn't get lost. I have no doubt that was the case.

Father Schneider joined us on Air Force One for the trip back to Washington. He played poker with his new friends, the Secret Service agents. And he won a few rounds. At one point, the president wandered back to where the game was going on, and he seemed surprised to see his old friend shuffling and dealing. A few minutes later, Johnson sent back a double deck of playing cards, in a box stamped with the presidential seal and inscribed with the words "Air Force One" and "LBJ." Father Schneider was so impressed he kept the package sealed as a memento.

The president continued to give Father Schneider the red-carpet treatment even after we landed back at Andrews. Father Schneider, Allen Dulles, Marvin Watson, Dean Rusk, and some others flew with the president from Andrews to the White House on an Army chopper. Father Schneider later wrote down his memories:

> We landed right at the back door of the White House. And then something happened, which I was so amazed. We got out of the plane. And believe you me, [the president] took my bag, which I had my belongings in. He carried my bag and said, "Come on, I'll show you your room." He carried my bag and I walked behind! I was so embarrassed. But he wouldn't let me have it . . . the people in the White House were all standing around. They were coming in for the reception, all those high-class people, and he wouldn't talk to anybody. He just walked through carrying my bag. We went into the elevator, and we went upstairs into the quarter where the rooms are for visitors . . . We went into the room and he looked around and said, "Oh, that's not a nice room. Let us look for another one." Then we went to another room. There was a suite of rooms: a sitting room, a bedroom, bath, telephone, and TV, and he looked around and said, "I think that's better. I hope you will be comfortable."

Before the president left, he got down on his knees to adjust the television to a station. "Mr. President," Father Schneider said.

Johnson answered, "What do you want, Father Schneider?"

The humble priest replied uneasily, "There are hundreds of people downstairs. They are waiting for you. They are more important than I."

Johnson answered, "You are more important to me."

Later that night, Father Schneider met some of the president's guests, but then tried to unobtrusively slip away to his quarters. He was worried he would take the spotlight away from the president. Johnson, noticing his friend was uncomfortable with all the dignitaries, told him, "Father

Schneider, if you'd like to go out sightseeing, this is night, all the fountains and memorials are lit up. Go out sightseeing." Johnson's secretary, Marie Fehmer, served as the priest's personal guide. Later, when someone noticed the priest was missing, Johnson brought laughter from his guests when he said, "Oh, yes, Father Schneider went out sightseeing with my secretary." And Father Schneider always told the story with a few chuckles himself.

The next day, Father Schneider flew back to the ranch on a plane with Lady Bird and Lynda. When the plane landed late at night, a chauffeur-driven car was waiting to drive the priest the rest of the way home. The driver told Father Schneider, "The president phoned from Washington to see that we would take you home."

Father Schneider was impressed. He never forgot that last act of thoughtfulness. "That shows you the kind of man he is, honestly," Father Schneider recalled years later.

A POPULAR REALITY TELEVISION SHOW THESE DAYS drastically renovates the inadequate home of a needy family in just one week. But I was involved in an extreme home makeover for Lyndon Johnson that leaves that television construction crew in the sawdust. In just seventeen hours, our presidential team transformed a house to make it majestic enough for a key summit between Johnson and Soviet leader Aleksei Kosygin. It was a superhuman effort.

In June 1967, Chairman Kosygin visited the United Nations in New York City. President Johnson sent word through our U.N. Ambassador, Arthur Goldberg, inviting Kosygin to visit the White House. But Kosygin, in his Cold War arrogance, responded by saying he was not visiting the United States, he was visiting international territory at the U.N. President Johnson didn't want to set a precedent by knuckling under to Kosygin's demands to meet only at U.N. headquarters. Johnson also worried about war protestors and other complications that might turn a meeting in New York into a circus. To defuse the standoff, the president suggested a compromise—finding a suitable location somewhere between New York and Washington.

I was part of a staff team meeting with the president in the White House family quarters on the afternoon of Thursday, June 22, 1967, when Johnson phoned New Jersey governor Richard Hughes, a Democrat, to ask whether he could suggest a midway location in New Jersey for a summit. Governor Hughes suggested Glassboro State College, south of Philadelphia. The college president and his wife lived in a large house on campus called Hollybush Mansion.

Johnson insisted that he didn't want to inconvenience the college or its president, but Governor Hughes assured him that college president Thomas Robinson would be delighted to offer his home for such an historic occasion.

"Where's Glassboro?" Johnson asked me after ending his call with the governor.

I searched each of my aviation charts and couldn't find it anywhere. Finally, I picked up a New Jersey highway map and we put a ruler down on it and Glassboro showed up as almost equidistant from New York and Washington. It was about thirty miles or so southeast of Philadelphia International Airport. We could land Air Force One there and use the presidential helicopters to land on the college campus.

The initial meeting with Kosygin was scheduled to begin at 11 A.M. the next day, so our advance team had to get going immediately. Communications and security systems had to be put in place, and there was no telling what modifications might be needed in order to make Hollybush worthy of an international summit.

While still in the president's bedroom, chief of staff Marvin Watson phoned presidential assistant Sherwin Markman and assigned him to lead the advance team of technicians.

"They're going to be in at eleven o'clock tomorrow morning. This is what the president would like: He wants to meet in some comfortable surroundings, have a chance to have lunch. He wants to have adequate security. He wants a place for the press to meet. He wants facilities for private meetings with his own staff. He wants Kosygin to have his staff. He wants to be able to meet in a small room, if possible, with Kosygin.

"We don't know what we're going to do. You just set it up and be ready when we're there."

I jumped into action, too. I chose, of my own assistants, naval commander and engineer John Dick-Peddie to go along to help with any structural modifications that might be needed at Hollybush. I quickly scheduled a VC-131 Turboprop Convair to carry the advance team, which left Washington at about 11 P.M.

Markman and Commander Dick-Peddie and the rest of the team were met by Governor Hughes when they arrived around midnight. "Whatever you want, I'll make sure you have," he told Markman. "I've got my whole state at your disposal."

Commander Dick-Peddie kept me informed of the enormous amount of work it would take to renovate the Victorian-style Hollybush literally overnight. Walls had to be moved, doors installed, carpet laid, and a completely new kitchen installed with a quality stove, refrigerator, and freezer that could handle meal preparations for a large group.

The worst problem they encountered was an electrical system inadequate for powering all the equipment necessary for a summit. There was no air-conditioning in the mansion and anything stronger than a 100-watt bulb would short out the anemic wiring.

Word got out about the need for workers, and someone from the Atlantic City Electric Company appeared out of nowhere to help. "I brought a truckload of my crew because I thought you might need me," he told Markman. An air-conditioning company also came to the rescue. A large transformer had to be installed on the power line at the street with a special line running electricity across the lawn to the mansion. Fourteen window air-conditioning units were installed in the house, but a team of carpenters had to build special frames because the Hollybush windows were larger and longer than normal house windows.

It was a hive of activity. Five men from the local phone company came to install thirteen White House phones; six Glassboro college students even turned up to help do odd jobs. And at about 5 A.M. an interior decorator was rousted out of bed to install draperies to keep the prying press from looking in the windows. The summit had been announced, and television crews were already setting up and filming.

Throughout the night, Markman had to reassure Mrs. Betty Robinson that the changes being made to the 100-year-old home would not ruin it. She finally went to bed at 3 A.M. but was up again at 7 A.M., still fretting.

I flew the president and Mrs. Johnson and others to the summit the next morning, landing Air Force One at the Philadelphia airport. The Johnsons landed at Glassboro College by helicopter just ahead of Kosygin's motorcade, and President Johnson met the Soviet leader at the front door of the newly revamped Hollybush Mansion.

The Johnson-Kosygin summit went so well that when the president had to leave at 3 P.M. to catch Air Force One for a flight to a Los Angeles fundraiser, the two leaders agreed to meet again on Sunday at Hollybush. As I flew the president westward that day, I was filled with overwhelming pride. Not only was I fortunate to be the one to fly that magnificent machine on behalf of our country, but I was thrilled that the presidential advance team had practically rebuilt a house overnight in an effort to help ease Cold War tensions.

As I piloted Air Force One back to Philadelphia on Sunday morning, our descent carried us east of the international airport and over western New Jersey. As I gently turned left for our long, final approach to the runway, I looked down and saw a large display of whitewashed rocks arranged to say, "Welcome LBJ." I knew the president would get a kick out of that, so I got on the public address system and announced the unusual welcome mat. The president and I rode the same helicopter to Hollybush, and he said, "Well, I reckon I have at least one friend left in New Jersey."

When the summit meeting ended that afternoon, the president asked if he could be back at the White House by 8 P.M. I didn't think that would be possible because of the motorcades, helicopter rides, and plans to land at Andrews Air Force Base outside Washington. Then he told me he wanted to be back to hold a press briefing in the White House before Kosygin could get back to New York City to hold one of his own.

"Can you save any time getting us back to Washington?" he asked.

I told him I could shave off just enough time by landing at National Airport across the Potomac River from the White House. Rules at National Airport ordinarily didn't permit four-engine Boeing 707 airplanes such as Air Force One to land there, but I had done it on two other occasions when the weather at Andrews was bad. Air Force One needed 6,000 feet to land safely and the runway at National Airport at that time was 6,800 feet.

"Okay, do it," he said.

And that's how Lyndon Johnson beat Kosygin in the race to the press pulpit.

CHAPTER SIX

THE SHADOW OF VIETNAM

IT MAY BE HARD TO BELIEVE, BUT I WAS READY TO QUIT MY job as Lyndon Johnson's pilot at one point. It was 1965, and I was in anguish over the tense relationships that Johnson's favoritism caused me with my superiors at Andrews and with General Clifton, the White House military aide and holdover from the Kennedy administration. The whole mess was so upsetting to me that I actually started looking for, and found, a civilian job. I planned to give up the Air Force and go to work as a pilot for a private corporation just to get out of the hellish situation. Sure, it was exhilarating to fly the president of the United States around, but the whole working atmosphere got to the point where I just couldn't take it.

Then things began to happen fast.

In early July 1965, Jack Valenti, the president's special assistant, called me at my home in Camp Springs, Maryland. I was relaxing before flying with the president to his ranch the next day. "Jim, are you going to be on Air Force One tomorrow afternoon when it leaves for Texas?" he asked.

"The president always insists that I am to be in the cockpit when he's on board," I told him.

"Well, the president is thinking about making you his Armed Forces aide when General Clifton retires next week," Valenti said. I was speechless. The president had never mentioned this possibility, and I had never even considered it. Presidential military aides traditionally were drawn from the ranks of generals and admirals, and I was still a major.

Valenti told me not to breathe a word, because the president also was considering several other officers recommended by the Pentagon. "Don't tell the president," he warned. The suspense built later that evening at the Andrews Air Force Base Officers' Club. Colonel Harlan C. Wilder, who had replaced Ireland as Special Air Missions wing commander, approached me confidentially and asked if I were in some kind of trouble. He said agents from the FBI and the military's Office of Special Investigation were asking lots of questions about me. I knew this had to be a background check, but I played dumb like Valenti had instructed and said I couldn't think of anything I was guilty of.

I flew to Texas the following day in the co-pilot's seat of Air Force One. At Bergstrom Air Force Base in Austin, General Clifton asked me if I knew I was under consideration to replace him. I told him I knew, but I doubted if it would come to pass. Two days later, however, on July 11, the president officially nominated me to be his Armed Forces aide and director of the White House Military Office. He also appointed me pilot of Air Force One. A promotion to lieutenant colonel was part of the deal. I found out about it from a Reuters news report passed along by an Army enlisted man, and the president later approached me at the ranch and asked if I knew about my new job. I thanked him for having confidence in me. The White House flew my wife, Marie, to Texas for the official announcement. After being an unofficial military aide for so long, I now had my pedigree.

As it turned out, I performed my first official act as military aide within a few hours of finding out I had the job. It wasn't a pleasant task, but it is one I will never forget. The war in Vietnam was about to become a major part of my life.

In 1965, the Vietnam War for many people was only something they saw on television or read about in the newspaper. Unless you were a serviceman, or one of your loved ones was fighting over there, it was just another distant news event. Even though most Americans were detached from the fighting, they believed in what our country was doing. Almost everyone supported the war, and saw our fight in Vietnam as part of a larger battle against the worldwide Communist menace. We thought the war was necessary to keep Southeast Asia from falling under Red domination, one country at a time. Most of us thought we'd eventually be fighting the Communists in Honolulu or San Francisco if we didn't stop them in Vietnam.

Things, of course, got a whole lot less black and white the longer the war went on.

The war came home to Austin, Texas, in July 1965 when Mr. and Mrs. Tommy Johns got the news all parents pray they never get. Their eighteen-

year-old son, who had just asked for a box of homemade cookies in a letter
sent from a foxhole, was killed in action. Private First Class Nathanael C.
Lee, the seventh of thirteen children, a loving boy and high achiever who
dutifully sent money home to his mother, was the first Marine from Austin
to die in the war. He had joined the Marines only thirteen months earlier.

When word of Pfc. Lee's death reached Austin, I was out at the ranch
with the president and still getting used to my new title of Armed Forces
aide. The president decided that I should go to Austin the day after my appointment was announced and see Nathanael Lee's family personally. This
was the only time I delivered condolences in person for someone killed in
Vietnam. It was a heartbreaking task. It was difficult for me to express the
president's extreme sadness in the kind of language a distraught family
would understand. Mr. and Mrs. Johns were extremely proud of their son,
as they had every right to be.

"He didn't want anything else but the Marines, and they took him in
just as soon as he finished school," Mrs. Johns had told a local newspaper
reporter. "He only wrote how good the Marines were."

A moving account of Nathanael Lee and his parents was penned by legendary Austin newspaperman Nat Henderson, a decorated World War II
veteran who always had the perfect touch when it came to military reporting. He quoted from letters Nathanael had written home, telling of combat
and death and hard times.

Henderson wrote in the *Austin Statesman*:

"Dear Mom, You can call me a killer now . . ."

But in the next paragraph of a monsoon-soaked letter penciled
in a muddy foxhole in South Vietnam, an 18-year-old Austin Marine
begged his mother to send him a box of homemade cookies as if he
were still a boy wanting his share of a few good things a youngster
might get in a family of thirteen children.

No more letters will come to Mr. and Mrs. Tommy Johns telling
them to mail some "ready sweetened Cool Aid" [sic] or some "instant
coffee" to keep their son from "going to sleep" on the battle lines in a
tedious war they do not quite comprehend.

A longer sleep has made Private First Class Nathanael C. Lee the
first Austin Leatherneck to be killed in action in a long war that pro-
gressively has grown more vicious and costly during the past few
months.

In one of his last letters home, Lee told his mother he was glad the Marines sent him to Vietnam, even though it was a miserable place. "He wanted to do his share," Mrs. Johns said. Wiping at tears, she told a newsman: "I've got one consolation. He wanted to go and wasn't drafted."

As I prepared to make that visit to the Johns home, I thought of other times in my military career when I had seen death close-up. In 1945, I was flying one of seventeen brand-new C-46s across India on the way to Ledo. We'd picked the planes up in Savannah, Georgia, and had flown all the way across the North Atlantic to Europe and then to Tripoli and Iran and Pakistan, and now we were on the final leg of that long, long trip. We flew into a major storm, and all the planes made it except one. The pilot of that plane, Robert Doten, and the co-pilot, Robert Dalton, were close friends of ours. We never saw them again. It was several days before search planes found the wreckage. We were saddened, but there were hundreds of thousands of men lost in World War II. I was young then, and I guess we didn't dwell on death.

Then, in the late 1950s, I was a captain stationed at Dover Air Force Base, Delaware, the place where all the bodies of deceased U.S. servicemen and -women go first when they come back to the United States. Back then, the bodies were shipped out of Dover by train. It was customary that each body be escorted to its final resting place by a serviceman of equal rank. I was called upon to escort the body of a captain I had never met back to Rock Island, Illinois, where he was to be buried in a national cemetery. He had been killed in some sort of accident in France. I rode the train with his body. The casket was covered with a flag and placed in the baggage car. I read a book to pass the time as I sat in a passenger car. We changed trains in Chicago, and I had to stay right with the body when it was moved from one baggage car to another, making sure it was carried feet-first.

When we got to Rock Island, I met the captain's family members. There were only about four of them at the funeral home. I went to the funeral and, at the appointed moment, I handed the flag to the survivors and made a little speech. I extended the condolences of the president and the Air Force chief on behalf of this fallen comrade. The mortuary officer at Dover had given me a ten-minute lecture on what to do, and they gave me a little brochure, too. Then my duty was over and I caught the train and went on about my business.

I can't say that either my experience in World War II or the trip from Dover accompanying that captain's body really specifically prepared me for visiting the family of that dead Austin Marine. If anything prepared me for the task, it was just the cumulative effect of losing family and friends over the years, and learning what it meant to grieve over a family member.

It was a bright, sunny, hot-as-hell July day when I went to that poor black family's house about a mile east of what is now Interstate 35, the historic division line between rich and poor, white and non-white in Austin. That was especially true in those even more segregated days of the mid-1960s. The family lived about two blocks south of the street that later was renamed Martin Luther King Boulevard. The house was a shack, really. The press was already there in the front yard when I arrived. Press Secretary Bill Moyers probably had announced that I would be delivering condolences on behalf of the president, and that brought the media. The thing that bothered me more than anything else as I walked inside that rundown house was that these were such poor people, and now they had suffered a very terrible loss.

The only person I remember being there was the mother, this poor little woman. It was sweltering inside. And Mrs. Johns was sitting on the couch wringing her hands with tears in her eyes. The somberness of the whole thing just made me sad. It was a very difficult experience for me. I'm not sure she even knew who I was, just some strange fellow coming to her house on behalf of the president. I had tears in my eyes. I guess I was there about five minutes. That's not very long, but it seemed like forever. Naturally, the mother didn't have much to say, and so it was a very tough five minutes. It was hard to know what to say to this very sorrowful person who had just lost a son. I just extended the condolences of the president and told her how sorry he was for her loss and that he and the country were grateful for the brave service her son gave.

She didn't ask me any questions. I remember that very specifically, and I thought to myself, "What could she say other than thank you?" I think she said, "Thank you for coming." Then I left. I remember telling the president afterward that I'd been to Mrs. Johns's house and extended his condolences, and she was appreciative. And that was it.

Delivering those regrets in person, and witnessing firsthand the devastating effect the death of a loved one in Vietnam had on a family, introduced me in a very emotional way to the task that would consume a large chunk of my time and energy over the next three and a half years. As military aide, I was in charge of sending the presidential condolence letters that went to the next-of-kin of every service member killed in Vietnam until the president left office in early 1969. During the time I had the job, my staff, or in many cases I personally, prepared or looked at more than 30,000 letters.

No task was more somber and draining. Preparing the condolence letters that went out over the president's signature got grimmer as the casualties mounted. During the Johnson presidency, the number of servicemen killed in Vietnam totaled 35,541. Although some might have slipped through the cracks, our policy was to send a presidential condolence letter to the next-of-kin in every case.

We kept the letters brief, usually three paragraphs. We sought to be sensitive and sincere, just as the president wanted. Here's a sample letter:

Dear Mr. and Mrs. Doe:

It was with deep regret that I learned of the death of your son, Private First Class John Doe, United States Marine Corps, as the result of wounds received in action against hostile forces in Vietnam.

Yours has indeed been a deep personal loss, but you may take pride in the knowledge that your son's service to his country contributed greatly to safeguarding the freedom cherished so dearly by peace-loving nations throughout the world. Our Nation, which shares your loss, is grateful for your son's vital contribution.

Mrs. Johnson joins me in extending to you our heartfelt sympathy in the loss of your son.

Sincerely,

In 1967, a year in which nearly 10,000 servicemen were killed, I had additional mock-up letters prepared to supplement those we continued to use. The idea was to avoid the appearance of form letters, even though in reality that was what we were sending out. For example, the second paragraph of one letter might begin: "Your son gave of his courage and convictions in the defense of freedom. No man can give more, or be honored more for selflessness." The second paragraph of another letter might read: "Words, I know, are inadequate to express our thoughts at times like this, but I earnestly hope you will find some comfort in the knowledge that your beloved son's sacrifice will survive him."

We had letters for specific branches of service, for deaths at sea or in the air, for combat and non-combat deaths, for accidental deaths, for deaths that occurred stateside. I ordered up special condolence letters for the thirty-four Navy personnel killed June 8, 1967, aboard the USS *Liberty* during the controversial, apparently accidental attack by Israeli forces during the Six-Day War. We tried to tweak the Vietnam War letters, even when using a format, so they were more personal. Some of the letters were written by Pentagon staff members, but all the letters came to my office for rewrite or final approval. I suspect I reviewed about one-third of them personally and rewrote quite a number of them. Unfortunately, the mounting casualties gave us ample opportunities to get more skilled at our grim task.

The president put a great deal of importance on the letters, as I did. It was always a difficult, perhaps impossible, challenge to find the right words. Occasionally, bereaved family members would react angrily to a presidential letter and send back a bitter letter of their own. In those cases, I took special care to ensure that a sensitive, personalized response was prepared.

We wrote the father of a deceased serviceman on one occasion: "While the president fully realizes the limitations of our language in extending meaningful condolences to those who have lost loved ones, he does nonetheless, feel a compulsion to express his personal sorrow and empathy to the families of each serviceman who is killed in Vietnam." The family was especially troubled by a letter their son had sent them earlier, complaining of rules of engagement he thought had endangered the lives of American soldiers. The implication was that our soldiers had been instructed not to fire until fired upon, and now his son was dead. We tried to explain that such restrictions were not common policy, and that American soldiers in fact often were on the offensive. I don't know if our words were any comfort to the family.

It was only natural that family members sometimes lashed out at the president when their loved ones were killed or injured. When angry letters came in, I tried to sensitively explain the president's very difficult position. I tried to soothe one writer upset about his seriously injured brother, and explained that the president recognized the pain and anguish suffered by the families of the boys who were fighting in Vietnam, and that he understood why they would write him angry letters. But I explained that the nation's destiny rested on the president's shoulders. "However difficult and distasteful it is for him to send young men into battle, he has to suffer alone in the agonizing decisions that he must make concerning the safety of our people."

Sometimes we got positive replies to the president's condolence letters, and some were quite touching. I was moved when a Georgia woman, the recent widow of a serviceman, asked if the president could visit her young son who was having difficulty adjusting to his father's death. That was out of the question, but I promised her and her family a special White House tour if they ever came to Washington. And I sent the family photographs of the president's airplanes, noting her son's interest in the Air Force, the branch where his late father had served.

We took great care with the condolence letters, but no matter how hard we tried, sometimes mistakes slipped in. I winced when I composed a heartfelt letter of apology to a family after we misspelled the name of a deceased serviceman. I made it clear the error was mine, not the president's. I'm sure no journalist who has misspelled a name suffered any more than I did over that regrettable error.

We constantly grappled with exactly what should be said in a condolence letter and how long the letters should be. We tried to make the letters as consistent as possible without being assembly line productions. I also came up with a uniform policy of exactly who should get the single condolence letter that the president sent to each family. Before, the different branches had different policies about who should get the letters, sometimes causing confusion and bitterness among family members. Our new policy specified that the surviving spouse always got the condolence letter unless there was a divorce or a remarriage. After the surviving spouse, the order of next-of-kin was eldest child over 21, sons in order of seniority, daughters in order of seniority, father, mother, and so on. Sometimes relatives questioned why we sent only one letter, or why we sent the letter to a wife and not to the parents. I explained on more than one occasion, as sensitively as I could, that there was no intent to slight other members of the bereaved family, and that it was the president's hope that the letter would be shared, and be a source of pride and comfort to all members of the family.

One couple in Michigan got national attention by returning their sympathy letter to the White House, telling the president that he was "in part responsible" for their nineteen-year-old son's death. I have no way of knowing how most families felt about the letters. It's very difficult to write letters like this. What the hell did people think when they got a letter signed by the president, saying, "We're so sorry you lost your son"? They're probably madder than hell at the president. Perhaps some letters were wadded up and thrown away as grief overtook family members. Maybe the family members were just numb and didn't even think about the president's words. I must say we did get a lot of letters back saying, "Thank you, Mr. President. We of course hated to lose our son, but he thought and we thought that you're doing the right thing." I suspect many of the letters became part of the family archives, tucked in Bibles or kept with family heirlooms.

Although condolence letters took up much of our time, we had other mail-call duties. Any letter sent to the White House with a military-related theme or question or problem was sent to my office for the mandatory quick but thoughtful response. The president always said that he wanted every letter that came to the White House addressed to him answered within twenty-four hours. And he didn't want a form letter to go out over his signature. He wanted every letter crafted individually. And that admonition especially applied to any having to do with the military or military personnel.

One airman said he sent a letter because he had heard a rumor that any serviceman in Vietnam who wrote the president was guaranteed to receive a personal reply. By the way, he wrote, could the president send him a flag to display outside his tent?

The president of course did not answer all correspondence from servicemen personally, but my staff or I did. We took every letter seriously. We explained to this airman that policy allowed only one flag to be displayed on an outside pole at any Air Force base, so we couldn't set him up with his own Stars and Stripes. And we gently suggested that if he wanted to fly a small flag inside his tent, he could have a relative back in the States buy him one. The president wasn't in the business of purchasing flags for every one of his warriors, no matter how much he appreciated their service.

Sometimes a mother would send a missive to the president and ask if he could find out why her son hadn't written in a while, or why he was in the guard house. My staff knew automatically to make the necessary calls to the Pentagon and come up with information that we could craft into a reply. And we made sure the reply had the touch of care and concern that the letter-writer was looking for.

One of my favorite letters was from a seven-year-old boy who asked the president if he could "go to Vietnam and help fight." Little Carter Cook Gooding explained that his father, a doctor serving in Vietnam, already had taught him to fight, presumably saving the nation the cost of basic training. "I am a good boy most of the time," he wrote in the letter that his mother helped him type.

We wrote back that he was too young to go to Vietnam, but that he could help the war effort by studying hard, being a good boy, and not causing his mother any trouble. We hope he followed our advice.

I answered many more letters sent to the president from people wanting to avoid military service, or from relatives or congressmen who wanted to keep them from going to Vietnam. For example, Congressman Henry B. Gonzalez of San Antonio once asked the president if one of his constituents,

an Army private, could be exempt from Vietnam because of his vision—
20/200 in the right eye and 20/400 in the left. However, I found that the
private's vision was correctable and replied negatively to the congressman:
"You might be interested in knowing that many men with eyesight problems
worse than these are presently serving in Vietnam."

A few Americans viewed Air Force One as their personal airliner, and
they weren't bashful about writing the president to try to snag a seat or
two. I got those letters, too. A Maryland woman once wrote in and asked
the president if space was available to transport her daughter's new dog,
a gift from grandma. A Long Island couple wanted to hitch a ride to Chicago's O'Hare Airport, and a group of students from the University of Day-
ton wanted to be whisked to their homes for the Thanksgiving holiday.
A Washington, D.C., couple had heard Walter Cronkite report that the
president was going to Mexico City, and inquired whether there would be
room on board for "two extras." An Army sergeant "volunteered" to serve
as a security man on the president's plane if he made a trip to Australia. In
every case, we answered politely that Air Force One was already occupied
by the president's staff, and we wished them well in finding alternative
transportation. Another letter-writer suggested we name Air Force One
"The Pedernales," in honor of the river that bordered the president's Texas
ranch. No need to monkey with success, I wrote back, explaining that the
fact that the plane is unnamed signifies unity and national purpose. We
sent the helpful Louisiana man a color picture of the plane and thanked
him for his thoughts.

Sometimes we chose not to write letters. That was the case for three
American prisoners of war who were released by the Vietcong in 1967 after efforts by anti-war activist Tom Hayden. The Defense Department was
against the president sending letters to the men, fearing the Communists
might try to find some sort of propaganda lever they could use against us. I
agreed completely, and no letters were sent. We also had to be careful that
the president was not embarrassed by the anti-war faction, which became
larger and larger the longer the war went on.

War protesters shadowed the president as the war deepened. In Texas,
they liked to gather on rural Ranch Road 1 across the Pedernales River
from the Texas White House. Sometimes they camped out; other times
they came to hold signs all day long. One time, they had a petition for the
president. The president asked me to go out and meet with them and collect their document. They were talking hogwash as far as I was concerned.
I heard them out, though, and dutifully brought the petition and signa-
tures back across the river. They thought I would deliver their diatribe to
the president. They were wrong. I threw it in a trash can as quickly as I

could. I didn't want to read their garbage, and I knew the president didn't, either.

Protestors also liked to gather at the White House in Washington. Sometimes thousands showed up to stage a sit-in or rally. They always demanded to have a word with the president, but that was never going to happen. The president and the rest of us in the White House just went about our business when the longhairs camped out. But one White House protest still sticks in my mind.

In February 1966, we got word that a group of veterans, mostly from New York, was planning to picket the White House to oppose the war. What had me concerned was the veterans' threat to throw their military medals over the fence. We couldn't have the news media snapping photos of decorated veterans hurling Purple Hearts and Bronze Stars at the White House. I had to make sure the White House wouldn't be left with a pile of unwanted lawn ornaments. Medal wrangler, just another of the many odd jobs I performed for Lyndon Johnson.

If you're going to have protesters tossing medals, you've got to have a plan to catch them. I brainstormed with some military brass in the Pentagon. As a proud military man, I was appalled that any veteran would dare use a sacred medal to show disrespect to the armed forces, the presidency, and the United States of America. The White House had to stand up to such unpatriotic acts. We would just refuse to accept the medals. The Pentagon agreed to take charge of any medals given up by protesters.

The day of the protest, February 5, 1966, was bone-chilling cold. About 100 veterans marched in front of the White House with signs that said "Stop the Bombing" and "Meet with the Vietcong." There were young protesters as well as middle-aged veterans of World War II and the Korean War. The vets were armed with their military discharge papers and decorations. They demanded to meet with the president or someone on his staff. They were rebuffed. Just as we had scripted it, a Secret Service agent told them he would send any medals, commendations, or discharge papers straight to the Pentagon. The veterans didn't like that, and refused to turn over their decorations. Instead, one by one, they made a show of placing their items in a metal box and speaking a few words. One WWII veteran gave up his Bronze Star, but most of the other medals were low-level decorations. "We shall return again and again until President Johnson, the Commander-in-Chief and the man ultimately responsible for the war, agrees to receive us," said the Korean War veteran who seemed to be the ringleader.

I never saw the theatrics, and neither did the president. Before the protest was over, we were on our way to Andrews Air Force Base for a working trip to Hawaii.

Not all war protests went so smoothly. In mid-October 1967, the Washington, D.C., police notified us that a massive anti–Vietnam War demonstration was planned for the Lincoln Memorial, the Pentagon, the White House, and the Capitol. Tens of thousands of protesters were coming from around the country, possibly as many as 200,000. The October 21 rally would be the largest gathering of war protesters we had seen in Washington. The White House military office needed to be fully informed. I called an assistant Secretary of Defense, John Steadman, and asked that my three officer assistants and I be included in an intelligence briefing at the Pentagon. As I learned more about the size and scope of the protest, I knew serious trouble could break out. My main concern was that the president be protected—and insulated—from the angry activists. I warned everyone in my office and the various other units around Washington under my jurisdiction to keep a low profile during the demonstration and to avoid letting their curiosity get the better of them. National Guardsmen and paratroopers would be stationed out of sight as a precaution against the civil disobedience acts threatened by protesters. The demonstrators had a permit to gather at the Lincoln Memorial and march over the Potomac River to the nearby Pentagon. There, troops would repel them if they attempted to enter the building.

As advertised, on October 21 more than 50,000 demonstrators gathered at the Lincoln Memorial to denounce the president and the war. The trouble came later at the Pentagon. Thousands of protesters stormed the building and had to be forced back by armed soldiers. More than 250 protesters were arrested, and scores more pushed, yelled, screamed, and created a chaotic scene. It was an ugly mess that lasted far into the night and well into the next day.

Today's history books are filled with photos of so-called flower children placing daisies in the barrels of soldiers' rifles and bird's-eye views of the surrounded Pentagon. But one photo that appears to be lost to history absolutely enraged the president.

After the protest was over, I picked up the jangling red phone in my White House office. It was the president calling. "Who in the hell authorized my helicopter to fly over those protesters?" he demanded to know.

He told me there was a photo on the front page of the *Washington Evening Star* showing the presidential Marine One helicopter hovering directly over 50,000 demonstrators. The presidential seal was clearly visible, he said.

"Sir," I said, "I have no idea who did this. But I will find out."

It didn't take me long to find out that the president's regular helicopter pilot, Marine Lieutenant Colonel Donald Foss, had taken it upon himself to circle the anti-war demonstration at a low altitude just to have a look-see. Foss had screwed up several other times, and had even argued with me when I had admonished him for his failures. But using the president's helicopter to satisfy his curiosity in such a public and inappropriate manner was beyond the pale. I was livid. I immediately sent word that he was fired as presidential helicopter pilot and commander of the Marine One unit. But when Foss got the word, he called and asked me to reconsider. "The decision is final," I said.

Foss was a relative of Joe Foss, the legendary World War II flying ace and Medal of Honor recipient, and he had a few friends in the Pentagon. He must have contacted every one of them. First, he lined up Marine Major General Keith McCutcheon to intervene on his behalf. Foss went to McCutcheon's office, called me from there, and badgered me until I agreed to speak with the general. I told McCutcheon that my decision to fire Foss was final, but he insisted on coming to my office to further argue the case. "Fine," I said. "Come at 1:25." McCutcheon arrived right on time and argued that I didn't have the authority to fire Foss and that he was restoring the pilot to his former command. He tried to intimidate me with his rank. He had apparently forgotten that I'd been trained by a world-class intimidator, Lyndon Johnson. This general's threats rolled right off me. I wouldn't back down, but I politely assured him that Foss would no longer be allowed on the White House grounds and would never fly the president's helicopter again. "And that's that!" I added.

Word of that flare-up must have circulated quickly in the Pentagon. A day or so later, General Wallace Greene, Commandant of the Marine Corps and a member of the Joint Chiefs of Staff, called me. He asked me to immediately phone him if any of his general officers ever came to my office again to try to intervene in White House business. "In the meantime," he said, "I will issue direct orders that my senior officers stay away from the White House unless invited, in which case I expect to be personally informed by them."

Many years after that historic 1967 war protest at the Pentagon, it occurred to me that I had never actually seen the front page of the *Washington Evening Star* with the photo of Marine One. I'd only heard about it from the president. I've searched the *Star*'s archives and can't find any such photo. I'm not exactly sure how President Johnson found out about the wayward flight of his presidential helicopter. But he had a sixth sense, eyes in the back of his head, and a network of political informants second to none. He knew before I did, and I still marvel at that.

I had always tried to avoid politics, but I got sucked in sometimes because of the nature of my job. How could I avoid politics when I spent so many waking hours close to the president of the United States? I had a run-in with Joseph Califano, an assistant Secretary of Defense who later became a special assistant to the president. Califano had it in his head that I should answer to him instead of to the president. He called me over to his Pentagon office not long after I was appointed Armed Forces aide and tried to intimidate and impress me with how important his job was. When he moved over to the White House a few weeks after I did, he told me, "Well, you'd better run everything through me." He wanted to be a permanent middle-man. The reality was that the president didn't want any middle-man between me and him.

Califano and I finally came to a parting of the ways. I just told him, "Joe, you gotta start remembering this, fella. I don't work for you. I work for the president. Whatever the president tells me to do, I go and do it. And he didn't tell me to run this through you or that through you. If there's something indicative to me that needs to come to your office, you'll certainly hear from me. Otherwise, stay out of my business."

So Califano and I never did get along very well. I've seen him two or three times since then at gatherings down at the LBJ Library in Austin. Every time I see him, I always speak to him. And my sweet wife, Marie, says, "Why do you always speak to that guy?"

And I say, "Honey, I'm not a politician, but anytime you have to deal with politicians, you've got to love your enemies."

Shortly after I was named Armed Forces aide, some uncomplimentary articles found their way into print. The articles suggested that an unknown like me was unqualified for the job, and criticized the president for selecting me. Part of this drivel apparently came from military officers who were upset because the job had always been held by flag officers. And some in the Pentagon were bent out of shape because a lowly major like me had replaced a general. Nobody had the guts to tell me this to my face, of course. A couple of weeks after my appointment, the president caught me in the Rose Garden and made mention of the sniping. "Cross, what are you going to do about your friends in the Pentagon talking out of school about your qualifications? They're talking to the press and telling these stories about how you're some old dumb country boy from Alabama that really doesn't have any of the required qualifications. I know it's embarrassing to you."

I replied, "I really don't have any friends in the Pentagon, so I can't do much about it. If they want to talk, they're going to talk." The president made it clear he didn't like the situation, and said somebody ought to do something about it.

A few days later we were back at his ranch. In comes a JetStar carrying Secretary of Defense Robert McNamara for a meeting with the president. McNamara and I were not bosom buddies and didn't really care for each other. He thought I was dumb, and I suppose I am, by his standards. He's a Harvard liberal, an egghead. His plane landed, and I went to meet it on one of the president's golf carts and loaded his luggage. The president pulled up in his Lincoln, and the two of them went for a drive around the ranch. I took McNamara's bags to an upstairs bedroom in the ranch house and went back to the 8-foot by 35-foot house trailer where I had my office, command post, and sleeping quarters. About eight the next morning, Sergeant Robert Duffy, the Army sergeant on my staff who always traveled with the president, walked into my little office and said he had a top secret, for-the-president's-eyes-only message. Duffy and my other military staff never had direct contact with the president. I served as the president's eyes and ears when he was at his ranch, so I took the message on over to the house. I saw Marie Fehmer, the president's secretary, and told her I had an important message the president should see. She said he was in the swimming pool with McNamara, and suggested I take the message out there.

I walked out to the swimming pool, and there were McNamara and the president stretched out in the pool with their arms hanging on the splash trough, kicking their feet and talking about something. I excused myself and told the president I had a rather important message for him. He asked me to hand him his glasses and towel, and he dried off. I cleaned his glasses and put them on for him. He read the message, then handed it to McNamara, and the two of them discussed it for a moment or two. I stood and waited politely to see if the president needed me for anything else. He didn't seem to want me, so I turned to leave.

The president piped up: "Bob, do you know Major Cross?"

I had just been promoted to lieutenant colonel, and of course the president knew that, but he always liked to call me "Major," even later when he had promoted me to general. I think he liked to remind me that, without him, I'd be nowhere. Which was true. Anyway, McNamara, being the very proper, political guy that he was, said, "Oh, yes, Mr. President. I know the colonel."

The president launched into a little monologue. "You know, Bob, some of your people over there in the Pentagon have really been trashing old Cross's reputation. They've been talking about him to the press, saying what a poor old dumb country boy he is. And the press has been writing these stories that are embarrassing him to death. I just want you to see what you can do about it. Now I know Cross ain't too smart. He went to some little old cow college down in Auburn, Alabama. He doesn't have one of those Ph.D., summa cum laude degrees from one of those eastern schools like Yale or Princeton. [The president didn't mention Harvard, where McNamara got his MBA and taught. But he could have, and I suspect McNamara knew that.] Now, by God, what I want you to do is see if you can't stop all this talk coming out of the Pentagon that's embarrassing ole Cross."

The president paused, but he wasn't through yet.

"Now I want you to know that if I have my druthers when I'm hiring somebody to be on my staff, if I've got a choice between some poor old dumb country boy like Cross here who is loyal, or some Ph.D. from Harvard that's got one of those highfalutin' degrees but he's got his own agenda, by God I'll hire that dumb old country boy every time."

Now I don't know for sure what McNamara did, if anything, but there weren't any more negative stories about me coming out of the Pentagon.

And for the record, let me point out that McNamara and his Harvard credentials didn't last out the Johnson presidency.

But this dumb old country boy was there all the way.

CHAPTER SEVEN

THE ENFORCER

LYNDON JOHNSON LIKED TO BE IN CONTROL WHEN IT CAME to his airplanes, helicopters, and yachts. And I was his gatekeeper. Each time Vice President Hubert Humphrey or any other top government official wanted to use an aircraft or boat, he had to go through me. It probably humiliated Humphrey to have to ask me for permission, but that's just the way it was.

After President Kennedy was assassinated, Johnson served in the White House with no vice president to help—or, as he probably saw it—to hinder him. By the time the Democratic convention was held in August 1964, Johnson had enjoyed nine months as not only the top dog in the White House, but the only dog (not counting his registered beagles, "Her" and "Him," whom he once famously lifted by the ears on the White House lawn, angering animal lovers).

The president micromanaged Humphrey's travels from the moment he selected the Minnesota senator to be his running mate at the convention in Atlantic City. After the convention, I flew Johnson and Humphrey to the LBJ Ranch for strategy sessions. Their three-day weekend was dubbed the "Live Oak Strategy Conference," but it turned out to be a lot of play. They rode horses and cruised in a power boat on Lake Granite Shoals, and Muriel Humphrey even water-skied.

The president thought Humphrey had loose lips around news reporters. So when Humphrey was ready to leave the ranch for Washington, the president wanted me to hoodwink the press. Humphrey was flying out

on a JetStar that I had sent for. As usual, I was staying at the ranch with
Johnson's JetStar. Johnson wanted Humphrey's pilot to land at National
Airport along the Potomac River, instead of at the usual landing spot at
Andrews Air Force Base outside Washington.

Our behind-the-scenes planning was caught for posterity on the telephone recording system that LBJ used in his ranch house.

> LBJ: "I don't want any of these reporters now knowing that there's
> even gonna be a [refueling] stop. They're already calling wanting
> to know where they can contact the plane and have interviews
> and so forth, and some damn fools talk too much. So, uh, cover
> every possible angle out there and just tell them if the winds are
> favorable, they may not even stop."
> CROSS: "All right, sir."
> LBJ: "They don't know where they're gonna stop. If they do, they'll
> have to see how the winds are en route. And I'd rather think, I'd
> just tell him, if you can, go on and land at National and not even
> let them know that he's coming in there."
> CROSS: "All right. Fine."
> LBJ: "Let's avoid all the reporters on this that we can."
> CROSS: "Yes, sir."
> LBJ: "You just tell the pilot in the air to probably just go on to Na-
> tional if he can."
> CROSS: "All right, sir. Will do."
> LBJ: "So he can dodge them at Andrews. They'll be expecting them
> at Andrews, not to tell them until they just get out there. And say,
> 'They're going to Andrews.' 'Course, I guess Andrews would tell
> they'd gone to National, wouldn't they?"
> CROSS: "No, sir. Not if I talk to him direct."
> LBJ: "OK."
> CROSS: "All right, sir."

The plan worked. Reporters never got near Humphrey.

The system we used in the White House when Humphrey or anyone
in the president's cabinet wanted an airplane or boat worked like this:
The minute I got a request, I'd call the president or go see him in person.
If the proposed trip was not immediate, I'd write the president a very
short memo that noted what they wanted, when they wanted it, where
the group or individual was going, and with whom. The president often
wanted to know what kinds of foods were requested. I'm serious. In my

memo, I'd leave an option for the president to check—"Approved" or "Disapproved"—and he'd mark it and initial it. If the answer was "Disapproved," I had to think up some excuse why the plane or boat couldn't be used. I never said, "Well, the president said you can't have this."

The president acted as if he owned the four Boeing 707s for VIPs at Andrews Air Force Base, including the big, customized 707 that most people knew as Air Force One. Same thing with the three naval yachts in service to the White House, and a couple of the VC-140 JetStars.

Johnson frequently instructed me on how to turn away Humphrey and others.

"By God, you just tell them that the planes are out of commission or you've got them scheduled for something else. Don't tell them the president said that. You just tell them."

In other words, I was the Enforcer. Humphrey and others may have figured out that the president was behind the refusals, but they never let on. I took the brunt of their frustrations. I suspect that many of them disliked me.

The president could really play some mind games with Humphrey. One night, there was a social gathering at the White House and I was standing in the wings in my military dress uniform, as usual, in case the president needed me. Johnson was buttonholing Humphrey about how to win over members of Congress when he pulled me into the conversation.

"Cross, I've been talking to Hubert about trying to get some of these bills through over there that are just sitting there stagnated," he said. "Now, Hubert, I want you to get in touch with old Cross here. I want you to find out from him when that yacht's available over there, and you take that yacht, get some of these congressmen and senators over there that ain't exactly going along with our programs and see if you can't wine them and dine them and give them some of that good shrimp rice curry that we like."

(Johnson liked shrimp curry, but I doubt if Humphrey did.)

"And you get some of those big airplanes that old Cross has got over there. You take some of these congressmen around here, there, and yonder, and drop them off in their home districts and make some speeches around in their country. The ones that are trying to defeat us, you act like you love them. I want you to just keep after these programs, and let's see if we can't get some of these bills through."

"Yes, sir, Mr. President," Humphrey said.

"Now, by God, Cross," Johnson said, "I want you to take whatever care of the vice president that he wants. I want you to be damn sure that he is always taken care of with these planes and those yachts. You do it."

"Yes, sir, Mr. President," I said.

Humphrey took him at face value. But I knew better. The president didn't always mean exactly what he said. "Uh-oh," I thought, "this is a set-up."

Sure enough, the next day the president told me in no uncertain terms to keep the planes and boats away from the vice president. He was dead serious. He never even winked about the conversation the night before.

"Cross, now, by God, I don't want Hubert out there abusing those yachts and planes. Anytime he wants anything, you clear it with me."

Humphrey, as expected, contacted my office to use a plane or a boat. Immediately, I had to throw up a roadblock.

"Well, Mr. Vice President," I said, "I need to know who is going to be in your party, and what you want for supper, and we'll have to check the yachts out, check the plane out. They may be already committed for something else, and I'll need to know this twelve hours in advance."

I would then call him back later to say, "I'm sorry, the planes are all committed. The yachts are down for maintenance." There wasn't a thing in the world he could do about it.

The yachts, which I oversaw as the president's military aide, were a constant headache for me. The U.S.S. *Sequoia* was a 104-foot wooden yacht built in 1925 and used by every president since Herbert Hoover. Franklin Roosevelt installed an elevator on the *Sequoia* to accommodate his wheelchair, but Johnson had me call the Navy and tell them to tear it out and replace it with a wet bar for cocktails. He also ordered the ceilings raised by three inches so he wouldn't bump his 6-foot-3-inch frame, and he had the floor in the shower lowered. Johnson used the *Sequoia* as a sort of floating prison; he invited members of Congress aboard, twisted their arms, and wouldn't let them off the boat until they sided with him.

The other boats were the ninety-four-foot *Honey Fitz* and the sixty-four-foot *Patrick J.*

My job was to make sure the Navy maintained the three boats and had them ready for presidential use. That put me directly in the line of fire on Friday, February 18, 1966, when the *Washington Post* published an article by syndicated columnists Rowland Evans and Robert Novak. The reporters took a swipe at LBJ for spending $102,900 to refurbish the *Honey Fitz* and the *Patrick J.* after making "a fetish out of petty economies in the White House, turning off the lights and restricting the use of White House cars."

The column also criticized the Pentagon for secretly buying a $325,000 Beech King Air turboprop to use at the LBJ Ranch. I knew good and well we had congressional approval to buy it. Not only that, but the plane was part of the Special Air Missions unit at Andrews and available to any high-ranking government official.

The Evans-Novak column threw the White House into an uproar. I got to work before 8:30 A.M. and was hit immediately with phone calls and visitors. The president's press secretary, Bill Moyers, called me mid-morning, and I gave him the facts: The Navy was doing the boat overhauling, and the Pentagon had congressional approval to buy the eight-passenger King Air.

At 1:25 P.M., the president phoned me about the news article. The first words out of his mouth were "What is the story on your boats and planes?" As if I owned them! I told him the leak must have come from Rep. Melvin Laird, a Republican congressman from Wisconsin who was chairman of the House Appropriations Committee. Laird would become Secretary of Defense under President Nixon just three years later. Laird's committee staff had been nosing around about the president's travel costs.

"Get me a full report so we will know what they are putting out on us," the president said. "It looks like a sabotage job somebody did."

I told him I already had two staff members checking out the news leak and the facts. He said the Navy should take the responsibility for the boat expenditures, and I agreed.

"Now, on the plane," he said. "Have I ever ridden in it?"

"You rode in it one time, from your ranch to the judge's place," I said, referring to his close Texas friend, former Blanco County Judge A. W. Moursund. "No report was made of this."

In fact, the new plane, which had arrived at Andrews in November 1965, had been at the LBJ Ranch from November 21–30 and from December 21–29. Johnson had used it on occasion. But that was off the record.

Johnson asked how many hours the plane had flown. Two hundred, I told him. He asked whether Mrs. Johnson had flown in it. No, I said, and neither had Luci or Lynda. The plane had been used mainly by Air Force generals and cabinet members, I told him.

"The King Air costs $74 per hour to fly compared to the JetStar's $305 cost per hour," I said.

"They should just indicate that the president has nothing to do with the plane," Johnson said. "Just tell them the president has never gone out in a trip—he may have gone out and got in it, but he never made a trip in it at Washington or at the ranch. It's used for courier services and is cheaper than helicopters and crews."

The president, like a Madison Avenue public relations man, could always supply his staff with damage-control dialogue off the top of his head.

"I'll get all the facts, Mr. President, and let you know," I said.

In less than ten minutes, I was on the phone with Major General E. B. LeBailly, director of information for the Air Force. "Get the story straight," I told him, "and low-key the White House." I emphasized that the president had never flown in the plane and that it was not purchased for the White House.

I talked to several more high-ranking Pentagon officials, including Brigadier General James Kirkendall, executive officer to the U.S. Air Force chief of staff. "You never heard from me," I told them all.

The Enforcer was just doing his job.

Meanwhile, Marvin Watson, White House chief of staff, called and told me to start sending Humphrey up in the King Air "and fly it to death." The more VIPs we could get in the airplane, the more heat would be taken off the president.

I was still in my office at 7 P.M. writing a multi-page memorandum for the president that outlined exactly what kind of boat repairs the Navy was doing for $102,900. I also traced the congressional approval process for the King Air. My memo had five attachments, including letters from several key members of Congress to Defense Secretary McNamara approving the purchase of the airplane in August 1965.

"In researching all the records and all the history surrounding the boats and the planes," my memo concluded, "I find that the White House had nothing to do with either the decision to overhaul the boats, which is a routine and periodic occurrence, or to buy the King Air, as the column indicated. I believe the record will bear this out."

At 7:30 P.M., I hand-carried the memo to the Oval Office.

ALTHOUGH THE PRESIDENT CAREFULLY CONTROLLED Humphrey and his cabinet members' use of the yachts and planes, he sometimes went all out to offer planes to others. He could be incredibly generous when he chose. On January 16, 1967, he sent me to the U.S. Supreme Court, a place I'd never been, to talk to Chief Justice Earl Warren about his upcoming goodwill tour of South America.

"Cross," he said, "I want you to go down to the Supreme Court and see Earl Warren. You tell him that the president wants him to have one of the presidential jets and that you're going to send one of your assistants along to make sure everything goes right and that you're going to send your pilots from the presidential pilots' office."

I was wearing a business suit, as I usually did when working in the White

House. But Johnson asked me to change into my military uniform before going to the high court. The president easily could have just picked up the phone and called the chief justice, but he wanted to make a big ceremony out of the offer of the plane. My appearance in dress blues would enhance the aura of presidential prestige and import.

I was humbled to meet the chief justice in his private chambers. I knew the president held him in the highest esteem. Here was the man who had led the Supreme Court to the historic *Brown v. Board of Education* unanimous decision that outlawed segregated public schools and had overseen other landmark civil rights rulings. He also had led the national commission that investigated the assassination of President Kennedy. Warren, who was concerned about separation of the branches of government, reluctantly accepted the commission post only after Johnson invited him to the Oval Office and appealed to Warren's patriotism. Johnson warned that nuclear war was possible if the worldwide unrest over JFK's murder was not quelled.

I had a much easier sell. The chief justice was warm and friendly. This wasn't the first time Johnson had dispatched him in one of the big presidential airplanes. Warren headed the U.S. delegation to the funeral of Winston Churchill in January 1965, and he flew to London with former president Dwight Eisenhower in Johnson's plane.

Warren said he was pleased by the president's thoughtfulness, but that nothing he could do in South America warranted such special treatment. I told him the president disagreed and thought his visit was profoundly significant to U.S. interests. He finally agreed to use the plane on his cultural affairs trip.

Warren and his wife, Nina, left in late February to visit Bolivia, Colombia, Ecuador, and Peru. My assistant, Marine Major Haywood Smith, accompanied the Warrens as their personal aide and trip coordinator.

The chief justice held press conferences in each foreign country and was surprised when he was bombarded with conspiracy theories and other questions about JFK's assassination. (The Warren Commission's September 1964 report said the panel "has found no evidence that either Lee Harvey Oswald or Jack Ruby was involved with any person or group in a conspiracy, domestic or foreign, to assassinate President Kennedy.") Warren finally fought back in Lima, Peru. "Now let me ask you a question," he said to the reporters. "How many of you have read the commission's report?" No one raised a hand. "You could have read it had you so desired to, because we sent copies to your libraries and to some government officials."

A couple of months after the South American trip, the chief justice came under fire from Capitol Hill, where some viewed the trip to South America as a junket. Warren, who earned $40,000 a year as Chief Justice, was criticized for collecting $586 from the State Department as a "visiting United States specialist" and listing his wife as a "voluntary social welfare worker." Mrs. Warren was paid $362 for speaking to women's groups about American volunteerism.

I guess no one in Congress knew about the use of the presidential airplane or my assistant going along as Johnson's emissary. The Enforcer had it easy that time.

RUNNING THE WHITE HOUSE MESS WAS ANOTHER MATTER. An unpleasant episode that I call the "White House Mess Mess" occurred with no warning at the end of a workday in March 1966.

I supervised the White House Mess as part of my military aide duties. Dining in the White House Mess was a coveted perk, so most of my headaches involved keeping out staff members who weren't entitled to eat there. It was a constant power struggle. Mess membership was limited because only thirty seats were available and the kitchen staff was small.

To accommodate all of the senior staff, I created two lunch shifts. The early shift, 11:30 A.M.–12:30 P.M., was for the lesser luminaries. The VIPs, including the vice president, cabinet secretaries, chief of staff, national security adviser, and press secretary, took the later shift, 12:30–2 P.M. It seemed like a problem erupted every day: some lower-ranking staffers brought unauthorized guests, or overstayed their time period, or, worse, showed up later for the prestigious, A-list shift. Others phoned my office or dropped by to try to get a spot on the members' list. I had to referee all the commotion and emotion, and even collect meal charges from diners at the end of every month.

I put Navy stewards at the door to watch for dining room delinquents, but they were just enlisted men and didn't have the authority to turn anyone away. So I had them take notes. They wrote names down and gave me the list of violators. I couldn't send them to jail, much as I wished I could sometimes. Instead, I forwarded the list of troublemakers to Marvin Watson, the chief of staff.

If a situation got really out of hand, as it did on Tuesday, March 29, I reported it straight to the president.

I was getting ready to leave my office at the end of the day to head for Andrews, where I needed to put in some flight training hours in one of the presidential planes. I usually trained twice a week on top of everything else I did.

At 5:55 P.M., the phone rang. It was presidential assistant Jim Jones calling to find out whether the Mess was ready for a 6:15 P.M. legislative briefing for the president and a group of senators. What?! This was the first I knew about it. There was no way to prepare enough hors d'oeuvres and beverages for a high-level cocktail hour, let alone rearrange the furniture, in the twenty minutes remaining. I was so mad at Jones it was a good thing he was on the other end of a telephone instead of standing within reach. He knew we needed more time.

I called the naval officer who managed the Mess, and sent two of my assistants to dash over to the dining room. They arrived at 6:05 P.M. and began removing dining tables with the help of White House ushers. But Secretary of State Dean Rusk, Senate Minority Leader Everett Dirksen, and other senators already were mingling outside the Situation Room near the Mess.

At 6:20 P.M., the senators entered the White House Mess, followed by the president. No refreshments were to be seen. Johnson was furious. He went straight through the kitchen door and demanded to know where the drinks were. The beverages haven't arrived, the kitchen staff told him. Didn't they know about this function? he asked. No, they told him, not until 6 P.M. When the president asked who had caused the foul-up, no one said a word. He stormed out.

The president was so angry that when my assistant, Major Smith, detailed the kitchen scene in a memo for me, he added a plaintive postscript. "P.S. I don't want to go to Vietnam!"

I was in big trouble. Unfair trouble, but trouble nonetheless. The president was calling my office the next morning before I even arrived. When I called him back, he chewed me out for screwing up a very important meeting with congressional leaders. I told him we had had no notice of the legislative briefing until 5:55 P.M. The president said he thought we'd had three hours' notice. "No, sir, we didn't!" I said in my defense.

By mid-morning, I had a memo on the president's desk informing him that Jim Jones had not notified us of the legislative briefing in the Mess until 20 minutes beforehand and that my office had responded immediately. Refreshments were served at 6:25 P.M., I reminded him.

"To preclude such a recurrence, I've established a larger mess duty section," I wrote. "Hence, in the future the Mess can respond almost instantly when little or no advance notification is received, as in last night's case."

Jones called me just an hour after the memo hit the Oval Office. He was upset and said, "Thanks for putting me in the limelight." He said he wanted to "get the story straight." I told him that "as far as I am concerned, the story was straight, at least from this end."

I've never had much use for Jones. I've never forgiven him for his incompetence that day.

DAILY HEADACHES WITH THE MESS WERE OUTWEIGHED only by the petty problems of the White House motor pool. Most of the president's staff felt entitled to portal-to-portal transportation from the fleet of several dozen official cars in the White House garage. And I was the traffic cop who had to blow the whistle and write the tickets.

I did some wheeling and dealing with the big U.S. auto companies, which then agreed to lease us the newest models each year for one dollar. Or less! It was the greatest deal ever. For example, in 1966, I lined up 21 black Mercury sedans for 50 cents each. I got two Cadillacs for $500 each and several Ford trucks and station wagons for nominal lease fees. But sometimes I got special requests. That fall, Lynda Bird complained to me that the Mercurys in the White House garage needed more head room to accommodate her bouffant hairdo. She was having trouble getting in and out of the car, so I got her a Chrysler. Cost? One dollar per year.

The White House cars were tied up all the time, delivering messages, ferrying senior staff, and running the odd personal errand. Trouble was, the personal errand-runners abused their privileges. I sent out a policy letter that revoked cars and drivers for the frequent abusers, but they ignored it. They thought they were above reproach and went merrily on their way.

I had my own staff car and chauffeured it myself. When I became chief military aide in July 1965, there were several military aides in the White House who had staff cars and chauffeurs. I got rid of the aides but kept their cars and drivers. Even so, the fleet still wasn't big enough to meet staff demands.

One of Johnson's first acts as president had been to order federal government agencies to cut back on the use of luxury cars by 75 percent. Although the White House was exempt from the austerity measure, I knew the president depended on me to keep the use of staff cars to a minimum. Personally, I didn't like seeing so many White House aides stroking their egos by taking the cars when they should have been driving their own or walking.

Marvin Watson wholeheartedly supported my efforts to corral the cars. At his suggestion, I began compiling a monthly list of motor pool violators for him. When the infractions continued, I sent memos to the worst abusers. But the violations continued.

"Liz, I have recently been having difficulty maintaining outstanding transportation service to the principal staff members here at the White House," I wrote to Liz Carpenter, Mrs. Johnson's press secretary, on May 15, 1967.

She had averaged six violations a month by using White House cars to go to the hairdresser, hotels, and restaurants.

"I would be embarrassed if you called for a car and one was not available because someone on the staff was misusing one," I wrote. "I would also be distressed if anyone else called and we were unable to produce one because of your misuse."

The president's secretary, Juanita Roberts, also used a car to get to her hairdresser at least once a week, sometimes twice a week.

"While I realize that you must always look your best (and you always are very lovely) and that the president insists on this, I ask your assistance in helping me find a solution to this problem," I wrote to her.

Worse than staffers taking trips to the hairdresser were the White House staff members who used official cars for their families. Jack Valenti often used a White House car for his wife, the former Mary Margaret Wiley, who had been one of the president's favorite secretaries before her marriage. In one three-week period in 1966, Valenti had ordered a car fifteen times for Mary Margaret—almost every day. Joe Califano would do the same thing for his wife. And Harry McPherson, an assistant to the president, used the cars not only for his wife, but to get his child to school.

But who was I kidding? Even Marvin sometimes used the cars for his wife.

Try as I might, I never could stop the misuse of the White House motor pool. The Enforcer failed miserably in this endeavor.

AS IF BEING IN CHARGE OF FOOD AND TRANSPORTATION weren't enough, I also handled wardrobe.

If there was ever a man comfortable in his own clothes, it was Lyndon Johnson. And the clothes he loved the most were the Western-style clothes he wore at his Hill Country ranch. Johnson was famous the world over for those jaunty khaki outfits topped by a Stetson.

But the world didn't know that I was the one who ended up in charge of the pushy San Antonio tailor who made the khaki clothes. It's hard to believe how much time I spent trying to block this relentless businessman from pestering the president about his bottom line (that is, the tailor's financial bottom line, not the president's sit bones).

Irving Frank didn't just sew custom clothing. His livelihood was making tens of thousands of military uniforms. San Antonio, home of the famous battle of the Alamo, has always been a military town. Uniforms are big business there. And the well-connected Sol Frank Uniforms was a large operation. The company was started by Irving Frank's father, Sol, a Russian immigrant who arrived in San Antonio in 1908. The Sol Frank Company, known for its downtown window mannequins wearing U.S. military uniforms, fitted Hollywood stars like John Wayne. Sol Frank tailors also sewed the uniforms worn by the Mexican soldier actors in the Alamo film that starred the Duke.

Irving Frank was obsessed with making a profit. As the Vietnam War escalated, the need for American military uniforms skyrocketed. After Frank became the president's unofficial ranch tailor, he didn't shy away from seeking White House help on military uniform contracts. I had to be the gatekeeper.

The relationship with Irving Frank began shortly after LBJ became president. Frank sent Johnson a Western-cut suit as a surprise gift. The president loved the casual outfit. On January 2, 1964, LBJ phoned Frank from his ranch and the conversation was recorded by the secret taping system.

> LBJ: "Mr. Frank, are you the one who sent this suit up here?"
> FRANK: "Yes."
> LBJ: "I liked it very, very much and I just wondered . . . about what do those wholesale out at—that shirt and trousers?"
> FRANK: "I hadn't figured a price on it. How many would you want?"
> LBJ: "I don't know. I just thought I might put a few of the staff around here in 'em—a dozen or so."
> FRANK: "I'd be glad to figure out a price. Am I speaking to the president?"
> LBJ: "Yes."
> FRANK: "Mr. Johnson, it's a real honor to talk to you."

The tailor told Johnson it would be a "real privilege" to make the suits. He told Johnson it would cost $20–$25 per suit. Johnson invited him to come to the ranch that day and take measurements. The president also gave him driving directions from San Antonio and even detailed a shortcut so he could get to the ranch more quickly.

The last words the president spoke to Frank were "and stay out of the newspapers."

No recordings exist of Johnson's personal conversations with Frank during measuring, but I'm sure the conversation got rather earthy. The president's taping system did record a conversation between him and Joseph Haggar Jr., chairman of the Haggar Company, the Dallas clothier. The conversation captures Johnson's blunt style as he orders six pairs of summer-weight slacks.

> LBJ: "I want them a half-inch larger in the waist than they were before . . . so that I can take them up. I vary about ten or fifteen pounds a month."
>
> HAGGAR: "All right, sir."
>
> LBJ: ". . . Make the pockets at least an inch longer. My money and my knife and everything fall out . . . The crotch, down where your nuts hang, is always a little too tight . . . Give me an inch that I can let out there because they cut me. They're just like riding a wire fence."

The Sol Frank uniform company bent over backward to please Lyndon Johnson. They made clothes for Mrs. Johnson, the formal morning suit the president wore to Luci's wedding to Pat Nugent in August 1966, and clothes for the president's friends. They even sewed custom-made Western clothes for Johnson's toddler grandson, Lyn Nugent. When Luci and Lyn Nugent flew to Hawaii in November 1968 to meet Pat Nugent while he was on R&R leave from Vietnam, little Lyn was dressed in a replica of his father's military uniform. It was sewn by, you guessed it, Sol Frank Uniforms.

The president made his Sol Frank clothes famous around the world when he wore the khaki jacket and pants during his 1966 and 1967 visits to meet with American troops in Vietnam. Johnson even had the Sol Frank Company make a suit for Australian Prime Minister Harold Holt, a big man's man with an outsized personality to match. I even flew one of the president's planes to Texas to pick up the suit when it was ready.

The company's work was so good, even I started buying custom-made suits and jackets from Irving Frank.

One particular episode with Frank dragged on for more than a year. He had an overstock of 1,200 Air Force uniform pants in a shade of blue that was being discontinued—a color known as blue "1084." The inventory had a price tag of $13,200, and he would be stuck with the garments if he couldn't find a military need for them. He kept up a near-constant letter campaign to get the White House to help him.

Frank had a history of trying to ingratiate himself. He sent flowers and best wishes for every major occasion in the president's life. Lavender chrysanthemums for Easter. A telegram for his election victory. Roses for his inauguration.

Frank was desperate for White House help in unloading the 1084 blue trousers. He pestered me with phone calls and letters. He pestered Marvin Watson, too. But his boldest move was handing a letter to the president at the LBJ Ranch on Saturday, March 4, 1967. The one-page letter was folded in an envelope addressed in pencil by a hurried hand: "Mr. President, From Irving Frank." Without a word, the president handed the letter to me.

"During the early part of last year," the letter began, "the Air Force rather suddenly decided to change their uniforms to a darker shade blue. When changes such as this are made and this information becomes known, it practically kills the sale of any garments that are made out of the presently used color.

"I have hesitated for some months to trouble you with my problem. The quartermaster at Lackland [Air Force Base in San Antonio], at no loss to the government or taxpayers, could absorb this quantity of trousers into their inventory and use it in their issue system to incoming airmen."

I couldn't believe his audacity in bothering the president with his personal inventory problems. Marvin and I already had contacted numerous Air Force officials over the past year, including Air Force Chief of Staff General John McConnell, to try to help the Sol Frank Company sell most of the other clothing made with the outdated 1084 blue fabric, a blend of wool and dacron. McConnell had worked with Wright-Patterson Air Force Base in Ohio to get some of the 1084 blue clothing approved for optional use.

But the Air Force upper echelon had no more patience for Irving Frank. They stuck to the new color guidelines and wouldn't buy the shipment of pants. Brigadier General E. L. Ramme, director of supply and services for the Air Force, had even written Frank a personal letter, just a month earlier, suggesting that he sell his overstock as municipal police uniforms or cut his prices. He also reminded Frank that a phase-in of new styles causes leftovers in many consumer items, such as automobiles and civilian apparel, not just military uniforms.

Obviously, Frank was unmoved. He acted as though he didn't hear the Air Force telling him no. As long as he had White House connections, he was going to try to use them to get out of his hole.

I forwarded the letter that Frank had handed the president to Colonel Charles Bennett Jr., executive assistant to McConnell. Bennett was well aware of Irving Frank's regular requests.

"The subject that you and I talked about has hit me in the face again," I told Bennett in a short cover memo. "If there is any avenue that has been unexplored to date, another look—in more depth—might head off this gentleman continuing to pester the president."

I'm not sure what Frank ever did with those uniform pants. I just know that I talked to him about them until I was blue in the face. A nice shade of "1084" blue.

IF IT SOUNDS LIKE I WAS THE ODD-JOB MAN AT THE WHITE House, I was.

But I was also in charge of a high-stakes $2 million secret fund for the protection and comfort of the president. Congress allocated this "off the books" money, called the Presidential Emergency Fund (PEF), every year. But only a handful of top-level congressional and Pentagon officials knew it existed. It was hidden in a top-secret section of the budget.

The secret fund was created in the Cold War years during the Eisenhower administration to build five underground nuclear bomb shelters for the president and top government officials. The House Appropriations Committee shepherded it through Congress to counter a potential enemy attack. One of the shelters was in the basement of the White House. There was a desk and phone for me in it, though I never used it.

I learned about the PEF in July 1965, within a few days of being named White House military aide. If I was going to be custodian of millions of dollars of secret money, I figured I needed to know more about it. I went straight to the source—Texas Congressman George Mahon, the powerful chairman of the House Appropriations Committee.

During our visit, Mahon told me the fund's purpose had been expanded beyond maintenance and provisioning of the hardened bomb shelters scattered about the Washington, D.C., countryside. The money, he told me, could be used for any legitimate safety and comfort needs of the president.

Occasionally, someone accused the White House of misspending or abusing the fund. But I stand by what we did for President Johnson. Everything I spent the money on benefited the image and prestige of the presidency and the United States. I spent the money to spruce up the accommodations at Camp David, the presidential retreat in the Catoctin Mountains of Maryland; Blair House, the official guesthouse across the street from the White House; presidential planes and yachts; and, yes, even the LBJ Ranch. Heads of state and other dignitaries used these facilities too, and I didn't want any foreign leaders to stay in a shabby lodge or endure a poorly provisioned journey.

When the Air Force didn't have appropriated funds to upgrade the radio telephone gear on Air Force One, I didn't think it prudent to wait for Congress to allocate the money. That would have taken two or more years. So, I used the Presidential Emergency Fund.

We caught some heat when I used the secret fund to drill a new well at the LBJ Ranch. But the ranch's one good well providing water to the president's ranch house didn't have the capacity to serve the large military and Secret Service staff that stayed at the ranch when the president was there. We had aircraft ground crews, crash crews, airfield control tower crews, runners, drivers, messengers, and communications experts. It was absolutely necessary for me to provide a well for our water supply.

I also used the Presidential Emergency Fund to buy an irrigation pump and pipe at Johnson's ranch to bring water from the Pedernales River to the runway. The soil at the edge of the runway's pavement was badly eroded, so I needed to provide a grass cover that would hold soil in place. Word of the project leaked out and I was criticized, but I knew I'd be haunted for the rest of my life if an eroded ditch caused a jet to crash.

The Pentagon was reluctant to pay for a ready room or shelter for all the troops on standby when the president was at the ranch. There was a metal building sometimes used as a hangar for the Johnsons' private plane, so I asked the president about modifying that structure. Fine with him. So, once again, I dipped into the $2 million secret fund. I had a portion of the metal building enclosed, sheetrocked, and painted. I put in a bathroom with the same famously powerful multi-headed shower that I had installed for the president in the ranch house. It had a two-inch pipe instead of the usual three-quarter-inch pipe and a jet pump booster. Within an instant of turning on that shower, the water pressure would practically knock you over. (Johnson also had me get this same type of killer shower installed for him in the White House.) I found surplus furniture at Bergstrom Air Force Base in Austin and moved tables, chairs, couches, and even a pool table to the ranch for my men. I also put in heat and air-conditioning.

By then, former presidential aide Jack Valenti was president of the Motion Picture Association of America. He gave me a 35-millimeter projector and movies so the crews could be entertained during their long hours on standby. Of course, the projector could also be used for training films.

My hands were clean in operating the Presidential Emergency Fund, and I make no apologies for myself or for President Johnson. It's interesting to note that all the items I installed at the LBJ Ranch are now owned and maintained by the National Park Service because the president, before his death, willed that his ranch become a historic park open to the public.

I GUESS YOU COULD ALSO SAY I WAS THE CUPID WHO SHOT the arrow that matched up Lynda Bird and Chuck Robb. Robb was a social aide at the White House, and I'm the one who hired him. I thought he was a top-notch, mainstream, all-American young man. If I had rejected him, I guess the two lovebirds never would have met.

White House social aides were young military officers assigned to units in the Washington area. I, or one of my three assistants, interviewed each one of them. Most were men, but we had a few women. None were married. They came from every branch of the military. Social aides had to be the cream of the crop. They had to be very personable, physically trim, nice-looking young people. I was responsible for their behavior, so I watched them closely. I made sure they had the poise, dignity, and grace to be extensions of President and Mrs. Johnson. They had to be of absolutely sterling character. All competed fiercely for the prestigious part-time White House assignment.

The social aides were on-call to the White House from their regular duties. We chose dozens from each military service, so we could summon as many as we needed for an event. We used them at the White House as meeters and greeters at social functions, where they mingled with the crowd and kept the party moving. We also needed them at military ceremonies. We used an average of twenty-five social aides each week.

When we had an official receiving line, two social aides introduced visitors as they approached President and Mrs. Johnson. One aide stood behind the line of guests about three or four yards before they reached the president. That aide quietly announced the approaching guest's name to another social aide who stood directly behind the president. That aide prompted the president with the name just as the person was about to shake his hand. The aide behind the president was supposed to announce the guest's name in a strong voice. But Johnson never liked the way the aides did it.

"I don't know why in the hell it is that you can't get somebody to talk loud enough that I can hear what the hell they're saying," Johnson said.

Sometimes, it was just easier to perform the announcement duties myself. I never got any complaints from the president when I took over.

But then he'd find something else to protest.

"Cross, I don't know why in the hell it is that you pick all these good-looking guys and good-looking gals to work these social functions," he said. "The first thing they do, I mean the very first thing they do—these guys, these good-looking guys—they look around the room and they won't do anything but go to the prettiest women and dance with them and talk to them. And these poor little old ladies standing around with sore feet in the corner, little old wallflowers, wearing these flowery dresses, hell, they'll never talk to them. I don't know why it is that you can't teach these people the social graces to go pick on these poor little old ladies that never have anyone to talk to. You tell your people the president will entertain and dance with all the pretty women."

"Yes, sir, Mr. President," I said. "I'll sure get after that."

I'm not sure exactly when Lynda and Chuck caught each other's eye. It would have been at a White House social function. I had watched Lynda grow from a typical teenager into a lovely young woman. I'd always been close to Lynda, who whiled away many lonely hours at the Texas ranch by chatting with me and my staff in our little military trailer next to the ranch house. She had a good head on her shoulders. She also had an eye for handsome men.

Lynda and Chuck played bridge together. When Lynda needed an escort for a party at the Embassy of Peru in June 1967, Chuck was supposed to suggest some names of available young men. He suggested his own. They had a whirlwind courtship, most of it playing out at the White House.

When Lynda and Chuck decided to get married, I was the first person they told. They called me into the solarium on the third floor of the White House one evening in August 1967 and shared their engagement. I congratulated them, and I was tickled to be the first to know. Everyone in the White House supported their relationship. They asked my advice on how to break the news to President and Mrs. Johnson. "Well," I said, "just go on in there and tell them." I knew they would be well received.

They took my advice. After I left, they stayed in the solarium until the early morning hours. A giddy Lynda then sneaked into her parents' bedroom and woke them up with the news and climbed into bed to celebrate with them. Lynda and Chuck were married in the East Room of the White House on December 9, 1967. Of course I was there, and I wasn't even thinking about having to hire another social aide to fill the job opening. That could wait.

ONE OF MY OTHER WHITE HOUSE DUTIES PUT ME IN THE public spotlight like no other. As military aide, I was in complete charge of organizing and supervising the very public and very patriotic arrival ceremonies on the South Lawn of the White House whenever a foreign king, president, chancellor, prime minister, or chairman came for a state visit. The ceremonies always included an official review of the troops by

President Johnson and his foreign counterpart. And I was always right there with the two of them, making it a threesome that silently walked together around the contingents of Army, Navy, Air Force, Marines, and Coast Guard troops.

I always stayed on the president's left while the foreign dignitary would be on Johnson's right side. Our quiet stroll to inspect the troops would last only three or four minutes, but it always seemed much longer to me. I was deathly afraid that someone would faint and fall over in front of the president and his guest, or that some other unforeseen calamity would mar the ceremony. I held my breath, but made sure I showed a solemn and respectful face because the television cameras were rolling and the world was watching. In all my years working with Lyndon Johnson, I always tried to put on a confident face even when I was scared half to death.

At the same time, I was thrilled to be right in the middle of such an eventful moment at the White House. At heart, I still felt like a country boy who had somehow ended up in the middle of history in the making.

I worked very hard to make sure everything about the South Lawn arrival ceremonies went off like clockwork. I had to make damn sure the president was never embarrassed or that the United States' image was not marred by a foul-up. I was the guy on the hot seat.

My staff and I had to schedule the timing of the ceremonies, arrange the placement of troops, select and assign a band from one of the military branches, install the official review platform, cordon off the spectator and press seating areas, and get the artillery in place for the usual twenty-one-gun salute.

I was in charge of South Lawn ceremonies for President Ayub Khan of Pakistan, Chancellor Ludwig Erhard of Germany, Prime Minister Indira Gandhi of India, King Faisal of Saudi Arabia, President Ferdinand Marcos of the Philippines, President Cevdet Sunay of Turkey, President Gustavo Díaz Ordaz of Mexico, King Mahendra of Nepal, and others. My staff was well practiced, and I'm still proud today that each South Lawn arrival ceremony went off without a hitch. I didn't let my country down.

SOMETIMES, THE ENFORCER GOT TO BE OFF DUTY AND HAVE a little fun.

On one flight to the LBJ Ranch, while Mr. Johnson was still serving as vice president, we brought along Sarah McClendon, a Texas newspaper reporter well-known for her eccentric outspokenness. After we arrived, Johnson got off the plane, jumped behind the wheel of his Lincoln convertible, and said, "Come on, boys, let's go up to the Haywood place." We had about five vehicles in our mini-motorcade to his ranch and house on the banks of Granite Shoals Lake near Kingsland, about an hour away.

Johnson stayed in touch with the other cars by radio. We went by public highway toward Llano, Texas, then turned onto a gravel road leading to his ranch. Johnson saw a large rattlesnake slither from the road into a clump of prickly pear cactus. He slammed on the brakes, jumped out of the Lincoln, circled the cactus, and yelled at Secret Service Agent Rufus Youngblood, "It's a big rattlesnake, Rufus, get your gun and shoot him. Shoot him!" The other cars in the caravan had stopped as well, and everyone got out to check on the excitement.

Youngblood pulled out his revolver and took aim at the snake. But he missed with a couple of shots. "Give me the gun, Rufus. You can't hit the side of a barn," Johnson said. "Let me show you how to do it." He dispatched the snake with one shot. As he ordered everyone back in their cars, he whispered to Youngblood to bring the dead snake along. I suspected some nefarious scheme was being hatched.

At the lake house, Johnson invited Sarah and three or four other guests to come with him for a boat ride and tour of the lake. In the meantime, he had instructed Youngblood to take the dead rattler to a spot along the path to the boat dock, coil it into a life-like pose, and then keep quiet. The boaters spent a couple of hours enjoying the lake as sunset approached. The rest of us spent the afternoon having drinks and snacks on the ranch house patio.

After the boat docked, Johnson asked Sarah to walk up the path to the ranch house with him. Those of us on the patio could hear him joking with Sarah. Suddenly Johnson yelled, "Look out, Sarah, there's a big rattlesnake about to bite you!" Quite naturally, Sarah was frightened out of her wits. She yelled and jumped away. Soon she found out the snake was dead and harmless, and that the joke was on her.

"Lyndon, you son of a bitch, you scared me half to death," she told him. "Shame on you." Sarah never was one to be deferential. I was surprised she didn't call him a jackass, as she had on previous occasions.

Later, after a few more drinks and much conversation, a lot of it about the beauty and peace of the ranch and its Hill Country setting, dinner was served. I can still remember the meal—the best meal I ever had in my life. Simple Texas fare cooked to perfection: barbecued ribs, brisket, pinto beans, potato salad, and peach cobbler with homemade ice cream.

As the evening came to a close, Johnson assigned the seats for the trip back to his main ranch. Johnson drove the lead car, with his longtime friend, Judge A. W. Moursund, in the front seat, and me and my co-pilot,

Captain Paul Thornhill, in the back. Sarah McClendon and Yolanda Boozer, a secretary, were in another car with Mrs. Johnson. As we were leaving, the vice president said, "Keep your two-way radios on, everybody. I may need to talk to y'all on the way back home."

We pulled away from the lake house and topped a small rise in the road. Johnson picked up the radio microphone and told Youngblood, "Rufus, hold all those cars back there until I call you back. The judge and I need to stop just over this little hill and check out the plumbing." He and Judge Moursund emptied their bladders along the road while, needless to say, Thornhill and I sat quiet as church mice in the back seat. We were afraid to move, even though we both needed to check our plumbing too. We probably should have just jumped out and gone for it anyway, because it was a long miserable ride back to the main ranch at Stonewall.

CHAPTER EIGHT

VISITING VIETNAM AND SOUTHEAST ASIA

JOHNSON MADE HIS FIRST OVERSEAS TOUR AS PRESIDENT in October 1966, and it was a massive, spectacular event with bells and whistles, pomp and circumstance, fireworks and flash. Johnson was the first American president ever to set foot in Southeast Asia while in office. And of course the president had a surprise or two up his sleeve.

The trip was the biggest logistical challenge of the Johnson presidency so far, not only for me but for all the White House movers and shakers. The 27,000-mile trip to the Far East was the longest overseas journey made by a U.S. president since Dwight Eisenhower went on an eleven-nation jaunt in 1959. The centerpiece of our trip was a two-day summit conference in Manila, but we also visited five other supporters of the U.S. effort in Vietnam—South Korea, Thailand, Australia, Malaysia, and New Zealand.

As the president prepared to travel, reports of Vietnam peace possibilities were in the news daily. Almost every nation except Communist China was working on a peace plan of some sort, *Newsweek* reported. Some speculated that Johnson might announce a major new peace move himself. Others speculated that his trip was more political in nature, designed to put the president in the spotlight and boost the election hopes of Democrats in the 1966 congressional elections.

I had no time or patience for the speculation. The president's inner circle scrambled just to make the trip happen. Presidential press secretary Bill Moyers abandoned his plans to attend the World Series in Baltimore, and took off on a dry run of our itinerary, getting briefed at every stop and meeting with the host of the Manila conference, Philippine president Ferdinand Marcos. The White House, the State Department, the Pentagon, and all their counterparts in the countries to be visited took care of an immense quantity of logistical and protocol problems.

I had to make sure that more than two dozen American warships were moved into position throughout the Pacific Ocean to monitor the president's flights and provide navigational fixes. The flotilla was in constant contact with military commanders at Pearl Harbor and the Pentagon. Air Force bases and Seventh Fleet aircraft carriers provided jet fighter honor guards as needed for Air Force One, and air defense if necessary.

Preparations rippled around the world. To ensure the comfort of the president, with his 6-foot-3-inch frame, special beds were constructed—a seven-footer in Canberra, Australia, and a 6-foot-6-inch one in Manila. In South Korea, bands learned songs calculated to please the president, including "The Eyes of Texas." South Koreans promised a "Texas-sized welcome, Korean style" and made plans to shower the president with chrysanthemums instead of ticker-tape.

The president obsessed over some of the most minute details of the trip. He wanted an honor guard fit for a king when he deplaned Air Force One. At every stop, he envisioned two Army officers in full dress uniform hustling off his plane to first take positions at the foot of the departure stairs. They would come to attention, face each other, draw their ceremonial sabers, then raise and hold them in a salute to the president as he exited to meet the greeting party. He'd even picked out the two officers he wanted: my assistant, Army Major Hugh Robinson, and Army Colonel Joseph Conmy, a regimental commander at Fort Belvoir, Virginia.

The president's scheme bothered me. I thought the showmanship involved might be over the top, a little too majestic-looking. I wrote him a memo suggesting an alternative. But, if he insisted, I told him we didn't need to bring Colonel Conmy along, because another one of my assistants, Major Haywood Smith, would be with us anyway and could wear his dress uniform and join with Major Robinson to do all the ceremonial duties. The president didn't respond to my memo. But a day or so later, Chief of Staff Marvin Watson told me the president wanted to know, "Why didn't Jim Cross want me to have these two Army guys do this?" That question was code for "Tell Jim I'm doing it anyway." So I told Conmy to get his stuff together and be on board the plane. The salute of the sabers went just as the president wanted.

We took off early on the morning of October 17, loaded to the maximum with the presidential party for the first nonstop leg of the trip to Hawaii.

The president was a hit there. He concluded a formal dinner by using a felt-tip marker to autograph the forehead of a bemused waitress. Everyone had a big laugh. Then we were off to Pago Pago in American Samoa. The greeting crowd was huge and friendly, and the president was barely off the plane before he was bedecked with many seashell wreaths. He looked like a Kentucky Derby winner, the press said. He and Mrs. Johnson officially opened a new television-equipped school that had been renamed Lady Bird.

We ran into our first major logistical problem at our next stop in New Zealand, 2,300 miles to the southwest. Johnson briefly had visited this nation of 2.6 million people during World War II as a lieutenant commander in the Navy. We wanted to land at the airport in Wellington, but Air Force One was simply too heavy for the runway. We had to land at the O'Hakea military airbase, then transfer the presidential party to a smaller plane for the 90-mile trip to Wellington. I had wanted to send one of our small planes, a Constellation or a Douglas DC-6, to take the president those last few miles, but New Zealand authorities insisted we use one of their planes. When I saw the DC-6 they had provided, I was aghast. It looked war-weary and decrepit. It was hardly the kind of plane that I would want to put the president on. Hell, I didn't even want to ride on it myself. I worried about the mechanical condition of the plane, and I wasn't sure the New Zealand flight crew met the standards of our own crews. The nasty-looking weather between the military airfield and Wellington also made me fret.

But protocol forced me to overcome my anxieties and just make sure the presidential party got aboard. I also had to carry the presidential "football," the satchel with the nuclear codes, because my assistants were busy putting on their saber show as President and Mrs. Johnson climbed the stairs. After I boarded the plane and walked down the aisle counting heads, Liz Carpenter, Mrs. Johnson's press secretary, grabbed my arm as I passed. "Jim," she said, "I'm scared to death about this plane and the weather. Do you think it's OK?"

I replied, completely dishonestly, "Sure, Liz." Then she asked if I would sit in the seat next to her. I asked her to move over next to the window so I wouldn't have to step over her if I needed to get out. But she said she didn't like to sit by the window, so I climbed over her and buckled into the window seat as the plane started up, then smoked and leaked oil.

Liz was well-known as a reluctant flier, so I couldn't reveal my own concerns. At the beginning of the takeoff roll, she grasped my arm into a vise grip and didn't let go until we landed 45 minutes later. I spent the trip in a white-knuckle sweat worrying about the weather and the mountains. They loomed dangerously close every time I got a glance at them through the cloud cover. Although the plane was drafty and rattled and groaned in the turbulent weather, we made it.

In Wellington's civic square, a crowd of 200,000 gave the president an uproarious reception. The huge crowd chanted "LBJ, LBJ, all the way with LBJ," and anti-war demonstrators had their placards ("Hey, Hey, LBJ, How Many Kids Have You Killed Today?" and "Withdraw from Vietnam") ripped from their hands. A little old lady who said she had traveled 500 miles to see Johnson got a presidential kiss on the cheek. At one point, the president was taken with some red tulips growing in the square. Being October, it was springtime in New Zealand. The president squatted down and gave them a sniff before rising and yelling into a bullhorn: "Now that Lady Bird has seen these wonderful flowers, I know that all next year I'll be planting tulips nonstop."

The next day we took the rattletrap plane back to O'Hakea, and the trip was, thankfully, uneventful. We loaded up into the friendly confines of Air Force One and flew on to Canberra, Australia. Thousands of locals shouted a welcome, and crowds stopped Johnson's car nine times so he could visit with them on the drive from the airport into the city. "The Aussies have been my brothers since 1942," the president said, referring back to his wartime visit.

Melbourne was the next stop, and a crowd estimated at over half a million turned out. A Royal Australian Navy band blared "Deep in the Heart of Texas," and the president kissed babies, handed out ballpoint pens, and spoke with the people through a bullhorn. There was an anxious moment as well. As the president's car moved slowly down the street hemmed in by the crowd, a young man hurled plastic bags of red and green paint. The paint splattered against the limousine, the same car in which President Kennedy had been killed in Dallas. Secret Service Agent Rufus Youngblood, who had shielded Johnson with his body when the shots were fired at President Kennedy, was walking alongside the car and also got splattered. For a few moments, onlookers thought the paint might be blood and that an attack had occurred. Police hustled away the youth and a companion, and the president laughed off the incident.

The reception in Sydney the next day was even more massive—an estimated 1.2 million people lined the route of the motorcade. The crowds were overwhelmingly friendly, and the president pulled out his bullhorn every time his car stopped. When he was warned there could be anti-war demonstrators ahead, the president quipped, "Maybe we'll get a little more paint today." Twenty protesters were arrested after a clash with police. Later, the president ate a steak and relaxed in his cream-colored Stetson and gray coveralls emblazoned with a gold presidential seal on the chest. After a band serenaded us with "Waltzing Matilda," we were off to Manila.

As we left Australian airspace and headed north toward the Philippines, I gazed through the cockpit windows into the clear skies and marveled at the sandy beaches and tropical islands covered with jungle canopies. I remembered my time two decades earlier as a pilot flying to and from many of those Pacific islands. I couldn't help but wonder about a native in the village of Merauke, New Guinea, that I had seen using a broken shard of glass as a razor. It may not have been a Gillette, but the man did quite well and I marveled at his innovation. I wondered if he had ever enjoyed a real razor. And I wondered if there were women down there still wearing nothing but grass skirts. Were their lives part of the twentieth century, or were they still living in blissful ignorance?

A little later, my daydreaming was shattered by the fear of a midair collision. Four Philippine F-5 fighters appeared out of nowhere—two just off our left wing tip and two just off our right—as we approached Manila. These guys were much too close. I could see the whites of their eyes. I figured they were hotshots trying to show off a little, but I didn't trust them. I called Manila air traffic control and demanded the fighter escort be recalled or at least moved away from us to a safe 200 yards or more. Traffic control had the fighters on a different radio frequency than we were using, so I couldn't monitor their conversations. Apparently, the fighters got instructions to move away from us, but they didn't move more than a few feet. "Get those planes the hell away from us!" I demanded of the air traffic controllers.

We never permitted even our own fighter escorts to approach closer than 300 or 400 yards when we thought an escort was necessary. They finally moved away, but the little incident caused me to swing wide as we approached Manila International Airport and delayed our arrival about five minutes.

Manila was alive with activity in preparation for the summit conference, which brought together leaders of the United States and South Vietnam and their major allies in the war. Convicts were pulled out of prisons to paint government buildings, soldiers and sailors cut grass, laborers fixed potholes, and public officials made formal requests to prostitutes, pimps, and con men that they leave the diplomatic visitors alone, *Newsweek* reported.

The Manila conference resulted in no new proposals for ending the war, but rather was a show of unity among the allies and offered hope for more regional cooperation. The Johnsons kept a lower profile there than at the previous stops, seeking to advance the impression that it was a conference of equals. After the summit, the president on October 25 visited the island fortress of Corregidor, where American and Filipino troops had made a stand against Japanese invaders in the early days of World War II in the Pacific.

The president zipped rather quickly through the Corregidor visit; he had other places to go. I was waiting for him in Air Force One in a secret location. Sending Mrs. Johnson to a previously scheduled reception, the president kissed the First Lady good-bye—something he didn't normally do when leaving her for a short time. Then he climbed into a helicopter and flew to Sangley Point Naval Air Station in Manila Bay.

That's where I was hiding out. The president was going to Vietnam, but he wanted it to be a secret. Earlier that day, he had told me to move Air Force One from Manila International Airport, where it had been parked since we landed, and to meet him somewhere the press wouldn't find out about until he was ready for them to know. I considered moving Air Force One to nearby Clark Air Force Base, where I had been stationed in the late 1940s and early 1950s. But on second thought, the Navy's Sangley Point Air Base across Manila Bay seemed a better option. No one would think to look there.

I took off from Manila International using the ruse that I needed to test-fly the plane after maintenance. I immediately headed for the naval base, a flight of just a few minutes. We didn't even pull up the flaps or the landing gear. The naval folks in charge were very surprised to see that big airplane land. Before they realized what was happening, the president and his party flew in from Corregidor in the helicopters I had arranged. They hurried up the ramp into Air Force One, and we were airborne again toward Cam Rahn Bay, South Vietnam.

The surreptitious departure was planned only the day before. Speculation had been heavy that the president would visit Vietnam, but he had kept his intentions to himself. And the reasons were obvious. Announcing the visit in advance would have put not only the president in danger, but would have raised the risk to everybody involved, including our servicemen on the ground. They might have been targeted by Communists trying to get at the biggest prize of them all. And the president simply didn't want everybody knowing what he was going to do. He didn't want to be second-guessed. "If I say I'm not going, and then go, I'll be called a liar," he said. "And if I say I am going, and then don't go, I'll be called a coward."

No incumbent U.S. president had visited a foreign war zone since Franklin D. Roosevelt reviewed American troops in Casablanca in 1943.

When the other delegates to the Manila conference had left the Mala-canang Palace the day before, the president had stayed behind. He met with a group of his closest advisers: Moyers and Watson, Secretary of State Dean Rusk, and Assistant Secretary of State for the Far East William Bundy. Two unofficial confidants, Jack Valenti and Clark Clifford, were there, as was Henry Cabot Lodge, the U.S. ambassador to South Vietnam, and General William Westmoreland, the U.S. commander in Vietnam.

Westmoreland urged the president to visit Vietnam. He said the troops expected a visit and that Johnson would be as safe in Cam Ranh Bay as any place on the trip. The president said he wanted no large ceremony, and he did not want troops pulled away from their duties. Westmoreland said he could immediately prepare for the visit, and Johnson made the decision to go.

A few hours before we left, the group of about a hundred news reporters, soundmen, and cameramen accompanying the presidential party was summoned to the ballroom of the U.S. Embassy in Manila. Embassy guards and Secret Service agents locked the doors. Moyers told the media they would be going to Vietnam in the press plane, but they would be barred from contact with the outside world until the trip was over. No cell phones in those days, so this shroud of secrecy was easier to handle than it looked. Moyers said he felt like James Bond as he laid down the rules.

A few minutes after Air Force One was aloft, the president slipped into a lounging robe and spent the brief flight examining charts of the Cam Ranh Bay area with Rusk. Westmoreland sent a squadron of American fighter planes to escort us. Before we landed, Johnson slipped into what the press called his "cowboy" outfit—tan gabardine slacks and a matching zipper jacket. The clothes were made by the San Antonio tailor whom I often had to ride herd on as part of my "unofficial" duties. I'm sure I am the only Air Force One pilot in history to also be the official presidential haberdasher.

After we landed, Johnson climbed into the rear of an open jeep beside Westmoreland. The 7,000 assembled servicemen cheered as the jeep passed with Westmoreland and the president standing, hanging on to a brass handrail. A 900-man honor guard of suntanned veterans, some straight out of the battlefields, snapped to attention as the jeep rolled by. A band played "The Yellow Rose of Texas" before the president pinned medals for heroism on five men. He gave a brief but inspirational speech, and then, as *Newsweek* said, "moved through Cam Ranh Bay like a locomotive, pressing the flesh, yelling encouragement, and clearly having the time of his life." He handed out Purple Hearts at the Twelfth U.S. Air Force Hospital with tears in his eyes and ate pork chops at an enlisted men's mess hall. In an impromptu talk outside an officers' club, he said, "I pray the good Lord will look over you and keep you until you come home with that coonskin on the wall." And then, after a little more than two hours on the ground, we flew back to the Philippines.

On the flight home, we added some extra protection. When we flew from Malaysia to South Korea, General J. P. McConnell, the Air Force chief of staff, provided a fighter escort as we flew over the South China Sea east of North Vietnam. In fact, we had fighter escorts from different bases all the way to South Korea.

At one point, not far from mainland China, Dean Rusk walked into the cockpit and sat down behind me in the jump seat. "Colonel," he said, "you know at this time in their developmental history, the Chinese are very belligerent. We don't have any idea what they might try to do at any time. They, of course, know we are here today and might try to destroy this plane. We just really don't know what they might try." I shared Rusk's concerns and told him if he looked to his left he would see an entire squadron of U.S. fighter planes looking out for our welfare. The secretary sat with us for a while, speculating that the trip had been a major diplomatic success for the United States and our president. As we chatted, I felt I was in the presence of a true patriot and statesman, the likes of which might never pass our way again.

After our visit to Korea, we would go back to Washington by way of Anchorage, Alaska, via the Great Circle Route, a flight that would bring us within sight of the Kurile Islands. I feared some enterprising Russian officer might send a fighter force up to greet us. I called General McConnell and asked for another fighter escort, but he told me none was available. I knew that we constantly kept B-52 heavy bombers aloft, so I asked him to send me one to accompany us through the danger area. He told me a B-52 wouldn't help much if we were attacked by fighters. "Yes, sir, I know that," I said. "But at least if we were to be attacked and shot down, the B-52 could report our loss, so the world would know the Soviet S.O.B.'s did it."

He didn't hesitate. "You've got it, Jim," he said. We got the B-52 to fly with us to the Aleutian Islands.

Our homeward-bound flight took on a party atmosphere as everyone celebrated the successful journey to Southeast Asia. Passengers sipped champagne and even donned party hats. Some of them even performed a musical comedy with skits that spoofed the trappings and protocol of presidential travel. One song was called "On the Road with LBJ." And this was years before Willie Nelson's hit song about being on the road again.

After a refueling stop in Anchorage, we were on our final flight leg home. What should have been the most worry-free part of the long trip turned into an unpleasant flight. We hit very heavy turbulence, and try as I might, I couldn't find a smooth cruising altitude. We were bouncing up and down like a spastic yo-yo. I even slowed down because I didn't want to put any more stress on the airplane. A routing change didn't help, either. We weren't in a thunderstorm; there was no lightning or rain. It was just severe turbulence in the clouds. I had never been happy with the weather radar on this plane, and I was really peeved that night.

Several people from the cabin came forward from time to time to complain, and, of course, Liz Carpenter was sending some of them up. About an hour out of Washington, Marvin Watson came forward and asked, "Boy, what's going on up here? Can you get us out of this?" He knew Mrs. Johnson was frightened.

"Marvin, I'm doing everything in the world I can. We've changed altitude. We've changed our route." I told him I had done everything I could think of except crash the plane.

"Well, do what you can except that!" he snapped.

Mrs. Johnson described the flight in her diary: "Never in all my life and travel have I been on a big plane that tossed and twisted and plunged like Air Force One did then. Thirty-one thousand miles of good flying, and within an hour of home I was scared white. I looked at Ashton [Gonella, Lady Bird's secretary], and she looked ready to faint. Liz, who hates to fly, was sending inquiries to the pilot. I was holding on to the arm of the State Department man next to me. I am sure he had blue bruises the next morning."

No one was more relieved than I when we landed safely back in Washington. A couple of days later, the president announced he was going to undergo surgery to repair a golf-ball-sized hernia at the site of the incision made for his gallbladder surgery a year ago. But they couldn't blame our rough flight for that.

Cross and President Johnson walking near the White House Rose Garden, February 1, 1966. LBJ Library photo by Yoichi Okamoto, A1852-20a.

Cross, left, and cousin Harold Cross
on the occasion of their graduation
from Pleasant Home High School,
1943. Author's personal collection.

Jim and Martha Catoe at their country store in Pleasant Home, Alabama, 1930s.
Author's personal collection.

THE WHITE HOUSE

WASHINGTON

November 3, 1960

Dear Captain Cross:

I have been remiss in not thanking you, Captain
Waldrep, Sergeant Wainscott and Sergeant Palmer
for the many kindnesses showed to me and the members of my party when we went to Staunton recently
in an Air Force Convair. I suspect I have come to
take for granted the service accorded me by the
members of Colonel Draper's crew, service that
was in every way equalled by the four of you in
the smaller ship we used last Thursday. At any
rate, I want to make a record, by means of this
note, of my appreciation to all of you.

It is gratifying and reassuring to know that you
typify, I am sure, the fine group of people in the
1299th Air Transport Squadron of the 1254th Air
Transport Group.

With best wishes, and again my thanks,

Sincerely,

Dwight D Eisenhower

Captain James V. Cross
Aircraft Commander
1299th Air Transport Squadron
1254th Air Transport Group
MATS, Washington National Airport
Washington, D. C.

Letter of thanks from President Dwight D. Eisenhower, after Cross subbed for the
president's regular pilot on a flight to Virginia. Author's personal collection.

To Jim Cross
Competent, loyal and my friend

Xmas '64   Lyndon B. Johnson

Photograph of the president autographed and presented to Cross for Christmas 1964.
Official White House photo by Donald Stoderl.

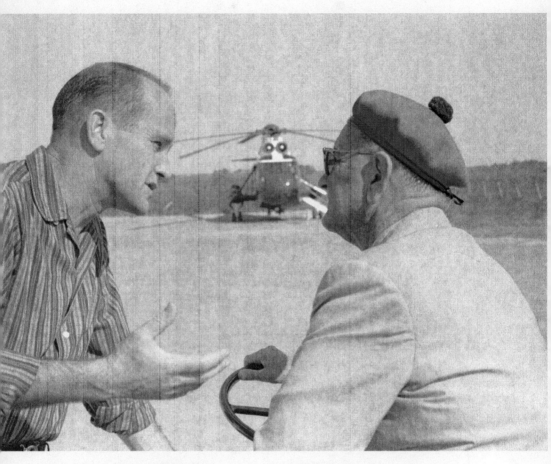

Cross and President Johnson on the airstrip at the LBJ Ranch, November 1965. LBJ Library photo by Donald Stoderl, C813-11-WH65.

Office of the White House Press Secretary
(Austin, Texas)
- -

THE WHITE HOUSE

Major James U. Cross, who will become a Lieutenant Colonel on July 15, entered the Air Force in 1944. He served in the China-Burma-India theater near the close of the Second World War. He holds the outstanding unit award, with bronze oak leaf cluster, the Armed Forces Expeditionary Medal, the Presidential Service Badge, and the Small Arms Expert Marksmanship ribbon.

He achieved his present rank of major in September, 1962.

Major Cross has commanded the Presidential Jet Star since February, 1964; prior to that time, he commanded the aircraft assigned to then Vice President Johnson. Major Cross has been a pilot of special mission aircraft for high-ranking officials of the U.S. Government since September, 1958. Prior to that he served as Operations Officer, Dover Air Force Base, Delaware, and Base Flight Operations Officer, Goose Air Base, Newfoundland.

Major Cross was born in Adulusia, Alabama, on April 25, 1925 and attended Alabama Polytechnic Institute in Auburn, Alabama.

He is married to the former Marie Campbell. They have four children.

#   #   #

After President Johnson announced that Cross would be the new director of the White House Military Office as well as Johnson's personal military aide, the White House issued this "backgrounder" press release on Cross's career highlights.

Cross takes notes during a meeting with President Johnson and Senator Ralph
Yarborough in the Oval Office, March 12, 1968. LBJ Library photo by Yoichi Okamoto,
A5797-5a.

MEMORANDUM

THE WHITE HOUSE
WASHINGTON

May 11, 1967
12:05 PM

MEMORANDUM FOR THE PRESIDENT

Governor Bryant wants one of your big jets on May 25th for his
trip out to Nebraska and Wyoming. He will be accompanied by the
Federal team and will return the same day.

On June 6th, he has asked for a big jet for a trip of the team to
Texas.

Respectfully,

JIM CROSS

APPROVED: _____ OK this time _____

DISAPPROVED: _____

Let's hold,
make hold
three

MEMORANDUM

THE WHITE HOUSE

WASHINGTON

Monday, 6 May 1968 - 5 PM

(9)

MEMORANDUM FOR THE PRESIDENT:

The State Department informs me that Ambassador Harriman
wants one of your planes for the peace talks. He thinks the
windowless C-135's are drafty and are not appointed befitting
his position and mission.

Respectfully,

Jim Cross
JIM CROSS

APPROVED: _____

DISAPPROVED: ___✓___

One of Cross's White House duties was fielding requests from government officials for
the use of presidential aircraft. These memoranda are typical of the system used by
Cross to communicate with the president. Author's personal collection.

Secret Service Agent Clint Hill, Cross, and President Lyndon Johnson on the tarmac at March Air Force Base, California, April 1968. LBJ Library photo by Yoichi Okamoto, C9604-10A.

President Johnson meets with Cross in the "little office" just off the Oval Office, about a month after LBJ stunned the nation by announcing he would not seek another term as president. LBJ Library photo by Yoichi Okamoto, A6163-10.

AUSTIN, TEXAS

Dear Jim:

Mrs. Johnson and I are going to try our best
to accept your invitation for April twenty-eighth.

So many last moment tasks and problems are
arising concerning the Library dedication that
I am hesitant to say a definite yes to anything,
but, we will be there if we can.

Meanwhile, know we're wishing you all the
good in the world.

Sincerely,

Brigadier General James U. Cross, USAF
75 Tac Recon Wg (C) (TAC)
Bergstrom Air Force Base, Texas 78743

April 12, 1971

I'm coming Hell or high water —

President Johnson's response to the invitation to attend Cross's retirement ceremony at
Bergstrom Air Force Base. The president wrote across the bottom, "I'm coming hell or high
water." Author's personal collection.

Cross, President Lyndon Johnson, and General William Momyer enjoy a lighthearted moment at Cross's retirement ceremony at Bergstrom Air Force Base in Austin, Texas, April 28, 1971. Official United States Air Force photograph.

LBJ Ranch

Stonewall, Texas

February 2, 1973

Dear Jim,

Walking through all the paces of last week, I
was so grateful that I had your strong arm to lean on,
literally and figuratively. It made it so much easier
on Lynda, Luci, and myself to be working with a real
friend and the very man that Lyndon would have had
us work with. Thank you for your steady assurances,
your good judgment, your many, many considerations,
and gentle sympathy.

Lyndon had a life of usefulness, of impact, and of
many happinesses. How can a man ask for more than
that. I'm so glad I shared thirty-eight of those years
with him.

Lyndon loved having his friends around him
during life. I know he would have liked the kind of
exit he made from this earth - with the balance of
dignity for the office and grace and warmth for the
man.

Most sincerely, and
always affectionately
Lady Bird Johnson

Letter of thanks to Cross from Lady Bird Johnson following the funeral of the
president. Author's personal collection.

Luci Johnson Nugent

2706 MACKEN STREET
AUSTIN, TEXAS 78703

February 12, 1973

Dearest Jim,

Few know better than you how deeply Daddy cherished the virtue of loyalty. You were there in sunshine and in our greatest sorrow, you were the first to rally and the last to leave. How proud he would have been to know you were by our side through difficult days and by his to take him on that last trip home.

Mother says that there are two words we must eliminate from our vocabulary - if only - and three we must concentrate on - aren't we glad. When I think of "aren't we glad" I recall the magical moments I spent with Daddy and so many of them were in your safe hands headed home. You never said the two words he despised, "I can't", for you were a can do man who always delivered for him - and when he was gone delivered for his family. My father said there were two types of friends, the talkers and the doers. You were a dawn to midnight doer, Jim and for the 1,001 assistances and sacrifices you've given us all, we love you.

Devotedly,

Luci Johnson Nugent

Personal letter to Cross from the president's daughter, Luci Nugent, after President Johnson's funeral. Author's personal collection.

CHAPTER NINE

AROUND THE WORLD, PART ONE

WHEN THE PRESIDENT TOLD ME HE INTENDED TO SPEND Christmas 1967 quietly in the White House, and that there would be no holiday traveling, I have to admit I didn't really believe him. I suspected I would get a last-minute call telling me his plans had changed and he wanted to return to his Texas ranch. Spur-of-the-moment trips had become so commonplace that I was never surprised and I was always ready to go.

Just as I suspected, those stay-at-home travel plans went in the trash can. But I never dreamed we would end up flying around the world in four-and-a-half days—and that Lyndon Johnson would become the first president to circumnavigate the globe. Our 26,959-mile trip took us to seven countries and territories, and we kept the president's jet in the air for fifty-nine hours of the 116-hour trip. Lyndon Johnson in orbit, the press said. "Lyndon B. Magellan," squawked *Life* magazine. It was a blur of a trip that exhausted everybody, except maybe the fifty-nine-year-old president, who kept up his strength by pedaling a stationary bicycle and grabbing airborne naps in his bedroom cubicle. He fortified himself with bowls of vanilla ice cream at all hours.

What made the trip an even more unnerving experience for everybody was that the president made up the itinerary as we went along. I don't think even he knew for certain when we started all the places we might end up stopping, although I suspect he had more of an idea than he let on. The secrecy the president insisted on gave the historic journey an air of the mysterious. No one—not the press, the Secret Service, or heads of state—could be certain where we would pop up next, sometimes unannounced, sometimes in the middle of the night.

The odyssey was triggered when the president's cherished friend and ally, Australian Prime Minister Harold Holt, disappeared December 17, 1967, in a swimming mishap off a jagged, rocky beach near his summer home in Portsea. A witness said he was lost in the swirling, fifteen-foot surf after the waves became violent and "boiled up into fury." His body was never found, despite a search party of 300. The president had a relationship with Holt that he shared with no other world leader. They were simpatico, sharing bottomless reserves of energy, down-home speech, and a flair for the spectacular. They were even the same age. Holt said his philosophy was never to waste a moment. He was sometimes described as Australia's answer to James Bond. He loved the ocean, and he loved to challenge it as a swimmer, spear fisherman, skin diver, and water-skier. Eight months earlier, a twenty-seven-year-old fashion model had saved him from drowning at the same beach where he disappeared. Doctors had advised him to cut down on swimming because of muscle trouble in his shoulders and back. But he could never stay away from the water.

The president and the prime minister spoke often by telephone. Earlier in the year, Holt had been the guest of the president at Camp David. Holt was a staunch ally in Vietnam. One of his first acts after taking office in January 1966 was to triple the Australian troop commitment. Holt's promise that he would "go all the way with LBJ" had become a rallying cry for supporters of his pro-American stance on the war. "We struck things off together," the president said after Holt's death. "He spoke plain, unvarnished, without any dressing . . . I don't think I have ever known a man whom I trusted more or for whom I had greater affection."

Knowing how close the president and Holt were, I shouldn't have been surprised that we would make the trip to Australia for the memorial service. But I still was caught flatfooted when the president called me at 11:35 A.M. on Sunday, December 17, just hours after he had learned of Holt's disappearance. "Cross," he said, "we may want to go to Australia tomorrow. You better get my big plane out and make sure it's ready to go."

My heart rate shot up. What he was asking was impossible. The "big plane"—the intercontinental version of the Boeing 707 (tail number 26000) specially equipped with creature comforts for long international flights—was scattered in pieces at the Lockheed hangar at JFK Airport outside New York City. The extra-long presidential bed was there too. During the Thanksgiving holiday at the ranch, the president had given me the go-ahead for the plane's overhaul, which was required every two years and was now overdue. He told me then that he didn't have any major travel plans and that it would be no problem to have the plane out of commission for a couple of months. I followed up our conversation with a short memo, and the president once again approved by checking the "yes" option on my note and initialing it. I tried to be diplomatic in refreshing the president's memory. "Mr. President, you'll recall, sir, that I sent you a note two weeks ago that the big plane is in the Lockheed Air Service contract facility in New York and it won't be ready for forty-five days."

That didn't faze him. "Well, go up there, get it fixed and get it back down here," he said. "We plan to leave tomorrow."

I had just been at the maintenance hangar two days before, and I could verify that that plane wasn't going anywhere for a long time. The plane had been practically dismantled, a complete Humpty Dumpty job. It had taken them two weeks just to take it apart. If it takes two weeks to tear it down, it takes at least four to put it back together. And so I chuckled, and said, "Well, Mr. President, it's impossible. There's no way."

He wasn't buying it. "Well now, why in the world did you let my airplane get off when I want to go somewhere?" I told him we could prepare one of the other presidential 707s for the trip, but he would have none of that. The backup planes were seven feet shorter than his favorite plane and had a wingspan of 130 feet compared to the bigger plane's 145-foot wingspan. The backup also held less fuel. "No, I don't like those planes," he said. "They don't have good sound-proofing and I don't like the seats and they don't have a bed in them like I'm used to."

The president finally gave in after I insisted that even a superhuman, around-the-clock effort could not put his favorite plane back together in less than a month. But he let me know that "you Air Force people always seem to be able to find some way to make me feel uncomfortable." Again, I offered to spruce up a backup plane to make it comfortable enough for an overseas flight. The backup plane (tail number 86970) certainly would have no problem making the trip. It would require a couple of extra fuel stops because it carried 50,000 pounds less fuel than our regular plane. I actually liked flying the backup plane more. We had customized it with more powerful engines. It was more of a hotrod than 26000, and fun to fly. The big objection—as far as the president was concerned—was that it did not have the niceties and feel of home that his favorite plane had.

Johnson rattled off a laundry list of things he wanted done to make the backup plane president-worthy. "Well, you better fix it up so it'll have a nice quiet bedroom, a place where I can sleep. Put some of your men on that airplane and fix all the windows so no outside light will leak in. Put a lot more sound-proofing in the walls and fix a projector in that thing and bring some good movies, and put one of my good beds in it because I need to rest. And don't forget to put on plenty of good food and Diet Fresca."

Once the president hung up, I thought to myself, "Oh, Lord. We'll never get that airplane ready." But we had to try. I quickly called Colonel Sid Hess, our maintenance officer at Andrews Air Force Base, and Colonel Lyle Thomas, the wing maintenance director. I told them to roll out the best and the brightest, the hardest working and most motivated maintenance people. We would have to practically rebuild the interior in one of the secondary planes. They were to spare no effort or expense. "Boys," I said, "we'll take seats out and we'll put a little partition here and a curtain up there, and we'll do this, and we'll do that, and we'll use plenty of Velcro tape and foam padding stuff to cover the windows to make it dark inside."

Over the next forty-eight hours, the maintenance team under Colonel Hess pretty well gutted the interior of the plane and reconfigured it the way the president wanted. My co-pilots, Lieutenant Colonel Paul Thornhill and Major Donald Short, and navigator Lieutenant Colonel Charles Rogers, joined in this speedy makeover. We stitched and sewed and hammered and knocked and banged and put beds, curtains, and whatnot in there, and took seats out, and changed other seats around. Where four seats had been, we bolted down the president's exercise bike. We also crafted padded covers for all eighty windows in the cabin with ⅜-inch foam edged with Velcro. These could be attached to the plane's windows by our cabin crew to keep out any cracks of daylight. Once they were in place, they were as good as any blackout window in London in World War II. As usual, our folks could and did perform miracles. When it was time to go, we had the interior of that thing practically rebuilt. While it was not really worthy of the presidency, it was quite comfortable. The president pointed out several times during the trip that he was well pleased.

From the beginning, the president was thinking about extending the trip from just a visit to Australia to a world tour. He told me he might want to visit the troops in Vietnam and come home by way of Japan and Alaska. Or, he said, he might want to come home through Rome and visit the pope. Either way, it was going to be a ball-buster. "I absolutely expect you not to tell one damn soul about this," he warned. He didn't want the world to know in advance. He worried about security, but he also feared the embarrassment of anti-American demonstrations. So he planned to keep everyone, including the news media and many of those of us flying with him, guessing all the way. On Monday, December 18—the day before we left—the president called his old adviser, Jack Valenti, and started him to work on setting up a visit with the pope at the Vatican. Valenti was Catholic and had met Pope Paul VI in 1965 in New York City. He had connections.

Even though we were just hours from takeoff, the Australia visit still had not been officially announced to the media. Press secretary George Christian, who had been at home with the flu just the day before, sent the president a memorandum on Monday urging the announcement be made immediately. Reporters going on the press plane had to get their immunizations, update their passports, and make travel preparations. (The State Department kept the passport office open until 10 P.M. to help with the rush.) Also, word would definitely leak anyway, since the president was taping an interview with the three television networks that would be aired after we were airborne. The networks had been told in confidence that the trip was on. Christian feared the White House would lose the trust and goodwill of other journalists if they also were not informed. Finally the White House relented, just before 5 P.M. Reporters were told for sure they were going to Australia, that there could be some additional travel but that they would be back in time for Christmas. They weren't told anything else officially. But speculation immediately began that we also would be going to Vietnam and Thailand.

Christian was caught in the middle of the president's passion for secrecy and the media's insistence on their right to know. Security, of course, was an issue, but the president always liked to keep his plans to himself. He reasoned that he did not like to announce travel itineraries unless he was certain he was going. He feared the creation of a crisis atmosphere if he ended up canceling plans for reasons the public did not understand. The press didn't buy into this line of thought.

I had a lot of last-minute coordination to do. I put in thirteen hours at the White House on Monday, fielding or placing ninety telephone calls from my East Wing office before leaving at 9:15 P.M. to go look at the airplane at Andrews. Everyone needed to talk to me: the president, White House aides, Pentagon officers, State Department diplomats, my crew at Andrews, and secretaries. Even my car mechanic from the White House motor pool was looking for me to discuss some needed repairs. The president called periodically to check on the plane's progress. He even called me during a break in the taping of the television special to ask more questions about possible routes and flight times. Our itinerary changed at least fifteen times. I was working nonstop to make sure everything was in order on our substitute Air Force One. I also had to arrange the chartered Pan Am plane that carried the news media, and I had to schedule a backup presidential plane to carry extra staff and equipment. We traveled with a backup Air Force One only on overseas flights. President Kennedy had used a backup on all of his official flights, domestic and international. But when Johnson became president, he did away with that. He said it was an unnecessary waste of taxpayer money, just like leaving lights on in empty White House rooms.

Before we could leave, we had to get overfly clearances from every country we would cross without giving away the possible Rome destination. We had the Navy set up a picket line of ships in case Air Force One was forced down at sea. Contrary to Hollywood's portrayal of Air Force One, there is no special rescue pod or emergency ejection equipment for the president or for the rest of the crew either. The Navy ships were the closest thing to a rescue plan we had.

Because I was military aide to the president in addition to my position as Air Force One pilot, I was in charge of all the president's transportation needs. I had the Air Force dispatch several C-141 cargo planes carrying advance security agents, limousines, and helicopters to different locations around the world where we might stop. Although I had no firm itinerary in hand, we had to have the required assets close at hand to be ready to go in whatever direction the president decided. I estimated our advance communications equipment would total 34,000 pounds; the TelePrompTer and other equipment used by the president during speeches weighed half a ton alone.

Among the twenty-eight passengers on board the president's plane were Christian; Valenti; Australian Ambassador John Keith Waller; Walt Rostow, special assistant for national security; Marvin Watson, chief of staff; Assistant Secretary of State William Bundy; and Charles and Jane Engelhard of Florida, personal friends of both the late prime minister and the president. Charles Engelhard, who had made a fortune in mining, was an informal adviser to the president as well as a close friend. The president always liked to have company around him, and since none of his family was going on the trip, the Engelhards were the stand-ins.

We had a large entourage, no doubt about it—more than 300 people on three planes—but we didn't take everyone who wanted to go, by any means. It never ceased to amaze me when mid-level White House workers who thought they were essential—but weren't—pushed to get on the manifest. Everyone wanted to bring their secretary and their horse holder. Hangers-on seem to appear out of nowhere when a trip on Air Force One was dangled. Just before we left for Holt's funeral, an Australian graduate student at Yale sent the president a telegram asking if he could hitch a ride on the flight. Marvin Watson's staff sent him a polite letter saying there would be no room for him.

One other unauthorized passenger almost breached security. As the president said good-bye to Lady Bird on the South Lawn of the White House, his little dog Yuki jumped aboard the Marine helicopter for the ride to Andrews. Yuki was no stranger to Marine One or Air Force One. He often flew to the Texas ranch with the Johnson family, and, even in the cockpit, I sometimes could hear him barking when he played with the president. Yuki thought he was going on this trip, but he was chased off before he could become a globetrotting stowaway.

We took off at 12:02 P.M. on Tuesday, December 19. I wasn't thinking about making history on the flight. I was just hoping everything would fall into place with no problems. I worried about the weather, the advance planes I'd dispatched, and whether there would be any unforeseen delays. But I kept my concerns to myself, and my crew sensed nothing out of the ordinary. The president went straight to his compartment. He said he hadn't slept in three days and wanted a nap. But he was too hyped up. Instead, he chatted with his guests and had his usual lunch: a bowl of chili, two glasses of buttermilk, some crackers, and one-and-a-half bowls of vanilla ice cream, which he couldn't seem to live without. We always tried to stock Air Force One with Blue Bell ice cream from Texas, the president's favorite brand. But this trip came up so suddenly, we didn't have time to order any. I usually ate whatever the president had—except for chili. He liked it so spicy I couldn't stomach it. I ate a sandwich in the cockpit.

Mrs. Engelhard gave the president an early Christmas present: a blue paisley bathrobe. He was so proud of it he immediately put it on and walked the aisles showing it off. He finally went to bed and slept most of the five-hour trip to northern California.

About fifteen minutes from our refueling stop at Travis Air Force Base near Sacramento, we learned there were 2,000 servicemen and servicewomen waiting outside to greet Air Force One. The president was awake by now, again wearing his blue bathrobe, and he was in a good mood. If the air crews wanted to meet him, he was willing to make their day. "We aim to please," he said. We also got word that there were forty-one injured troops from Vietnam who had arrived at a nearby military hospital just that morning.

We landed at 2:13 P.M. West Coast time, and the president went over to the crowd and shook hands up and down the fence. From the cockpit, it looked as though he reached every person in a uniform. The reaction was always the same: "He touched me! He shook my hand!" We were only on the ground for forty-five minutes, but the president made a quick visit to the hospital and visited the injured boys.

As we left California and crossed the Pacific, the three networks ran one hour of a taped interview the president had done the day before with Dan Rather of CBS, Frank Reynolds of ABC, and Ray Scherer of NBC. The president sat in a padded rocker in the Oval Office in a scene that some said was reminiscent of President Franklin Roosevelt's "fireside chats." The president outlined a new peace initiative for the Vietnam War, raising the possibility of more participation in peace talks by the National Liberation Front, the so-called political arm of the Vietcong. He also challenged America's businessmen to come up with jobs for unemployed blacks.

When we approached Honolulu about 6 P.M. for our second fuel stop, a heavy rain was falling. The air traffic controllers advised all other incoming aircraft to hold until we touched down. This was standard procedure when a presidential plane is making a landing. But the crew of a United DC-8 passenger plane elected to land on a shorter runway instead of waiting for us to clear the main landing strip. Unfortunately, the airliner ran off the runway, leaving the passengers stranded for several hours, unable to deplane, in a patch of mud and rock. No one was hurt. Later, a misleading press report said the airliner "crash-landed . . . as a result of President Johnson's unexpected arrival." When a congressman later asked the White House about the incident, the query was routed to me. I told his staff that it seemed to me the airline flight crew was grasping at straws to try to explain why they ran off the runway. Air Force One wasn't the problem; the other crew made the wrong decision.

A small crowd of politicians, including Hawaii's Governor John A. Burns, Alaska's Governor Walter J. Hickel, and Hawaii's Senator Hiram Fong, and dozens of Boy Scouts, Girl Scouts, and Cub Scouts greeted us in the tropical downpour. Of course there were the all-too-familiar war protesters, a fixture at every presidential appearance in the United States, even in the far-flung state of Hawaii during a driving rainstorm. The fifty protesters were far outnumbered by the 3,000 Johnson supporters, but they were an irritant nonetheless. The Scouts booed them, and the president glared at them. One mother who accompanied a Cub Scout troop later wrote the president that the boys' view of him was "blocked by a few of the raunchiest hippies I have ever seen." She said she sympathized with what the president was going through. The president stood under a red umbrella and delivered a brief but touching eulogy to his lost friend while the war protesters tried to shout him down. The journalists who accompanied us got soaked. They could come up with only one umbrella among them as they left the press plane, and they gallantly gave that to the only female reporter on the trip, Muriel Dobbin of the *Baltimore Sun*. By the time she got back on the press plane, her male colleagues had stripped off their soaked clothes, hung them all over the cabin, and wrapped themselves in blankets. She said the plane smelled like a steam laundry. We were on the ground for about an hour and a half, enough time for an Army dentist to come aboard and work on a sore tooth that had been bothering the president. The press never knew the president had to open wide before we headed to American Samoa, our next fuel stop.

Speaking of the news media, none of the reporters knew what a close relationship I had with the president. Fine with me. That meant they didn't pester me very often when we were on the ground with questions that I couldn't or shouldn't answer. And that was the way the president wanted it. He always told me, "Cross, don't you be going out there and talking to these damn press people. They're going to be asking you a lot of questions, so just keep your mouth shut."

That was my forte. I was friendly with all the reporters who traveled with us, but I didn't tell them anything. Kind of the old dumb country boy approach. They would ask me where we were going, and I would say, "Beats me. Ask the president." We didn't have to worry about what we said on board the presidential plane because the reporters were all on the press plane. Conditions on the press plane were not plush by any means. The reporters got to spend only one night in a hotel during the trip. The rest of the time they all had to sleep on the plane sitting up, with the exception of Dan Rather, who apparently wrapped himself cocoon-like in a blanket and stretched out below three rows of seats. None of the other reporters could ever figure out how he awoke after a deep sleep with his hair perfectly coiffed and his suit wrinkle-free.

The reporters' agony began before the trip ever started. Like the president, I stayed current on world travel immunizations—a gamma globulin and cholera shot every six months as well as regular boosters for typhoid, tetanus, yellow fever, and other dread diseases. But the reporters had to get five immunizations before we left, so they all departed with sore arms and perhaps sore butts as well. Many of them also had slight fevers and generally felt rotten from the shock of five vaccinations at one time. Then, en route, when we decided we were going to Vietnam and Thailand, they all had to get hepatitis shots—and that one definitely went in the rear end. There were a couple of casualties on the press plane. Cyril Rennie, the vice president of RCA who was assisting the electronic media, was hospitalized after suffering a heart attack in Australia. Charles Franks, a CBS sound technician, collapsed from sheer exhaustion while airborne and was hospitalized in Thailand. Two Navy medical corpsmen aboard the press plane were hailed by the media as well as the president for their quick actions in administering oxygen to Franks.

The leg of the trip from Hawaii to American Samoa established a pattern for the trip. It seemed we woke up people wherever we went. Or we kept them up later than they were used to. In Pago Pago, after a stormy and turbulent flight, we were met by the governor, Owen S. Aspinall, and his wife at 12:30 A.M. on Wednesday, December 20, at the Tafuna International Airport. The reception in Pago Pago was the wildest of the trip. About 1,000 natives, many of them shirtless, held up torches as we arrived. The dancing flames and the passionate greetings could have been a scene straight out of Hollywood. A crowd of natives came right up to Air Force One to escort the president. There was drumming and dancing and celebrating, and I caught snatches of ukulele music bouncing off the lush mountains. It looked like every single inhabitant of the island had shown up. Everyone was joyous and wide awake. Some wore a traditional headdress of colorful feathers; others wore matching white uniforms. The president received leis of shells and flowers before making his remarks. It was a sight to behold, more intoxicating and evocative of an island paradise than when I saw Pago Pago in daylight the year before on the president's trip to Asia. The spectacle ended with a children's choir serenading us with the U.S. National Anthem and the Samoan Anthem, "Amerika Samoa." The president came back on board grousing about the muggy island air and declaring himself incompatible with the tropics. "I have trouble breathing," he said.

When we took off from Pago Pago at 12:55 A.M., we had a couple of new passengers: two Australian news correspondents. Despite the president's penchant for keeping the media at bay, he knew how to take advantage when it suited him. He'd get more column inches in Australia by having these two ride into their home country aboard Air Force One.

At 2:25 A.M., we crossed the International Date Line. Suddenly, it was Thursday, December 21. I'd been so busy racing the clock to get the plane ready and all the equipment launched that the days had run together. Now I had proof that this trip was making hours disappear. I wasn't a coffee drinker, but I had to go to the galley to pour a cup before we got to Australia so I could stay awake. I didn't leave my commander's seat in the cockpit too often on any trip with the president. He had caught my co-pilot at the controls on one of our earliest flights together and told me, "Cross, I hired you to fly this airplane. Not that other fellow." As long as I had to sit in the left-hand seat, I made it comfortable. A cockpit can get chilly when you're flying 600 miles an hour at 30,000 feet with nothing much between you and the frigid atmosphere except a thin aluminum skin. So I had our technicians install a heating unit at my feet in the president's bigger plane because my toes always got cold. But there wasn't a heater in this backup plane, and I felt the difference. My Air Force dress uniform socks did nothing to keep my feet warm.

I started my descent just before 4 A.M., about 100 miles out of Canberra. We took it gently. I just eased the throttles back ever so slightly, and nobody in the back could even tell we'd reduced the power because I did it in little bitty increments. As we arrived just after daylight, the president came up into the cockpit to have a few words with me. "Well, Cross, you look like a really tired fellow." I admitted I was a little tired. It had been twenty-five hours since we had left Washington. The president made reference to his busy schedule and then said, "I won't be needing you for about twenty-four hours. You find yourself a hotel room somewhere and just go to bed and get plenty of rest." Of course, he probably knew that our advance people had made hotel reservations for all of us and I was just a door or two down from where he was staying because, as the presidential military aide, it was my job to be close at hand. He often feigned ignorance about the mundane things like accommodations, but he knew everything that was going on around him. In fact, we were all booked at the Canberra Rex, the same hotel we stayed in during the president's trip to Asia just the year before. The president even had the same room.

Before the president got off the plane, he gave me my marching orders, sort of. "We'll leave here in about thirty-six hours. You make some plans to go maybe up to Vietnam. Maybe we'll go to Thailand." He said he also might want to go to Pakistan to see that country's leader, Ayub Khan. "And we might want to go see the pope."

I wasn't totally surprised, since the president had told me before we left Washington that we might extend the Australian trip. As the president got off the plane, he left me this admonition: "But now don't go telling anybody." And I didn't. I didn't tell the pilot of the Pan Am press plane, Captain Doug Moody, who is a fine lad and a longtime friend. I didn't tell Mr. Rostow. I didn't tell my wife when I talked to her on the phone. I didn't tell a soul.

There were no large crowds to greet the president in the early morning hours, only a small entourage led by interim Prime Minister John McEwen, Governor-General Lord Richard Casey, and Ed Clark, the U.S. ambassador to Australia. They stood "pasty-faced and bleary-eyed" in the forty-eight-degree sunshine as the president read a statement to a handful of newsmen. Our traveling party outnumbered the greeters about ten to one at that early hour. The president was gratified to clearly hear from McEwen that Australia planned no change in its support for the U.S. effort in Vietnam.

Dog-tired and with my head full of thoughts and logistical worries I could not share, I got to the hotel room about 8 A.M. I was carrying the "football," the black bag to be used by the president in case of nuclear war. It weighed about ten pounds, most of it pre-prepared executive orders and strategic operation plans. I just wanted to snooze. I drew all the blinds, took a shower, went to bed, and headed straight into a sound sleep. I was in deep slumber when the phone rang. I fumbled for the phones. There were two of them—the regular hotel room phone and the special White House phone that was always installed when I traveled with the president. In my groggy state, I picked up the hotel phone first, and then I realized it was the other one that was ringing. I finally got the right phone and said, "This is Colonel Cross."

The voice on the other end that I knew so well said, "Where are you?"

I told the president I had been asleep, and he said, "Well, come on over here, I need to talk to you." I slipped into a pair of pants—I already had on a clean T-shirt—and put on a pair of those house slippers that hotels provide. I walked the few steps down the hall to the president's room. The Secret Service agents waved me on in.

The president was sitting up in bed in his pajamas and a robe. Jack Valenti, Walt Rostow, Marvin Watson, and George Christian were all standing around in suits and ties. I'd come in on a discussion about the press and communism in Italy, and it was obvious that the president was talking over the ramifications of a visit to the pope. The president wanted to enlist the pope's help in getting talks going with the North Vietnamese. "I've tried every damn thing I know to get them to talk, and I just can't get Ho Chi Minh to ever sit down and talk," he said. "We'll go anywhere, anytime, to talk to anybody to get this damn war over." But he was worried that the Communist Party in Italy would stage a big demonstration if word got out that he was coming.

The president said he hadn't made up his mind for sure he was going to Rome at that point, or even what our next stop would be. He threw a bunch of questions at me, things like, "If we decide to go back to Manila and go home through Alaska, how much time is it gonna take?" I had a pretty good idea of the answers. I knew there were lots of possibilities, and I had stuck in my head the approximate times it would take to go to Manila, to go to Thailand and Vietnam, and from Vietnam to India, or from

Vietnam to Karachi and then on to Rome, and what it would take to be in Rome on Christmas Eve, and so on. We even talked about flight times for Japan and South Korea. That was my business. I understood distances and airplane speeds, and I could figure out flying times roughly within half an hour or so. This went on for about forty-five minutes. I stood the whole time. Unless I was invited to sit when I was around the president, I never took the liberty. The conference sort of broke up when the president got up to go to the bathroom. At that point, even though he hadn't said so, I knew in my heart we were going to Rome.

After a few hours' rest, the president plunged into a breakneck schedule that included lunch with South Korean President Park Chung Hee and dinner with South Vietnam's president, Nguyen Van Thieu. The president and Thieu issued a joint communiqué on the war, carefully worded to minimize Thieu's objection to the idea of including the National Liberation Front in any peace talks. Throughout the day, the president squeezed in visits with the other Asian and Pacific nation leaders who were allies in the war: New Zealand Prime Minister Keith Holyoake, Thailand Premier Thanom Kittikachorn, Laotian Foreign Minister Sisouk Na Champassak, and Philippines President Ferdinand E. Marcos.

I spent the rest of the day planning options. I already had airplanes all over the Pacific hauling Secret Service people and limousines and helicopters and cars for the president. We had to be ready for wherever the president decided to go. I must have had eight to ten planes in the air. And I had one C-133 sitting on the ground in Spain, loaded with partly disassembled Huey helicopters and other equipment ready to go to Rome if the president chose that option. I had them stand by in Spain so as not to tip our hand that we might be headed for Rome. We had to take the rotors off so the copters would fit on the plane, but it was a simple matter to unload and reassemble them.

With those details out of the way, I grabbed a little rest before we flew to Melbourne the next morning, Friday, December 22, for the prime minister's funeral. I didn't know it then, but those few hours of sleep at the Canberra Rex would be the only sleep I would have on this trip. Every time I tried to catch a nap on the lower bunk directly behind the cockpit, someone always saw me and had to ask a question or two. I couldn't sleep anyway, so I never even drew the curtain around the bunk. I had too much on my mind. I was in charge of all logistics—from the airplane, to the advance teams, to the communications, to the lodging, to the flight clearances, and even to the food on board—so there was no way to relax. I didn't want to go down in history as the ignoble fellow who missed a detail that ruined a historic presidential trip. The pace was nonstop. But I was forty-two years old and in excellent physical condition, so I could stay awake and perform.

The next morning, the first thing the president did when he woke up was call me. It was 4:45 A.M., and I was already on the plane. We had a problem. Air Force One weighed 240,000 pounds, and it took a toll on the tarmac. The plane had been parked in the heat for so long that some of the asphalt was stuck to the main landing-gear tires. When we tried to taxi, chunks of asphalt about the size of half a watermelon rind peeled off and I felt a slight bump-bump. We had to scrape all of it off before we could depart.

We had another problem, too, but not one I could remedy. Press reports were already surfacing in Washington that the presidential party might go to Rome to visit the pope. Before we left Canberra, the *Washington Evening Star* reporter on the press plane, Garnett Horner, filed a front-page story with a headline that announced we "Might Visit Pope in Rome on Way Home." Someone had leaked something to the press, but I was just glad it wasn't me. At that point, it wasn't my problem, but I felt bad that the president's secret had been uncovered.

In Melbourne, we were scheduled to land at Essendon Airport, one of three airports in Melbourne and the closest to the city's center. But Essendon was also the oldest airport, and its landing strip was almost too short for Air Force One. We had to dump fuel before we could land. I had ordered a regular load of 60,000 pounds of fuel just in case our plans changed once we were airborne. But nothing came up, so we started pumping out fuel as soon as we got to 20,000 feet. At that altitude, dumped fuel just vaporizes. We let about 30,000 pounds of fuel go before we landed.

The prime minister's funeral—coupled with the president's visit—drew the largest number of high officials ever to assemble in Australia, and it was the biggest top-level Asian-Pacific confab ever held at that time. The visit drew to Australia the presidents of the Philippines, South Korea, and South Vietnam; the premiers of Thailand, New Zealand, Singapore, Taiwan, the Fijis, and Western Samoa; and the foreign ministers of Laos, Cambodia, and Indonesia. In the church, the president sat behind nineteen-year-old Prince Charles, who was there to represent Great Britain.

President Johnson was a hit in Australia. It's true what they say—Australia is a lot like Texas. A security guard at the airport in Melbourne said of the president: "That bloke is 100 percent." Many Australians were gratified that the president made such a long trip to honor their fallen leader. They also were pleased at the way the president's trip centered world attention on their country and turned a domestic misfortune into an occasion to be remembered.

While the funeral was going on, I had to get Air Force One to Tullamarine Airport across town. The runway at Essendon wouldn't accommodate
a fuel load heavy enough to get us to Darwin or any other far-flung spot. So
we merely hop-scotched the plane to Tullamarine while the presidential
party was gone, and loaded up with fuel. As we did at all refueling stops,
we checked the fuel for purity and possible sabotage before we loaded it on
the president's plane. By this time, our plans were firmed up for the Thai-
land-Vietnam leg of the trip. But we kept mum. We kept the press in the
dark because we didn't want the world—especially the North Vietnamese
and Vietcong—to know the president was coming their way. The president
had told the press the night before in Canberra: "Y'all get a good night's
rest. I'm gonna get you home by Christmas Eve, if I can." But he did not tell
them how he was going to do it.

CHAPTER TEN

AROUND THE WORLD, PART TWO

BEFORE WE TOOK OFF FROM TULLAMARINE AT 2:45 P.M., I did not even inform the pilot of the Pan American Airlines press plane, Captain Doug Moody, where we were going. I acted like I didn't know. Only after the press plane was airborne did I radio Doug to say we were going to land somewhere in Thailand. I told him to generally head northwestward to Bangkok, and to slow down so he wouldn't get too far ahead of us and out of radio range. The press plane was equipped for international flight and could fly nonstop all the way to Thailand, but we would have to refuel. It's interesting to note that the press always wanted their plane to take off after Air Force One departed and to land just ahead of us. I always suspected that their philosophy, a bit macabre perhaps, was intended to ensure their immediate coverage if Air Force One crashed on takeoff or landing.

Just after takeoff, the president changed out of his morning dress—tails, striped pants, black tie, and a black top hat—and called a meeting at a table in the front of Air Force One. He wanted to plan the rest of the trip, so I was summoned from the cockpit. My co-pilots, Major Donald Short and Major Carl Peden, took over for me. We were flying to Darwin to refuel, a trip of almost three hours. But the planning around the table went on for two hours. Rostow, Bundy, Valenti, Watson, Christian, and special counsel Harry McPherson, who had boarded in Melbourne, were all in on the meeting too. I answered more questions about flight times and possible air routes. "You figure it out, Cross," the president kept saying. After about twenty minutes, I headed back to the cockpit.

In Darwin, on the north central coast of Australia, the president hopped off the plane for a brief walk around the terminal. Our substitute plane didn't carry the usual presidential seal, and apparently no one recognized the tall man in ranch khakis. He bought some cufflinks for his sons-in-law, Chuck Robb and Pat Nugent, and a stuffed koala bear for his six-month-old grandson, Lyn. In just under an hour, we were back in the air, and I told Doug Moody in the press plane to just stay up there in front of us and await further instructions.

What happened next was one of the most infuriating episodes of my entire Air Force One flying career. We were headed for Thailand, with our exact landing spot still undecided. General William Westmoreland, MACV commander, and General William Wallace Momyer, commander of the Seventh Air Force in Vietnam, couldn't agree on where they wanted the president to visit the troops. I had filed a flight plan to Bangkok just to get something in the works. But just as senior staff aboard Air Force One were communicating with U.S. authorities who were tracking and passing along military and diplomatic intelligence, our secure presidential radio/telephone network went dead. Some unauthorized user somewhere had preempted—stolen, really—the secure phone system, code-named Soft Talk. We had no idea what had happened. For almost four hours, Air Force One flew without a top-secret phone line. The president didn't know about it, but I did, and I was furious. It could have been catastrophic if a nuclear war or other disaster had occurred and President Johnson couldn't conduct business in secret. Without Soft Talk, any foe or crackpot with the proper equipment could have listened to presidential conversations.

Only after I was back in Washington did I find out that a self-serving, trouble-making Secret Service agent was the culprit. He had been aboard one of the C-141s (tail number 70008) full of staff and equipment that I had dispatched ahead of Air Force One. The little sneak had picked up the radio/telephone microphone, called Clark Aeronautical Station in the Philippines, and said, "Priority One with a DV-1 on board, requesting a continuous patch to Crown." The president of the United States, of course, is a DV-1—distinguished visitor—and entitled to radio priority. And Crown was code name for the White House. Later, after a White House investigation led to the meddling Secret Service agent, I called him into my East Wing office and dished out my own version of the "Johnson treatment." The president often criticized certain of the Secret Service agents, and sometimes referred to them as "those little Mexican generals who couldn't protect anyone from a threat." I got right down in the agent's face and yelled so hard and for so long I thought my eyeballs were going to burst. I was just madder than hell. I still am, four decades later.

Fortunately, his shenanigans didn't mess up our trip. As we approached landfall in Thailand, Air Force Chief of Staff General John P. McConnell got a call through to me on a military network and said we should land at Korat Royal Thai Air Force Base, an American-built installation 120 miles northeast of Bangkok. The Air Force conducted F-105 Thunderchief bombing operations around the clock from that base. I then called Doug Moody in the press plane, and Lieutenant Colonel Thornhill, who was piloting our backup 707, and instructed them to land just ahead of us. We had an escort of fighter planes as we made our approach. Before we landed, two F-105 fighter bombers took off for a mission over North Vietnam. It was just after 10 P.M. when we landed, bathed by a huge tropical moon. Even many passengers on Air Force One did not know where they were when they deplaned.

The usual VIP greeters were awaiting the president, who also managed to get over to the fence to shake hands with some airmen. There wasn't a limousine in sight, but there was plenty of pandemonium. People and trucks and combat planes were everywhere. General Momyer, Seventh Air Force commander, accompanied the president to his quarters for the night—a group of trailers set in a circle. The president was given Trailer Number One. He barely had time to survey his room before he and Momyer climbed into a weapons carrier truck and were driven to a nearby mess hall, where the president gave a Christmas pep talk to some of the airmen. The air crews crowded around as the president stood near a bar decorated for the holidays. "I realize that an old man is a poor excuse for your wife and your loved ones, but I wanted so much to be with you at Christmas, I wanted to look each of you in the eye and tell you that right will prevail," he said.

Then the president was supposed to get about four hours' rest in his austere mobile home, which had a weak air conditioner and far from state-of-the-art plumbing. He was not happy. He seemed tired and discouraged and disgusted and uptight. I think he was worried about his security, although he would never admit it. Here we were almost in the middle of a combat zone. North Vietnamese sappers occasionally attacked our bases in Thailand, and he knew it.

The president's metal "hotel" was apparently the mobile home Momyer stayed in when he was at Korat. It had two bedrooms, a living room, and a kitchen. There was a large double bed for the president, and it filled one of the little bedrooms. The trailer wasn't much, but it was one of the best places on the base. And that's not saying a lot. It certainly had no niceties like presidents are accustomed to.

I had a jillion things to do to get ready for the trip to Rome—if the president should decide we were going there. I was out at the plane, trying to use the phones to reposition some of our advance planes and work through other logistics, when Marvin Watson called me. "You better get over here," he said. It didn't sound good. I jumped in a security vehicle and hustled over to the mobile home. When I walked in, the president was just madder than hell. I never did know for sure what he was mad about. Maybe it was a combination of the facilities, bad food, the stress, everything. The president was eating on Marvin Watson's ass and on anyone else who was handy. Now it was my turn.

Then he said he wanted me to find General Momyer. It was the middle of the night, but somehow I tracked down Momyer, and he walked into an ambush. The president just ate him alive, I mean just ate him in little bitty pieces and spat him out. Momyer's no shrinking violet. In World War II, he led the 33rd Fighter Group in action over North Africa and shot down eight enemy aircraft. He won the Distinguished Service Cross and three Silver Stars for bravery. And in just a few weeks, he would coordinate our devastating air response to the Tet Offensive.

But after the president lit into him, he just shriveled up. I really felt sorry for the man. Of course, I had been chewed out equally badly myself by the president, but I was used to taking it and it didn't bother me. The president just had to have an outlet, and there were people like me who were there for that purpose. I knew that he didn't really mean what he said.

General Momyer was not accustomed to the "Johnson treatment." He was a four-star general and not really used to getting torn to pieces. So afterward, when things cooled down a bit, the general and I got off by ourselves outside, and I told him not to worry about it, just go on about his business. He looked like he wanted to cry. Right then General Momyer wasn't a fan of the president, but he wasn't the first to feel that way.

I went back to the plane and tried to grab a catnap, but I couldn't sleep. I had too many to-do lists in my mind, and I was thinking about my family, too. The best part of landing at Korat was seeing my eldest daughter, June, and her husband, Randy McCann. Randy was working in Bangkok on a one-year assignment for Philco-Ford. June and Randy found a late-night taxi driver willing to make the 120-mile trip to meet me at Korat. I was tickled to see them, and we got on the plane's phone and called Marie back home in Maryland. "I've got someone here who would like to say hello," I said. Marie got to say hi to the kids, and then I had only about half an hour to visit with them aboard Air Force One before I had to get back to work. I hated to say good-bye, especially knowing they would be back in a taxi for another five hours, a ride that was costing them more than $200. But I had to make sure the plane was ready for takeoff.

After his miserable night, the president was up at 5 A.M., dressed in khaki shirt and pants and battle jacket. While it was still dark, he was driven to a hangar where he awarded some Silver Stars and Distinguished Flying Crosses and addressed a crowd of early rising enlisted men, saying U.S. air power was creating havoc with the enemy's guerrilla warfare. Those enlisted men never knew that the president had created a little havoc of his own with their commander a short time earlier.

There was little time for dawdling or relaxation on this trip. Entertainer Bob Hope was in Thailand and Vietnam for the fourth time entertaining the troops, and he hoped to connect with the president. He never made it, and later sent a telegram from Bangkok to the president saying, "You travel a little too fast, even for me." If the quick-witted entertainer had caught up with the president, he might have needled Johnson that he drew crowds of 25,000 soldiers, much larger than the attendance at the stops during our security-shrouded tour. Of course, the president probably would have shot back that the troops came out to see the very buxom Raquel Welch, not Hope.

It was a great day for flying when we took off just before 6 A.M. from Korat and headed for Cam Ranh Bay, 170 miles northeast of Saigon in South Vietnam. We flew south, headed for the coast, and went around the Indochina peninsula, then turned northeast to Cam Ranh Bay. Four Phantom fighters escorted us, two just off each wing tip. I requested that they be there, even though the North Vietnamese did not have anything that could attack from the distances they would have to go. But I just felt like we were in a war zone, and why take a chance? I was enjoying the sunrise when Marvin Watson walked into the cockpit, tapped me on the shoulder, and asked, "Have you got the medals?"

I replied, "Sure, Marvin. I've got plenty of Purple Hearts." I always carried a briefcase with some Purple Hearts in it when we expected to be near a military hospital, just in case the president wanted to visit and make some impromptu presentations.

"No," he said. "The president told me you had the Distinguished Service medals he intends to award the admirals and generals commanding this war when he sees them in Cam Ranh Bay." I nearly had a heart attack. No one had told me of this development earlier, and I had no way to manufacture medals while flying at 30,000 feet off the coast of Vietnam.

About this time, I turned the plane northeast toward Saigon, and I could see the city fifty or sixty miles ahead over the nose of the plane. Fortunately, I had two very good friends in Saigon: Brigadier General Bill Knowlton, chief of staff for General Westmoreland's MACV headquarters, and Colonel Ernest Triplett, commander of the military airlift detachment at Tan Son Nhut airbase. I told my radio telephone man, Master Sergeant Bill Justice, to contact both of them and keep everyone else on our plane off the phone until I could talk to these men. I told him if Walt Rostow or Assistant Secretary of State Bill Bundy or even the president wanted to use a circuit, just tell them atmospheric conditions were bad and we had no reception at the moment.

I talked first with Knowlton, told him the problem, and he said he could come up with the medals. I got Triplett on another line, and I put Knowlton on hold. I told Triplett to stop the first plane in Saigon that he had on the runway and hold it for a priority package from Knowlton, and then send the plane on to Cam Ranh Bay posthaste. Both these men were outstanding "can-do" officers, and I figured if anyone could pull off this maneuver, they could. Well, lo and behold, I got a call back from Triplett. He said he had put the medals on a plane, and that it should be landing about ten minutes behind Air Force One. Then, as we passed over Saigon, I fretted about everything that could go wrong for the rest of the forty-five-minute trip to Cam Ranh Bay. But I knew I had done everything I could to put the medals in the president's hands.

After we landed, I stopped a public relations officer, Colonel Jack Giannini, and asked him to personally meet every plane coming in from Saigon and stay there until he found the one carrying the priority package with my name on it. And I told him to race the package to me at the makeshift speakers' platform where the president would make the presentations. I figured I would have about thirty or forty minutes before the president began to award the medals.

As the president deplaned, he was met by General Westmoreland, Ambassador Ellsworth Bunker, and Major General Nguyen Cao Ky, vice president of the Republic of Vietnam. They climbed into a jeep and went off to visit wounded troops in the hospital, where he awarded twenty Purple Hearts. These medals came from the local base supply, so I didn't have to worry about them.

Next, I saw General Westmoreland and the president leading a group of dignitaries over to the stage. When "Hail to the Chief" was played, all I could think of was the "hell from the chief" that was sure to come my way if those special medals didn't arrive. I was able to buy a little more time when, instead of mounting the steps to the stage, the president and the general got into an open jeep to review the Army, Navy, and Marine personnel assembled on the tarmac. When they returned to the speaker's platform—a "low boy" assembled from two flat-bed trailers and a set of wooden stairs—everyone stood at attention for the U.S. national anthem and the South Vietnam national anthem. It was the first time I wished that a song I'd saluted a million times had about three more verses.

Still no medals. I was starting to soak my shirt. The president awarded Exemplary Service medals to sixteen heroic servicemen, some of whom hadn't even been told why they were being flown back from their fighting positions in-country. One soldier even had to borrow fresh fatigues to meet the president. We had plenty of service medals, just none for the big boys. But I was able to buy a few more minutes when some confusion erupted from the stage. The president had some prepared remarks he wanted to make, so Westmoreland asked the troops to come forward. Nobody moved. I'm sure the servicemen and servicewomen didn't really believe they were supposed to come in so close to their Commander-in-Chief. So the president stood up and raised his arms to beckon them closer. That was all it took. They fell out of formation and rushed the stage. All 2,450 troops representing the Army, Air Force, Navy, Marines, and Coast Guard. The airspace around Cam Ranh Bay had been even busier than usual earlier, when the troops arrived on thirty-five C-130 transports. And now, jets flew overhead to provide security for the president while infantrymen patrolled the area outside the base.

The president told the enthusiastic troops that he wished he could have brought them a Christmas gift that would reflect the pride, care, and concern of their families and loved ones. "All that debate you read about cannot obscure that pride," he said. "The slogans and the signs cannot diminish the power of that love." He noted that "it's not the shortest route back to the White House through Vietnam, but because it is almost Christmas, and because my spirit would be here with you anyway, I had to come."

In his rousing eight-minute speech, the president said that the Vietcong and North Vietnamese knew they had met their master, even though they were not yet beaten. He portrayed the enemy as trying to buy time while hoping the will of the U.S. public would prove weaker than theirs. "But we're not going to yield," he said. "And we're not going to shimmy."

I, however, was shimmying and shaking and sweating blood as I kept my eyes peeled for Colonel Giannini and the box of medals. I had almost given up when I saw him running my way. I ran down the tarmac to grab the box. I ran back as hard as I could in my full-dress blue uniform and got back to the platform stairs seconds before the citations were to be read. Marvin Watson and I both tore into the package, and pulled out the small individual boxes containing the medals. As each man's citation was read, Watson and I pulled out a Distinguished Service medal matching his branch of service and I ran it up to the president and helped him pin it on. Fortunately, we got them all right. When the last of the medals was presented, I breathed a huge sigh of relief, thinking we had pulled off a last-minute miracle successfully.

But then the president intoned into the microphone, getting across that he was coming to the climax of the ceremony: "And now, Ambassador Bunker, it is my privilege and pleasure to award you the Medal of Freedom. Your devotion to duty and unselfish work as United States ambassador to this war-torn country has been above and beyond the call of duty. This medal is the highest civilian award our nation can make to those civilians who devote their lives to the search for peace."

At that point, the president turned and looked straight at me, standing at the foot of the platform's steps. I guess I was standing there just looking dumb. He gestured as if to say, "Okay, Cross, you're my medal custodian. Get it up here!"

Now I certainly knew what the Medal of Freedom was, but I had never seen one, and I didn't know which department of the government issued them or kept them. And I certainly knew that at that moment I did not have one. The only thing I could do was shrug and silently mouth my dis- may to the president that I was empty-handed. The president's eyes threw some little bitty daggers my way. Then he turned back to the microphones and announced to the ambassador, the troops, and the press corps: "Well, Mr. Ambassador, my military aide has failed me once again." He said that certainly the medal would be sent to the ambassador when we returned to Washington.

When the ceremony was over, someone in the rear ranks shouted, "Three cheers for the president of the United States!" and the troops let out a thunderous chorus of "Hip, hip, hooray!" But I was crushed. I under- stood that someone had screwed up and the Commander-in-Chief had to blame someone and I was handy. A moment later, when the president came down the steps where I was standing, he turned toward Air Force One, parked about fifty yards away, and said, "Come on!" I fell in with him as we walked to the plane, and he asked me what had gone wrong. He got right down in my face and let me have it: "I don't know how the hell it is, every time I want to do something, you can manage to screw it up."

I told him I was not trying to make excuses, but I had no idea he was going to award the Medal of Freedom to Mr. Bunker. "In fact, Mr. President, the White House military office has no authority over that medal." I promised to find out what had gone wrong and let him know.

But he had the last word. With his voice dripping with feigned self-pity, he said, "Well, dammit, Major, you could have saved me a lot of embarrassment if you would've at least brought up an empty box I could have given him."

I simply hadn't had the presence of mind to think of that, even though there were plenty of empty boxes lying around that had contained the military medals. The president never brought up the matter again.

If the president was miffed with me, he had to be gratified by the warm letters he later received from relatives of the boys he visited. Some of the parents forwarded to the White House letters from their sons. "Just had the most thrilling moment of my life," a Wisconsin soldier wrote his parents. "He was shaking the hands of everyone in the crowd. I inched up and got right next to him and shook his hand. Just then the photographers told him to pose, and he put his hand on my shoulder and asked me where I was from and he shook my hand again ... I'm too excited to write any more."

Some people might have criticized the president and said he was mingling with the troops just to get favorable publicity for himself. But there was no doubt he genuinely was touched when he was among the soldiers, whom he often called "my boys." The fighting men didn't seem to doubt the president's sincerity. "This visit and the genuine warmth and friendliness you expressed in smiles and words is deeply appreciated by all," wrote one injured sailor who received a Purple Heart from the president.

The wife of one serviceman wrote that her husband was excited to have stood within fifteen feet of the president. "The world situation now seems to be in a mess, and I know you get a lot of criticism," she wrote, "but you're doing a good job and doing what you feel is right."

One Air Force colonel wept while the president spoke at Cam Ranh Bay. An Air Force sergeant said he did not wash his hand for a full day after shaking the president's hand, and was letting his buddies "shake that hand as a Christmas present."

One of the letters, written by a twenty-year-old soldier, was poignant as well as insightful in its description of the president: "He seemed like a very lonely man. He started talking to us just like a father talks to his son and giving encouragement to us. He was dressed in light tan pants and shirt, no tie or hat. He looked like a normal old man talking with his gray hair waving in the wind. You could tell by his face that he wasn't normal, though. He was so tired, torn, and troubled-looking. I'll never forget the way he looked, and for some small reason I all of a sudden admired him."

We took off from Cam Ranh Bay and headed for Karachi, Pakistan—an intermediate stop on our circuitous and surreptitious flight plan to the Vatican. Walt Rostow sent word ahead to the Embassy in Karachi to "arrange spread of rumor that we plan overnight" by inquiring about "massive hotel space." This little bit of subterfuge was designed to hide our real plans to head for Rome. I pulled a feint of my own shortly after takeoff by calling a friend of mine, Colonel Jim Swindal, at the U.S. airbase in Torrejon, Spain, outside Madrid. Swindal had been President Kennedy's pilot on Air Force One, and I flew as his co-pilot after Kennedy's assassination until I was fully qualified in the 707s. I had contacted Swindal before we left Washington so he could help me disguise our flight to Rome if we indeed were to go to the Vatican. He knew how to keep his mouth shut. I knew he wouldn't tell even the U.S. ambassador to Spain. Swindal had promised to babysit a C-133 cargo plane loaded with two Huey helicopters and crews that I had dispatched from Washington for possible use in Rome. Now I needed those helicopters up and running in Italy. "Jim," I said, "send that airplane to Aviano Air Base and tell the crews to start putting the rotors back on the helicopters and start test-flying them so they'll be ready. Don't let anybody else know what the deal is. I'll be in touch."

Karachi was going to be just a one-hour fuel stop, but the president wanted to squeeze in a quick visit with Pakistani President Ayub Khan. Rostow messaged our diplomats to adroitly arrange the situation with Ayub so he wouldn't be offended by the brevity of our in-and-out visit. "President delighted to meet Ayub if he comes to the airport, but does not wish to inconvenience him and will of course understand perfectly if this is impossible on such notice," Rostow messaged. "Above all must not, repeat not, give an expectation that President can stay longer than a minimum refueling time, which is crucial to safe meeting [and] onward schedule."

As we flew toward India en route to Karachi, Air Force One had to deal with an unexpected problem—three Indian fighter planes approached, and we were told we could not proceed over their country. Someone in India had not received word that we had overflight clearance. It's standard operating procedure to arrange this kind of permission every time a foreign plane flies over another country. I had the hard copy of the clearance in my briefcase. The Indian fighter planes were within a mile of our plane, and an air traffic controller radioed that we had to land and could not proceed. I wasn't sure whether something had slipped through the cracks or whether the Indians were offended that a U.S. president would be flying over their country to land in Pakistan, their avowed enemy. It was tense for a few minutes. Walt Rostow sent a flash message to Bromley Smith, one of his staff back in Washington. And Bromley apparently got the prime minister, Mrs. Indira Gandhi, or someone high up in the Indian government on the phone and told them, "Hey, some of your air traffic control people are telling our president that he has to land, and it's urgent we correct this situation." Immediately the fighters backed off, and we went on our way to Karachi without further excitement. The president was even relaxed enough to ride his exercise bike. He opened the door so everyone could see his exertions. But he stayed in the saddle for only ten minutes.

When we got to Pakistan, the president walked down a hastily laid red carpet and met for an hour in an airport building with the Pakistani president. Johnson was determined to keep his every move close to his vest, despite resentment and anger among the press party that occasionally spewed out onto the president's advisers. On the flight from Cam Ranh Bay to Karachi, the president stewed over a report from deputy press secretary Tom Johnson, who was on the press plane. The press was exhausted. They said the trip was turning into a carnival. And they were mad that the president was deliberately trying to mislead them.

In Karachi, the veil of secrecy got Jack Valenti into a shouting match with Hugh Sidey of Time-Life, a hundred yards from where the president was meeting with Ayub Khan. Valenti wouldn't confirm that our next stop was Rome, and Sidey didn't like it. Valenti later described the scene as resembling two bottled scorpions surveying each other. "The tension was stretching to the snapping point," Valenti said. "Patience was in pitiful short supply." As usual, I was too busy to worry or, frankly, to care what the press thought. I filed a flight plan to the U.S. airbase in Torrejon, Spain, outside Madrid, and we took off toward Iran and Turkey and the Mediterranean Sea. It was only when Air Force One was crossing the boot tip of Italy that I switched flight plans to land at Rome's secondary airport.

By that time, we had press aboard Air Force One. The president had heard about the shouting match before we left Karachi, and he decided to relent. He allowed six American correspondents to come aboard Air Force One as a press pool. We picked up Sidey, Frank Cormier of the Associated Press, Merriman Smith of United Press International, Frank Reynolds of ABC, Pat Heffernan of Reuters, and Garnett Horner of the *Washington Evening Star*. The reporters visited with the president in his compartment for more than two hours. Then they did something their colleagues on the press plane would have loved to do. They went to the back of the plane to sleep in the bunks. They were beyond bushed.

The president later asked Valenti about the confrontation with Sidey. Valenti explained that the arduous trip and not knowing where we were going next had put Sidey and the other reporters in a bad mood. The president told Valenti, "As of now, I am running the president's plane, not Sidey." When Valenti replied that the press probably had good reason to complain, since they were not given advance notice of the travel plans, the president just glared. He pulled a message from his pocket that said Communist mobs were planning a vocal reception for the president if he landed in Rome. "You want me to advertise where we land and have an international crisis on our hands? Now, if I explain to the press where we are going and when we get there, don't you suppose we would be helping enlarge our greeting when we get there?" Valenti said he couldn't disagree with that reasoning.

William P. Bundy, assistant secretary of state for Far Eastern affairs, transferred from Air Force One to the press plane in Karachi. He had the unenviable task of trying to make peace with the press, who were becoming grouchier and louder as the trip wore on. As Valenti had pointed out, their number-one complaint was secrecy. They felt like they were a captive audience on a trip to the unknown, which wasn't far from the truth. Bundy convened a background meeting on the plane. He began with an apology for the "very difficult and arduous trip." In an understatement, he added, "I can only say it hasn't been a cinch for us, either." With the reporters safely in the air and away from telephones, Bundy explained that the entourage was indeed headed to Rome. In fact, Bundy acknowledged that it was the president's hope from the beginning that he could extend the trip to include Vietnam and Rome, but the details did not come together until the trip was under way. He said a key to scheduling was how long the presidential party had to stay in Australia. No one knew how long it would take the president to hold the informal meetings with other world leaders that were so important to him. By necessity, the scheduling had to be last-minute.

Bundy explained that details of the Vietnam and Thailand legs were kept hush-hush because of fear for the president's safety. "If Hanoi knew exactly where we were going to go and when, it was the considered and earnest advice of our military in Saigon that the risks of the president coming to Vietnam would be significantly increased," Bundy said. The same held true for Thailand, he said.

The stop at Rome would not significantly increase the length of the trip, Bundy said, and the president did not want to miss an opportunity to discuss Vietnam with the seventy-year-old pope. "It was the president's firm feeling that a serious conversation with the pope on a subject in which His Holiness is deeply and widely informed was an important and worthwhile thing to do," Bundy said.

While Bundy was trying to appease the press, Walt Rostow was working relentlessly to thwart anti-war demonstrators in Rome. He instructed the U.S. Embassy in Madrid to spread the rumor that the presidential party planned to refuel there, and possibly stay overnight. As part of the ruse, Rostow told the Embassy to check on possible hotel accommodations for a party of 100 in a secure location. The idea was for the demonstrators to think the president would overnight in Madrid and come to Rome on December 24. In reality, we would go to Rome late on the 23rd and be long gone by Christmas Eve, when the demonstrators were expecting us. As George Christian put it, "So when Johnson landed in Rome on the night of December 23, hundreds of thousands of demonstrators were enjoying their wine and their intrigues, planning for the big bash on December 24."

We landed at Ciampino Airport, a military field on the outskirts of Rome. This was part of our strategy to maintain secrecy and foil the protesters. Almost all international traffic came into the much larger Fiumicino Airport. That's where any protesters would have expected us to land. Security and secrecy were much easier to maintain at Ciampino. It was dark when we landed, and the area was cordoned off by security forces. We had absolutely no ground support at Ciampino. We didn't even have a stairway to get off the plane. No ground crewmen, nothing. We couldn't have the president just jump out of the plane onto the tarmac, so Chief Master Sergeant Joe Chappell, my flight engineer, threw an emergency escape rope out the front door, clambered down, and hot-footed it over to a maintenance hangar. He found an old yellow maintenance stand with steps on it and rolled it up to the airplane. And that's how the president of the United States disembarked in Rome on his way to meeting the pope.

Getting the president off the plane was just the beginning of our troubles. He was to fly first to meet Italy's president Giuseppe Saragat at Castelporziano, Saragat's 5,000-acre walled-off hunting lodge retreat and summer residence. Our president would then go on to the Vatican, using helicopters to avoid a highly visible motorcade, which would advertise its presence to protesters. Our best-laid plans to bring our own Hueys from Spain had met up with a hitch. Bad weather had delayed their arrival, and Major Pete Rice and his crew were working like fiends to reassemble them and test-fly them before we put the president aboard one. As frantically as they worked, they would not be ready to go in time to meet the president's tight schedule.

Marvin Watson and I started looking for alternative transportation around the airfield. We spotted a Navy commander standing over by a fence. I asked him if there was a U.S. military presence on the airfield. He said there was a little rescue outfit with some old helicopters. A dirty old faded Navy dark blue, they were shopworn birds that looked as if they had seen their best days long ago. They had ratty bucket seats with strap nets for backrests, and there was no sound-deadening insulation in the cabin. That meant they were noisy as hell. We had to have them anyway. Marvin and I told the commander we wanted a couple of his helicopters to fly the president and his party over to meet President Saragat and later to fly Johnson to the Vatican.

The Navy commander was not with the program. "Oh, well, you can't do that," he said.

I quickly set him straight. I told him with all the force of my authority (something I'd learned from the master): "Commander, get those helicopters over here with some pilots right now." I think the commander knew that it would not be good business to get crosswise with an Air Force colonel traveling with the president. He got the helicopters ready to go in about ten minutes. At 7:12 P.M., the choppers took off and headed for the Italian president's hunting lodge. The president, Rostow, Valenti, and Frederick Reinhardt, U.S. ambassador to Italy, were aboard one. On another were Marvin Watson, the Engelhards, and Marie Fehmer. The press pool hitched a ride, too.

The party was on the ground at the hunting lodge for less than an hour. The president had a forty-minute private meeting with Saragat, then Valenti rounded everyone up. Luckily, by that time, Major Rice had the two Hueys put back together and test-flown. We had the Hueys fly to the villa and pick up the president and his entourage and head for the Vatican. We thanked the Navy pilots and sent their rickety old choppers back to their base.

The landing at the Vatican was without a doubt the president's edgiest airborne experience of the entire around-the-world trip. Major Rice, the Huey pilot from San Antonio, of course, had never landed there before, and he had to set the copter down blind at night in an inner garden. Vatican officials were worried the bird would sink in the grass and ruin the garden, so Rice and his crews hovered for twenty minutes trying to work things out. Valenti later described it as "a hairy experience, a virgin landing in the dark, putting down on the head of a pin! God!"

The president did not know all this, but he figured something was amiss when Rice kept circling around and around the Vatican. He leaned over to

Valenti and asked, "Does this pilot need a road map?" Valenti later said he wanted to blurt out that what the pilot really needed was a seeing-eye dog. Finally the chopper fluttered above a small opening in the foliage and Rice set it down, to everyone's relief.

Pope Paul VI met with the president from 8:50 P.M. until 10:17 P.M. Valenti—the man most responsible for the meeting taking place, through his excellent behind-the-scenes logistics—sat in for its entirety. They sat around an ancient marble-topped, claw-footed table near a fireplace in the pope's study. They talked mostly about the Vietnam War. The pope offered to be an intermediary for the United States, an offer the president graciously accepted. They talked of bombing halts and American POWs, of peace talks and patience and perseverance. The president stressed that peace in Vietnam, if it was to last, had to be made among the Vietnamese. "In my home state of Texas, a lot of Ford automobiles carry a sticker that says 'Made in Texas by Texans.' I would like a slogan in Saigon that says 'Peace in South Vietnam made by Vietnamese.'" Valenti noted the warmth of the meeting, and that both the president and the pope seemed to regret that it was ending.

The pope presented the president with a wedding gift for his daughter Lynda, who had married Chuck Robb just two weeks earlier, and a Renaissance painting of the Nativity for Mrs. Johnson. The president presented the Holy Father with a large package wrapped in brown paper and tied with a rope. The pope had a problem pulling the rope loose, and the president pulled out a jackknife. According to one account, the president flipped open the blade, ripped into the package, and excelsior spilled all over the Oriental rugs. The president's gift to the pope was a five-inch bronze bust of himself.

I worried the entire time the president was gone. I wanted his meeting to go well with the pope. I knew he believed with all his heart that Pope Paul could bring the North Vietnamese to peace talks in Paris. He had tried so hard, and in so many ways, to initiate productive discussions with the North Vietnamese, but often didn't even get a response or acknowledgment. He was hoping for a breakthrough, and I didn't want anything to stand in the way. And I was worried to death that the old Navy helicopters wouldn't make it. I could just see myself as the fall guy in a fiasco if something went wrong with one of the birds or the weather soured or we missed a diplomatic warning because we didn't have any better communication than a Secret Service radio patched into the Rome telephone service. So many things were out of our control that I was beyond tense.

The president was bone-tired but elated when he came back aboard Air Force One at 10:45 P.M. on the 23rd of December. He told me his visit with Pope Paul had been useful and historic. He wanted to know what time we would be back in Washington and what the weather would be like en route. He then immediately went back to the passenger cabin, and I assumed I wouldn't hear from him again until we landed in Washington. The backup plane and the press plane—with the pool reporters back on board—were already headed home by way of Shannon, Ireland.

We had just reached our cruising altitude and were passing over the Straits of Gibraltar when the president suddenly walked into the cockpit and sat down in the jump seat behind me. I was startled for a moment by his presence, and I thought he might be upset about something. But it turned out he was jubilant. His face was flushed, and he couldn't sit still. "Major, this has been a great trip! A roaring success!!" (I was a full colonel, but he still enjoyed calling me major, reminding me, once again, that he was my benefactor.) I think he must have been feeling the same thing that a race car driver feels if he sets a speed record or a diver feels if he sets a depth record. Or maybe it was just the thought that he had completed a trip that relatively few people on earth have—a circumnavigation of the globe. And he was the first and only president to do it. He was just effusive in his praise. He admitted that he'd driven us all at a man-killing pace, but he didn't quite apologize. He sat with me and gazed out into the beautiful clear night. He was pumped full of adrenaline, which rubbed off on me just as I most needed a shot of energy. I was thrilled by his euphoria. I felt eighteen feet tall. I found out later that the president stayed up for three hours in his cabin with Valenti, Rostow, and the Engelhards, reliving his visit with the pope.

The president asked me if we were heading straight home, and I explained that we had to stop at Lajes Air Force Base in the Azores for fuel. The U.S. base on the Portuguese islands was often used as a military fuel station during transatlantic flights, and I had flown in there numerous times in my military career. The president wanted to know if I had done my Christmas shopping. Of course, I had not. He had intended to give his top staff two days off to do Christmas shopping before he learned of his friend's death in Australia. But any last-minute shopping had been scratched by this airborne voyage. Considering the hectic pace, I had hardly thought about the subject. I think the president knew what my answer was going to be. "Well, I haven't done my Christmas shopping, either," he said. "See if you can't call the commander down there and ask him to open up the BX for us when we arrive." Of course, the commander agreed to open the base exchange for the president of the United States, even though we showed up at 1:30 A.M. local time.

As I parked the aircraft in front of the passenger terminal, the president peeked out of the window and noticed a military officer of some sort—not one of ours—standing on the ramp, decked out in the full regalia of a high potentate. He had medals, fringed shoulder boards, a purple sash, and scrambled eggs on his hat. And he was surrounded by his personal staff of minions. Johnson assumed correctly that it was the civil governor of the Azores, and he didn't want to spend any time visiting with him. By that time, I think the president had had all the dignitaries he could handle, and he just wanted to shop for Christmas presents in peace. I guess after meeting the pope, he couldn't get too excited about meeting the leader of some Portuguese islands with less total land area than Rhode Island. So he sent Marvin Watson out to explain that the president was asleep, ill with a cold, and wouldn't be deplaning. Watson told them it was nice that they had come out, but that they should go on home.

Marvin came back aboard and said the governor was adamant about seeing the president and wouldn't leave. Johnson sent Marvin to see me in the cockpit. "The president wants you to put on all your braid, your scrambled-egg hat, and anything else you can think of and see if you can't get rid of that guy," he said.

So, looking as snobbish, official, and stern as I could in my full-dress uniform, I walked stiffly down the stairs, saluted the gentleman smartly, and tried to tell him the president was asleep, ill, and under a doctor's care and absolutely unable to see anyone. The governor didn't speak much English, and his interpreter wasn't much better. I didn't know one Portuguese word, but I could tell my message was not getting through. Desperate, I began to pantomime someone sleeping. I put my hands together and laid them aside my face and closed my eyes. "El presidente is asleep." Then I said, hoping Portuguese was a little like Spanish, "El presidente is mucho malo," which in Spanish means ill or sick. All the while, the president was peeking out from a crack in one of the window shades. Fortunately, I was able to convince the gentleman to leave with his entourage.

When the coast was clear, U.S. Air Force personnel drove a school bus around to the plane. The presidential entourage and the entire flight crew climbed aboard for the short trip to the BX for a two-hour shopping spree. But the president stayed behind. Later, an Air Force car brought him to the BX, where he shopped for thirty minutes. He wandered the aisles, checking out what everyone else was buying. I bought my wife, Marie, a new bottle of her favorite perfume, Shalimar, and some trinkets for the kids. The president picked up a few gifts for his baby grandson—a pair of red britches that cost $1.58; a red, white, and blue crib toy; a sterling silver cross; and more clothes. He also bought some round brass trays made in French Morocco and several silver bracelets.

He spoke to all the BX workers as well as to the base officers, who had gathered inside the front doors to watch the nocturnal shopping spree. The president was in a joyful mood, still buoyed by his trip to Rome. He didn't want to leave anyone out of the merriment. When he saw the Portuguese cooks and waiters peering out the mess room window, he went down to greet them. But they were terrified of this tall, strange man coming from nowhere on Christmas Eve. They fled in all directions.

Later, the Portuguese dignitaries learned the president actually had deplaned, and our Air Force officers in the Azores described the governor as grief stricken that he had missed the president. The governor apparently did not know that the president had purposely dodged him. After we got back to Washington, the Air Force suggested we do something to smooth over the situation. I prepared a letter for the president's signature expressing his regret that he did not "have the opportunity" to meet with the governor and his companions.

After our stop in the Azores, we flew an uneventful straight shot back to Andrews Air Force Base. It was 4:18 A.M. on Christmas Eve when we landed. The first around-the-world presidential flight in history was over. But at that moment, the president was only wondering aloud if Yuki would be on the South Lawn to greet him. He wasn't, but Lady Bird, Lynda, Luci, and Pat were there.

I went home to sleep in. Marie and the kids were thrilled to see me, and I got a kick out of handing out the perfume and trinkets I'd picked up along the way. Marie had had to rely on newspapers and television reports to find out where I was for the past four-and-a-half days. She had clipped all the articles for me and put them in a scrapbook. Being home was the best Christmas present anyone could have given me. I had flown around the world only once before, as the third pilot on Defense Secretary Robert McNamara's 1964 trip to Spain, Switzerland, India, Pakistan, Vietnam, and Panama. But we had had ten days to circumnavigate the world then, not four-and-a-half days. I was wearier than I ever remember being.

I slept as much as I could because I knew the president wanted to go to his Texas ranch within a day or so. What I didn't know was that he planned to award me the Legion of Merit and the Air Medal once we got to the ranch. I swelled with pride when he presented the honors. It was hard to believe that a poor farm kid from Alabama had just set a world record as chauffeur of the flying White House.

The epic trip got more negative sniping from the press than it should have. A particularly mean-spirited evaluation came from Sidey, Time-Life's White House correspondent, who called the trip "another Texas-sized operation to build up Lyndon Johnson." His article in *Life* magazine was sarcastically headlined "Around the World with Lyndon B. Magellan." Sidey has been a longtime friend, but I still could almost see him sneering when he wrote of the president: "Along that 26,959-mile trail, he elbowed everybody else out of the way, and at the end he stood center-stage alone, a marvel of speed, sound, and energy."

Sidey's feelings probably dated back to his heated discussion with Jack Valenti at the very hot Karachi airport. Sidey really let Jack have it then: "This is a flying circus, and you know it. And the president knows it. The best thing you and the president can do is start up this airplane, turn it around, and head back home right now in the same direction we came from."

Jack told Sidey where he could place his opinion, and said, "I find it damn short-sighted of the press to define the president's trip as grandstanding when none of you know what the hell you're talking about. We are not on the same wavelength. There is no point arguing."

Sidey wrote in *Life* magazine that "a continuing tragedy of the Johnson administration is that there are relatively few people on its wavelength." But not everyone was on Sidey's wavelength, either. An editorial writer in Erie, Pennsylvania, said the trip showed the president was "a formidable figure, much on the order of John Wayne." An editorial in Texas's *Abilene Reporter-News* took a shot at *Life* magazine and those other "powerful segments of the eastern and northern press." *Life* magazine, the editorial noted, probably would have found a "gimmick" or phony drama if it had reported on the Lord taking time for prayer in his last days in the Garden of Gethsemane. To Sidey's credit, he later told the White House staff that many readers saw the trip positively. He said his article drew more irate reader response than any he had written about the president. "I have never had them eat me alive like this one," Sidey said.

Some members of the public thought the trip wasted taxpayers' money. One California woman heard that the president had taken along with him his own personal swivel chair and bed. She saw this as unnecessary, since the Australians "have adequate chairs and beds, even for the president of the United States." The woman's whining letter was printed in a California newspaper and prompted critical letters to the White House. I answered one of them, explaining that the president was always attuned to economy. I pointed out that it was not just Lyndon Johnson who was flying around the world, but the Office of the Presidency. I said that every expense was necessary to maintain the safety of the president, and to keep him in constant communication. And I also pointed out that the president did not bring his own swivel chair and personal bed.

But what caused the biggest uproar was a critical article in *Newsweek* that said the president's visit with the pope was "impersonal" and "ended as a frigid meeting" at which "everyone left unhappy." Jack Valenti, who was present at every second of the meeting, called the article "totally 100 percent, from stem to stern, beginning to end, false." I wasn't at the meeting, but I also doubted the truth of the article because I'd never seen the president happier than when he got back on the plane that night in Rome. He exploded when the *Newsweek* article appeared. He fired off a scorching telegram to Katherine Graham, owner of the *Washington Post* and *Newsweek*. "This is the first wire of its kind I have ever sent, but for the sake of American relations abroad, I cannot let go unanswered the completely false account of my recent discussion with the Pope printed in *Newsweek*," the president wrote. "Your reporters were obviously misled, and I am surprised you would give credence to these un-named sources on a matter of importance to the world. Yesterday in my news conference, I denied the account, but of course this does not undo the damage."

The trip came at a time when the president was increasingly under fire from the media, mostly over Vietnam. And Vietnam figured into everything written about the president. James Reston of the *New York Times* critically said the president was trying to give something to everyone on the trip: "He wanted to express his sorrow about the human tragedy of the Australian prime minister's death. He wanted to visit the American troops in the Vietnam War. On the way, he wanted to talk to the Pope in Rome about peace, and obviously he was playing politics on the way and trying to keep on his side both the people who were interested in the bombers in Thailand and the people who were interested in the principle of peace in Rome. The trouble is that in trying to convince everybody the President convinces no one."

Petty criticism aside, I always felt the world trip was a high point of the LBJ presidency. I'll never forget the relaxed but excited glow I felt from the president when he came up in the cockpit during the homestretch and talked about what a great trip it had been. The trip around the world put the president on top of the world for a few days.

But it would not be long before the Johnson presidency hit its low point.

CHAPTER ELEVEN

MY TURN TO SERVE IN VIETNAM

I HAD BEEN TRYING TO GET TO VIETNAM FOR A LONG TIME. Even though it was a thrill and a privilege to be the personal pilot for the Commander-in-Chief, I was a military aviator at heart. It was tough to watch from the flight line while other pilots fought the war and I ran sorties as the president's aerial chauffeur.

When the U.S. Marines were under siege for two-and-a-half months at Khe Sanh in early 1968, I had to speak up. I tried to talk the president into letting me fly over there and address the embattled Americans. More than 200 Marines were killed during the siege, and General Westmoreland estimated that the North Vietnamese lost between 10,000 and 15,000 men. National TV showed scenes of C-130s blown up and on fire.

President Johnson had been adamant that the base would not fall under any circumstances. Khe Sanh was isolated geographically in the far north of South Vietnam, and the press and some members of Congress were comparing it to Dien Bien Phu. The fall of that isolated French garrison in May 1954 during the French Indochina War spelled the end of France in that conflict. The president worried about Khe Sanh all the time. He even required that the Joint Chiefs of Staff give him a guarantee in writing that Khe Sanh would hold.

"Mr. President, sir, why don't you just let me go over there and stay for a few days?" I asked several times. "Let me fly in on one of those C-130s that are keeping the base re-supplied. Let me get a chance to speak to the men, and tell them their president thinks of them every minute of the day and wants to be sure that they're getting everything that they need. I could go as a direct representative of you."

"No, no," he said each time. "You can't go, Cross."

Maybe he was afraid I would be put in too much danger. No question, it was a hot spot. The president must have figured he had enough on his mind without worrying about his pilot barnstorming into a firefight at Khe Sanh.

But in the spring of 1968, I finally got my turn to go to Vietnam. It came in a most unexpected way, one that saddened and elated me at the same time.

The Vietnam War was taking a toll on Johnson. The mood of the country was changing. There were too many deaths, too many demonstrations, too many dissenting voices, including that airhead actress Jane Fonda. During February and March, I got mixed signals from the president about his future. I hardly knew what to think. On some days, he told me to make sure my office was prepared for a difficult campaign in the fall. "You know, you better get yourself fixed up and living out there in one of those Andrews houses. We're liable to be traveling all over the world the next four years, and your family is going to need to be taken care of." Yet in other, more frustrating moments, he said, "I may not run again. Or if we do decide to run, we could lose and we'll all be looking for a job next year. Major, you had better get your personal affairs in order."

I took the conflicting comments as a warning. My future was as much up in the air as his. I couldn't tell whether he was committed to running for president again or to sitting it out and letting those who thought they knew better try to handle Vietnam and all the other incurable headaches of the presidency. But by selling my house, I would be ready to react either way. And I knew that even if he did run and was reelected, there was no guarantee I'd be retained as his pilot and Armed Forces aide.

The president was scheduled to address the nation at 9 P.M. on March 31 on the topic of the war in Vietnam. I left the White House about 8 P.M. and drove home while listening to radio commentators speculate on what the president would say. My wife had supper ready when I got home, so I ate quickly and headed to my easy chair in front of the television. My kids and Marie joined me to watch the speech.

I was shocked to hear the words the president tacked on the end of his speech. They were twenty words that changed my life: "I shall not seek, and I will not accept, the nomination of my party for another term as your president."

I was truly amazed. There had been no indication whatsoever among the White House staff and inside channels that the president was going to say anything like that in this speech. But I wasn't unready. My household was in good order. We'd been painting and fixing up the house to put it on the market.

Later, after midnight, the president decided to accept an invitation to address the National Association of Broadcasters that day in Chicago. We left at 9:30 A.M. in Air Force One. Soon after takeoff, the president came to visit me in the cockpit. This was common for him; he would just pop in to say hello as he wandered the plane. (The next day, the *New York Times* ran a story about the trip to Chicago with an accompanying photo of the president in the cockpit with me. But the cutline identified me as Colonel Charles Ross. I wonder if the *New York Times* ever ran a correction.)

"Well," he said, "what did you think about my decision that I announced last night?"

"Mr. President," I said, "I think the country needs you, but certainly I'm with you. Whatever you think is fine with me. But I'm disappointed, because in my humble judgment I think our country needs your leadership. And at this point, I certainly don't see any of the potential presidential candidates who could lead us in these troubled times."

"Ah, Jim, nobody is indispensable." He paused. "Well, what are you going to do, now that you don't have me to look after you?"

"Mr. President, I'm a big boy. I'm a full colonel in the Air Force, and I expect I'll make out all right."

He laughed but didn't say anything.

His real response came two weeks later. In mid-April, the president called me to his bedroom early one morning. It was about 8 A.M., so when I got to his room he was still lying in bed reading the morning newspapers. He immediately started rattling off a long list of chores he wanted me to take care of. It was a true smorgasbord: call Charles Maguire, one of his speechwriters, and remind him that simplicity, clarity, and brevity were the hallmarks of good writing; jack up the commander of Camp David about the air-conditioning in the bowling alley; touch up the paint on the presidential yachts; order the staff mess attendants to improve the chili; install more sound-proofing material in the aircraft; and jump on the White House social aides about their continuing inattention to the less attractive and older lady guests at the frequent evening social events at the White House. With a twinkle in his eye, he reminded me that he would be the one to entertain the younger, prettier ladies.

Then his tone changed, and he continued the conversation we'd had in the cockpit.

"Well now, Cross, what are you going to do after I've left the presidency? Who's going to take care of you?"

"Mr. President, you needn't worry for my welfare. I'm a big boy now and a full colonel in the Air Force, thanks to you."

"Oh, now, goddamn it, don't get so noble. You know when I get retired down in Texas, I'm going to need a friend down there. I'm going to need a general and somebody that's my friend."

I never anticipated his next statement.

"Oh, by the way, McConnell told me they're going to make you a general."

"Well," I managed to spit out. "I thank you for that, Mr. President. I know that the Air Force wouldn't be making me a general unless you told them."

I knew there were lots of colonels ahead of me in line to be promoted. I wasn't in the eligibility zone. I was too young, and I hadn't been a colonel long enough, just over a year. But the president, as Commander-in-Chief, could make anything happen.

"Oh, no," he said. "Hell, you've earned it. Now they're going to make you a general."

"Again, Mr. President, thank you."

"Your wife's from Austin, isn't she?"

"Yes, sir."

"Her folks still living down there?"

"Yes, sir."

"Are they retired?"

"Well, no. Her daddy works at the post office; he's not retired."

"Well, how would you like to go down to Texas as commander of Bergstrom Air Force Base there in Austin?"

I couldn't believe my ears. It was a dream come true.

"Yes, indeed, sir. I cannot imagine another assignment in the United States Air Force I would rather have. And I know my wife will be overjoyed. It would be wonderful to be down there in the South. That's where we want to live when we're retired."

"Well, I need a friend down there, and I need me a general that'll help me out. I'm going to be poor, and I won't have any airplanes or helicopters, and I'll need somebody to get me in that [air base] hospital down there if I get sick. By the way, you need to fix up that hospital down there now. You might get sick too sometime, and you'd want a nice suite down there for yourself. If you go down there, would you let me use your hospital if I get sick?"

"Yes, sir."

"How about your commissary?"

"Yes, sir." I saw what he was getting at.

"How about your BX?"

"Yes, sir, I surely will. If I'm the commander down there, you can have anything you want."

"And you'll need your own private airplane to travel around in," he said. "Tell the Air Force that you want to send one of those Convair turboprop airplanes down there."

"Yes, sir."

"You'll need a helicopter down there for yourself too, won't you, to travel over your facilities and look at them and so forth?"

"Yes, sir."

"When you get that helicopter, use one of those Hueys like we used out at the ranch. Be sure and put those nice seats in it like Mrs. Johnson likes and the colors and fabrics."

"Yes, sir."

"Would you let me use the plane and helicopter after you get down there?"

"Of course, Mr. President."

"When you get down there as general, you'll need a private suite," he said. "What you need to do is get a nice corner location in that hospital, modified into a suite with a little dining room and a sitting room and a bedroom. Be sure and use those nice fabrics that Mrs. Johnson likes."

"Yes, sir, Mr. President."

I had been researching what aircraft and military support were available to former presidents, so I knew there wouldn't be a problem with using Air Force assets for his post–White House needs.

"After I'm no longer president and back there living on my ranch in Stonewall, I won't have a friend in the world. If you are commander down there, would you be my friend and help me out once in a while when I'm in need?"

"Yes, sir," I said, "and, if you've got a moment to spare, Mr. President, I'd like to tell you a little story about my longtime connection to Bergstrom that I am sure you don't know about.

"In the summer of '42, my dad was the general superintendent of construction when Bergstrom was built. I was seventeen, and Dad gave me a job as water boy making forty cents an hour. Later, I talked him into letting me upgrade to lumber-truck driver at fifty cents an hour. I worked ten hours a day, seven days a week, and drew overtime, so I suddenly felt rich.

"After high school graduation in 1943, I was drafted into pilot training and, much to my surprise, after I had my commission and pilot's wings, my first training assignment was Bergstrom. Dad was elated that his oldest son was assigned to an airbase he had built. And that's when I met a sweet Texas girl and married her."

Then the president told me I would be promoted to brigadier general and be posted permanently to Bergstrom in February 1969.

"Get yourself ready," he said. "You need to leave next week. General McConnell tells me you need to get down there right away so you can retrain to fly those photo reconnaissance airplanes [RF-4C Phantom jets]. He also tells me you should fly some combat missions in Vietnam before you take command of the recon wing at Bergstrom."

I was elated. But I knew I couldn't leave in a week. I had to sell my house and wait for the kids to get out of school at the end of May. I didn't want to look a gift horse in the mouth, but I told him I couldn't possibly leave for Texas before the first of June.

"OK," he said. "But tell me, who's going to fly my planes after you leave?"

I told him the only man for the job was Lieutenant Colonel Thornhill, who had been our co-pilot for more than seven years. He was my close friend and an eminently qualified pilot with 15,000 flying hours.

"Do I know him?" the president asked.

I knew he was acquainted with Thornhill. He'd seen him on every flight. The president was being disingenuous again, a quirky habit he had of often playing dumb to give the impression that he never gave us worker bees a thought.

"Yes, sir, Mr. President," I answered. "He has been our co-pilot for all the years of your term as vice president and president."

"OK," he said. "You tell Paul."

That gave it away right there. He knew all along who Thornhill was. He even knew him by his first name, Paul.

"Now one more thing, Major, who do you recommend to be my new Armed Forces aide?"

Of course, I was well aware that both the president and Lady Bird knew and liked my assistant, Marine Lieutenant Colonel Haywood Smith. Their daughters Luci and Lynda were likewise fond of him. So I told the president that Smith was a loyal ally and worthy of the appointment.

The president replied, "Yeah, I like Smith, but under the circumstances, since the air force will soon announce your promotion to flag rank, I think it will look better in the press release if we put a general in there. You find a good general that won't rock the boat or will not start acting like a big-shot, and put him over there." I then suggested Brigadier General Robert Ginsburgh, who was already in the White House working for Walt Rostow.

The last thing he said to me that morning was "Now, Cross, don't you forget to take my funeral plans with you when you head for Texas."

Two months later, with the house up for sale and the kids out of school, we took off by car for Texas. We pulled a twenty-three-foot ski boat and traveled with a mutt named Dog. We couldn't wait for our Lone Star State adventure to unfold.

When I reported for work at Bergstrom, I was led to a small office set up for me in the flight operations building. The office was a nice surprise, but what was in the office was a shock. Obviously, the president had been talking to someone. Next to the regular base telephone was a phone with the familiar White House Communications Agency (WHCA) logo. Maybe I wasn't going as far away as I had thought. Sure enough, a few days later, the president called. I could tell he was upset about something from the strained tone of his voice, so I waited through the chitchat for the real reason of the call to become clear.

"Cross, that general you put over there in your old office is just not working out," the president said. "He's acting too much like a big shot, speaking to members of the press and otherwise getting involved in matters in which he has no business. You [emphasis on *you*] need to get him out of there."

Here we go again into deep water, I thought. No longer a staff assistant in the White House, I had no authority to remove Ginsburgh from my old job as Armed Forces aide. But then I remembered that this wouldn't be the first one-star general the president had asked me to dispatch. I had been ordered to fire General McHugh after he buried an Air Force jet in the mud at the LBJ Ranch back in 1963. This time, the president thought Ginsburgh was grandstanding. Since Ginsburgh had been on Walt Rostow's staff, I called Walt and told him of the president's displeasure. Walt agreed to tell Ginsburgh the workload in the situation room was so heavy that he was needed back in his old intelligence job. After the president finished talking about the need to remove Ginsburgh, he asked whom I would recommend to replace him. I again reminded him that Haywood Smith, already on board, was an outstanding, loyal, and capable Marine officer who deserved this appointment. The president concurred, and Smith was confirmed by the United States Senate.

Before I could take command at Bergstrom, I had to get some combat experience. Every RF-4 pilot at Bergstrom had already done a tour in Vietnam, and I wouldn't have their respect as a commander unless I did the same. I would have to be checked out in the Phantom RF-4C before being assigned to a Vietnam unit. That would be quite a change after a long career flying heavy transport aircraft. The first day, they put me in the back seat of a T-33 trainer and the young lieutenant instructor really wrung me out. I've never been so sick in my life. I suppose he'd been told to really work me over because I was the incoming commander. We were doing loops and spins and rolls and everything else I had not been accustomed to since my days as an aviation cadet. I was forty-three years old, and I thought, "Man, if it's going to be like this, I can't take it." I wanted to vomit, but I didn't want to give the instructor the satisfaction.

I toughed it out, and in a few days I started flying the RF-4C reconnaissance plane that I was scheduled to fly in Vietnam. I probably had three times as many flying hours as anybody else in the whole damn wing, so it didn't take me long to get toughened up and master the techniques to fly that airplane. I had to get used to wearing G-suits and oxygen masks, but had no trouble getting all the required hours and passing the tests. The exhilarating moments came when we got down to what was called defensive combat training, which involved tight maneuvers. Dog-fighting, really. By that time, hell, I was better than the young guys. We'd go out on a defensive combat mission, and I'd wax their butts. We didn't have guns, but we had cameras. I would fool around and get on their tails and shoot them down—with a lens, of course.

During training, I got a less-than-warm welcome at Bergstrom from the officers whom I would later command. I suspect they resented my relationship with the president. Maybe they didn't like the fact that I had a White House phone in my office. Or maybe they didn't like the idea of a new guy coming in and upsetting their world. They may have thought my military career was too lackluster and that I really wasn't worthy of a command position of this caliber. Admittedly, I had spent most of my career flying the less-than-glamorous multi-engine transport planes, and had done nothing in fighter planes or bombers. I had no combat medals or history of bravery. I had always earned the highest performance marks, but there was nothing particularly noteworthy in my military career other than flying the president and being White House military aide. I think some of the Bergstrom officers hoped something would happen that would keep me from becoming commander—not necessarily me getting killed, but something that would send me elsewhere.

One night, there was a party at the Officers' Club and I took my wife, Marie. The festivities had the jovial atmosphere of a typical O-club celebration. Drinks were flowing, and the chatter was loud and, at times, crude. But there was a secret purpose to all the merriment. The senior leadership, including the commander, Colonel Pat Malone, strung up a crude replica of an Air Force colonel to hang from the ceiling by the neck. It wasn't just any old colonel, either. It was me! The very officers I soon would be commanding were hanging me in effigy. It was supposed to be funny. But Marie was horrified. She said we should leave. But I whispered to her that we couldn't run from this. We couldn't give anyone the satisfaction of knowing how much the prank wounded us. I knew I was going to be commander, and things would change once I had my general's star. Of course, they did.

After training at Bergstrom, I went through survival school at Fairchild Air Force Base in Washington. The simulated prisoner-of-war training is still vivid in my memory. They put us in black boxes with black hoods over our faces. We were in a simulated prison camp for forty-eight hours. It was not something I ever wanted to experience for real. Survival school steeled your resolve not to get shot down and captured when you got into a combat situation. We were taught what to do if you had to bail out and you got wounded. We learned that, if you ended up in the jungle with maggots in your wounds, you'd better just leave the maggots alone so they could clean out the wound. Then, if you're starving to death, eat the maggots. They're pure protein. "My God!" I thought. I'm not the squeamish type, but that scenario got to me. I was more determined than ever to fly my missions so well that the enemy couldn't get close.

After survival school, I went back to Bergstrom for a few days before shipping out. Then I flew to Washington and caught a ride out of Andrews Air Force Base on a C-135 piloted by one of my friends, Keith Garland, who later became pilot for Vice President Hubert Humphrey. We flew to Clark Air Force Base in the Philippines, where I went through another survival school.

I had been stationed at Clark in 1950 when the Truman administration sent some surplus B-26 light bombers to aid the French in Indochina. I was a young operations officer and had a small role in sending the planes on to Saigon after their stop at Clark for refueling. Then, French authorities asked for rocket munitions for the B-26 planes, and my unit, the 6200th Troop Carrier Squadron, got the mission. I was selected to pilot the C-46 cargo plane carrying the rockets to the French in Vietnam. I was greeted warmly by the French, whose intelligence officers briefed me on their desperate need for any kind of help they could get. Within a few years, Dien Bien Phu collapsed anyway, in spite of the United States's help.

I finally arrived in Vietnam on October 1, 1968. I was sent to Tan Son Nhut, the major airbase outside Saigon. It was the home of "Pentagon East," the headquarters of our military effort there. I outranked my squadron commander, but it didn't matter to me. I wasn't there to look over anyone's shoulder or to be a spy for the president. "I'm here just to fly combat," I said.

I had a lot of people worrying about me when I was in Vietnam, and not just my loved ones and friends. On everybody's mind, whether they said it or not, was what would happen if I were shot down. Everyone in the military feared it would be a major propaganda coup for the Communists if they captured the president's pilot and the director of his military office. And I'm sure everybody involved was afraid their heads would roll or their careers would be sidelined if I were captured. And the thought that I would be tortured for information if I were captured crossed my mind as well. The enemy might have thought I had all kinds of secret information they could ferret out of me by torture. In reality, I knew a lot of things, but I doubt if any of it would have been useful to the enemy. I didn't know anything about war plans. I couldn't even say I knew how many missiles we had with nuclear warheads on them. But a determined enemy might very well think I had all kinds of top-secret information to divulge. They might think that my dumb old country boy demeanor was an act rather than reality.

The one thing they teach you in survival school is to keep your mouth shut. Give away nothing more than name, rank, and serial number. That wasn't much different from what the president had told me in dealing with the news media. But whether or not you would be able to withstand the pressure to talk is really something you could not determine beforehand. I would say to myself, "I'll never talk." Would I be tortured into talking if I were captured? I never knew. If I had talked, the Communists might have been disappointed to hear only about how the president loved Fresca, or about how many times he woke people with his middle-of-the-night phone calls.

I brought my own special handgun to carry on missions. I had had my White House aide, Chief Clerk Sergeant Bill Gulley, acquire it through the Secret Service for $40. It was a lightweight .22-caliber Ruger with an extra-long barrel. The Air Force issued us snub-nosed .38 caliber revolvers. But I liked the .22-caliber because it was lightweight and I could carry more ammunition. I carried a box of 200 rounds. I knew damn well I couldn't compete against .50-caliber machine guns, but if it ever came to the point where I was trying to kill something to eat or kill a single soldier who was trying to capture me, my little gun would be just as effective as the .38.

I wasn't in Vietnam that long, only two-and-a-half months. My tour of duty was more or less routine. I flew seventeen combat missions in an RF-4. We ran recon over South Vietnam, usually two- or three-hour missions, and never ventured far into the North. I flew over Cambodia a couple of times, too. We flew both day and night. Most of the time, the missions were uneventful. I would fly over the lush Mekong Delta and see little villages and rice fields, and I'd think, boy, that sure looks pretty down there. The mission I remember most was a night flight. I had been briefed that there was a lot of enemy activity in the area where we were headed, and that it was particularly dangerous. But there was no way I would be able to hide. My recon plane automatically dropped flares that lit the sky like fireworks. Each flare provided enough light for the camera to take a photo. Then you fly on another 500 or 600 yards and another flare pops out and another photo is taken. We went in at a speed of 420 knots at an altitude of 500 or 600 feet and then kicked the speed up to stay ahead of any ground fire. I came out of the run doing 600 to 700 knots. On this run, the shooting didn't really get close, so I felt fortunate.

Sometimes the firing got a little closer, and I recall a daylight mission along the Mekong Delta when I saw some tracers come arcing up over the vicinity of the wings. For every tracer you can see, there are five more slugs that you don't see. But nothing hit. We usually flew the photo missions alone. In fact, the motto of the recon guy is "Alone, Unarmed, and Unafraid." Bullshit. Anytime you get shot at, you are afraid. Anybody who isn't afraid is nuts. I would have loved to have gone over there and flown fighter planes. Hell, that would have tickled me to death. But I suspect someone high up in the Defense Department—maybe Secretary of Defense Clark Clifford— put in the word that they didn't want me assigned to fighters and placed in a real danger area where guys were getting shot down on a pretty regular basis. So recon it was.

When I was on the ground at Ton Son Nhut, I tried to keep a low profile in the single-story wood barracks we fliers lived in. I was the oldest guy in the barracks, at forty-three, but I was accepted as one of the guys. There were ten rooms on each side of a hallway, and a wall phone in the center of the hall. That phone got me the most attention I received in Vietnam. I would be asleep in the middle of the night, and sometimes when the phone would ring it would be for me. Of course, it was the president, waking me up just like he always did in the States.

I'd hear a knock on my door and someone would say, "Colonel Cross, the president wants to talk to you."

"The president?"

"Yes, the president of the United States."

I would climb out of my cot and just go padding down to the phone barefoot and in my shorts. Sometimes officers stuck their heads out the door to see what they could hear. Some people wondered why the president would be calling a lowly Air Force colonel in the middle of the night. I never went around broadcasting who I was or where I'd been, so I was a bit of a mystery.

Sometimes the president called because he'd received word of some reconnaissance planes that had gone down. I could tell he was worried.

"Well, now, goddamn it, don't you get shot down over there," he said.

"No, sir," I said. "I won't."

He usually wanted to know if I'd seen Pat Nugent, his son-in-law. Pat was in a transport unit assigned to Vietnam, and was a loadmaster on a C-122 cargo plane. He came to visit me two or three times in the barracks. He was just a kid, full of piss and vinegar. He just wanted to see someone he could talk to. I was always happy when I could tell the president that I'd seen Pat and that he was A-OK.

Pat wrote the president after seeing me during a layover from China. This excerpt is from that December 17, 1968, letter, handwritten on military stationery:

> On our return from Taiwan we stopped in Saigon to make the appropriate connections to Phan Rang [AFB]. I had a few hours to spend in Saigon so I decided to give Jim Cross a call. Jim came to pick me up and it was like an old time reunion. He gave me every indication that he is enjoying his work and is making the most of it while he is able to do so. I believe he returns to the States around 15 January. I tried to convince him that he should take me on a reconnaissance mission, but being the responsible individual that he is [he] turned down my request. I hope to visit with Jim once more before he returns to Bergstrom.

While I was in Vietnam, I didn't go around and make any speeches or do any stumping on behalf of the president because I didn't feel like the people I was in contact with would appreciate it. If someone would ask me, of course I would say, "The president is behind you 100 percent." But I didn't make a big deal out of it. I had been sent over there to get some combat experience, basically to punch my ticket so I could become the commander at Bergstrom. I hadn't been sent over there as a personal messenger for the president, and I didn't want to act like one.

The entire time I was there, I didn't feel particularly welcome. General George S. Brown, the commander of the Seventh Air Force in Vietnam, was blunt about that. He told me to my face, "I don't know why the hell they ever let you come over here in the first place. I don't think they ought to have let you come." The tough old pilot, who had earned his battle stripes leading bombing runs on Romanian oil fields in World War II, wasn't one to cushion his words. Late in his career he got into hot water for saying publicly that Israel was "a burden" to the United States and that the British military was "pathetic." Brown became chairman of the Joint Chiefs of Staff, but not before he took a lot of flak over the issue of secret bombings in Cambodia in 1969 and 1970. That time Brown was just following orders. President Nixon had ordered the secret bombing of Cambodian bases in March 1969 to keep the pressure on the North Vietnamese to negotiate an end to the war.

My time in Vietnam ended in mid-December. General Brown phoned me at 5 A.M. on December 16 and ordered me to be in his office at 7 A.M. I didn't even have time to say, "Yes, sir," before the phone went dead. I couldn't go back to sleep, so I arrived on time for my appointment. I saluted, and Brown ordered me to sit down.

"Cross, how long would it take you to get out of here and get home?" Brown asked. "A former Armed Forces aide to the president and pilot of Air Force One has no business over here flying combat. I don't like getting calls in the middle of the night from the White House. General McConnell called me this morning and told me to get you home. You get your butt out of here.

"I want you out of here today! Go home!"

I was supposed to stay until February 1969. I didn't want to leave until I had a few more combat missions on my ticket, but I suspect the president intervened to get me sent home early. He may have gotten a little concerned after the Air Force lost two or three recon planes over the North in a short time period. Maybe someone high up in the Secretary of Defense's office or the Secretary of the Air Force's office called the president and suggested he bring me home before something bad happened. My short career as a combat pilot was over.

I then served as Wing Commander of the 75th Tactical Reconnaissance Wing at Bergstrom for more than two years. I retired from the Air Force on April 30, 1971, and the former president honored me with his presence at the ceremony. Air Force General William Momyer, then commander of Tactical Air Command, came as well. I was pleased to note that both enjoyed a warm reunion on the parade ground that day—unlike at their last meeting in 1967, in that austere mobile home at Korat Air Force Base in Thailand.

During all my time as the president's pilot and his military aide, Johnson rarely discussed Vietnam strategy with me, although I certainly saw his frustration in many private moments. Several times during his presidency he asked me, "Major, what in the world can I do about that god-awful war in Vietnam?"

While I suspected the question was more rhetorical than anything else, I nevertheless stepped up to the lick log each time and gave him my best advice: "Mr. President, having been a military man for some twenty-five years, I am a hawk when it comes to confrontations with an enemy. I would start straightaway with a huge bombing campaign, targeting Haiphong Harbor, all the bridges leading into North Vietnam from China, all the electric power facilities, every single rail yard and terminal, and all their governmental infrastructure. And, Mr. President, I would continue such a campaign until every last ounce of their resistance was crushed." It was the Cross version of what General Curtis LeMay, the former Air Force chief of staff, said about bombing North Vietnam back into the Stone Age.

The president wasn't impressed with my opinion, and I remember him telling me, "For Christ's sake, Major, you would have us in a nuclear war with Communist China."

But the president never forgot my hawkish advice. Years later, after he was retired and living on his Texas ranch, he often invited Marie and me to come visit. One night in 1972, we were having dinner with the president, Lady Bird, and several of their friends. That was the year President Nixon had ordered the Linebacker I and II bombing operations that were credited with returning the North Vietnamese to the negotiating table. I remember President Johnson saying to me, "Well, Major, you finally got your wish." Once again, I was reminded of the nearly total recall this remarkable man possessed.

Sadly, the president would not live to see the signing of the Paris Peace Accords on January 27, 1973.

CHAPTER TWELVE

FAREWELL TO A FRIEND

ON THE AFTERNOON OF MONDAY, JANUARY 22, 1973, I WAS repairing a pasture fence about a quarter-mile from our ranch home near Austin when I heard a truck coming. It was my wife, driving our old ranch pickup, and she looked distraught. Through tears, she said an emergency call had come from the LBJ Ranch telephone switchboard. "I'm afraid it's the president," she said. "Something bad has happened to the president."

We feared the worst as we drove back to the house. Johnson was sixty-four, and all of us who knew him had been concerned about his health. We had been since his heart attack the previous April. He had begun smoking cigarettes again for the first time in sixteen years, and he was putting on weight, contrary to doctor's orders. It was no secret that he would grab an extra two or three cookies off the table when he thought Mrs. Johnson wasn't looking. The only hour she allowed him to spend alone every day was the one devoted to his afternoon nap. He liked to joke that his body was just aging in its own way, and besides, he was just an old man and what difference did it make? Of course, his life made a lot of difference to the millions he had touched in his long political career. It wasn't easy watching a giant among men slide ever closer to mortality.

I dialed the ranch switchboard as I had so many times since Johnson had left the presidency exactly four years before. I guess I expected to hear his voice needling me with a complaint or barking a demand for me and Marie to come visit. Instead, I was told the president was dead. A fatal heart attack had felled the bigger-than-life man whom I loved like a father. My heart broke in a way I didn't know it could.

The president, I was told, had eaten a lazy lunch and put on his pajamas for an afternoon nap as he often did. About 3:50 P.M., he called the ranch switchboard from a bedroom phone and asked that Secret Service Agent Mike Howard come immediately. That's all he said. Howard wasn't available at that moment, but two other agents ran the hundred yards to the president's room. He was lying on the floor, his right eye and cheek bruised by the fall he'd taken when his heart stopped. Secret Service Agents Harry Harris and Ed Nowland administered mouth-to-mouth resuscitation and gave him oxygen from a portable unit they brought with them. When Agent Howard arrived, he tried external heart massage. But it was too late. The president's body was already turning blue.

Dr. David Abbott came from nearby Johnson City, arriving just after the president was placed on his private plane. Dr. Abbott jumped on board, and the plane took off toward Brooke Army Hospital in San Antonio. First, the plane landed at San Antonio International Airport, and there Dr. Abbott pronounced the president dead.

Mrs. Johnson had been spending that Monday afternoon at the LBJ Library. She was a passenger in a car leaving the library and had traveled just one block when she was notified by Secret Service radio of the president's heart attack. She immediately returned to the library, where a helicopter arrived to fly her to San Antonio.

By the time I talked to the ranch switchboard, the operator told me that Mrs. Johnson was already on her way back to Austin from San Antonio. I figured she would head for the downtown apartment atop the KTBC radio and television station the Johnson family owned in Austin. I took a quick bath, shaved, put on a black suit, and broke the speed limit driving the ten miles to Austin. I carried with me the official funeral plan for Lyndon Baines Johnson that I had been the custodian of for more than seven years. I kept the six-page document in a safe in a storage room just off the family room at my ranch.

The Johnsons' apartment was in the shadow of the pink-granite state Capitol dome, and I arrived there just ahead of Mrs. Johnson. Already there was a gathering of some of the president's closest friends and most trusted advisers, including George Christian, the president's press secretary; longtime friend and University of Texas regent Frank Erwin; Jesse Kellam, general manager of the Johnson radio and television interests; and Tom Johnson, the president's adviser and former assistant press secretary.

We weren't crying, but the mood was somber. All of us had been caught off guard. Just two days before his death, the president had helped plant a tree near his ranch as part of Mrs. Johnson's highway beautification program. The president had devoted himself to his ranch since he had returned to Texas in early 1969. He loved the Hill Country lifestyle—everything from going to livestock auctions to discussing the price of hogs and eggs. Once an old friend jokingly complained, "He's become a goddamn farmer. I want to talk Democratic politics. He talks only hog prices." It was hard to believe that that irascible personality had been silenced just as it was mellowing.

The phones in the penthouse suite were kept busy with outgoing calls. Fortunately, someone had instructed the station's main switchboard to screen out all but the most urgent incoming calls. Messages of condolence flooded the switchboard all evening, I found out later. But in the family quarters high atop the building, we couldn't hear the commotion.

Mrs. Johnson arrived about 7 P.M. She was composed as she greeted us, one by one, and thanked us for coming. We were the president's closest friends, and she looked relieved that she could lean on us. She joined us in discussing how to carry out the official funeral plan. It was just like a typical military plan, an hour-by-hour sequence of things that would happen over the next several days. "D+1," it said, beside the instructions for what to do an hour after the president's death, and "D+2" and "D+3" and so on. We ended up changing a lot of things. Instead of the president lying in state at an Episcopal church a couple of blocks from the apartment as originally planned, Mrs. Johnson decided the president's body would instead lie in the Great Hall at the LBJ Library. It was Frank Erwin's suggestion, and Mrs. Johnson liked it.

The last funeral plan detail to be reviewed seemed the easiest. I had no idea it would thrust me into the spotlight and test my ability to be a pillar of emotional strength in public while, inside, my heart was heaving. According to protocol, Mrs. Johnson was to be escorted by an active-duty military general. I told Mrs. Johnson that the general would meet her in the morning and escort her through the events of the next few days, concluding with the funeral and burial. But Mrs. Johnson balked. "Jim," she said, "I don't know this general. Could you escort me? Would you mind putting on your uniform again and being my escort?"

I said the only thing I could say: "Yes, ma'am."

I didn't quite know how to deliver the news to the general, but I knew he was at Bergstrom Air Force Base on the eastern outskirts of Austin. I had to meet with the funeral coordinators who had flown in from Washington to the base anyway, so I decided to seek out the general in person rather than by phone. I arrived there about 1 A.M. and found the three-star Army general from Fort Sam Houston in San Antonio. He was wide awake, still putting the finishing touches on plans for the huge military procession and the honor guard needed to escort the president's body to the library.

I had to tell him delicately that he was going to be bumped from his official duty. I took a deep breath, and just walked up to him and said, "General, sir, I'm sorry to have to tell you this, but Mrs. Johnson has asked me to be her escort, since I was military aide to the president. I've been visiting with Mrs. Johnson ever since the president died. And this is what she wants."

He kind of hemmed and hawed a little bit and said, "Well, I'm supposed to be her escort." I told him I understood his feelings, but that I could not let Mrs. Johnson down at a time when she needed me more than she ever had. He was a gracious fellow and accepted the change and went on about his business. I walked out of there feeling kind of embarrassed. He was a lieutenant general, and here I was, a former one-star general, now retired. I thought of the other times that the president had put me in the position of "pulling rank" on someone who outranked me. Even in death, I was breaking rules because of Lyndon Johnson.

There really shouldn't have been any last-minute changes in the plans for Lyndon Johnson's funeral. The president himself had actually started preparing for his funeral a decade earlier. When he was still vice president, in 1962, Johnson took me driving around his ranch one day in his white Lincoln convertible. We ended up at the tree-shaded family cemetery by the Pedernales River. Out of the blue, he pointed out the exact spot where he wanted to be buried. I wasn't prepared for that kind of talk. We had just been killing time on a lazy afternoon and all of a sudden we're contemplating death. "Now, Cross, one of these days I want you to bury me right here," he said. It was weird—why would I, a military pilot, have anything to do with burying him? But I just went along with it and joked that he probably would live to be 100 and that I would die before he did.

But later, when Johnson was president and I became the presidential military aide, I learned that one of the responsibilities that went with the job was overseeing funeral plans for the sitting president as well as for all former living presidents. It was a joint responsibility of the military aide and the commander of the military district of Washington to maintain and fine-tune the plans. So I kept funeral plans for the ex-presidents living during Johnson's term—Truman and Eisenhower. And I continued to keep Johnson's plan up-to-date after he left the presidency, even though it wasn't my official duty. I knew he was depending on me to handle things. In fact, the president had reminded me to take the plan with me when I moved to Texas in 1968 to prepare to command Bergstrom.

During my many visits to the ranch, both during Johnson's presidency and for years after, it became a habit of Johnson to wheel by the cemetery when we were out for a drive on the ranch. He'd remind me again that he was counting on me to make sure he was buried next to his mother and father. He always told me to keep that funeral plan current and accessible to his family. I can't count the number of times we had this conversation. I dreaded these moments and tried to steer the conversation in another direction. But he persisted, insisting each time that I get together with Mrs. Johnson and his daughters to work out the details. So I dutifully, and repeatedly, called Mrs. Johnson and explained that the president wanted us to meet and discuss the arrangements for that horrible day. She was as uncomfortable with the subject as I was. So, as gently as I could, I told her I was available anytime she wanted to get together. But each time, she put it off. This went on for years. Dodging a delicate subject was uncharacteristic of Mrs. Johnson. She was a strong, disciplined woman who didn't shy away from getting a tough job done in an organized way. But refusing to think about the passing of her husband was, obviously, her defense against an inevitable grief. In fact, we never discussed the arrangements for the president's funeral until that awful night after his death.

On Tuesday, the day after the president died, my first official duty as Mrs. Johnson's escort was to accompany her to the LBJ Library. I arrived at the Weed-Corley Funeral Home that morning wearing my old Air Force uniform which I had retrieved from storage. Somewhere along the way, I had lost the ribbons and the necktie that were supposed to go with it. I asked my former secretary at Bergstrom, Patsy Darby, to buy the ribbons and tie out at the Bergstrom BX. But she forgot to send the necktie to the funeral home. I asked Patsy to send someone to the BX to get me one, but it never arrived. There was no way I could appear in public in a high-visibility role without a complete uniform. That would violate military protocol as well as the honor of the president. I had had to break military rules before to satisfy some of Lyndon Johnson's demands over the years, but I wasn't going to do it now. In desperation, I looked around the funeral home and noticed a young airman standing guard near the flag-draped, silver coffin. I just marched over and asked him to lend me his necktie. He dutifully agreed, and I was tying it just seconds before I met up with Mrs. Johnson for the trip to the library. I don't think she even noticed. She reached for my arm and hung on to me pretty tight.

I could hear a military band strike up "Hail to the Chief" as the president's coffin was brought out of the funeral home and placed in a hearse. We stepped into the waiting limousine. Several hundred soldiers stood in respect along the procession route to the library. Thousands of people were waiting outside the library when we arrived. I opened the car door for Mrs. Johnson, and she surprised me by immediately taking hold of my right arm. Protocol called for her to take my left arm so my right arm would be free to make military salutes. I didn't want to rattle her, though, so I didn't say anything.

A military honor guard serving as pallbearers carried the casket into the library as a military band played. The president's casket was placed on a bier at the top of a long grand staircase to the library's second floor, in front of a wall of bronze friezes depicting scenes from the president's life. One of the most poignant moments at the library came during a brief service around the coffin. Mrs. Johnson recognized one of the reporters, Norma Milligan from *Newsweek*, and called her over. Their eyes welled with tears. Mrs. Johnson managed a smile and said, "Oh, but didn't he live well!"

Two Austin ministers, the Reverend John Barclay and the Reverend Charles A. Summers, offered words of prayer. Longtime friends of the Johnson family and a few dignitaries paid their respects before the doors to the library were opened to the general public. About 32,000 people filed past to view the body as it lay in state from noon Tuesday until 8 A.M. on Wednesday, January 24. The mourners represented a broad cross-section of the people the president had touched over the years. There were blacks, whites, and Hispanics. There were rich people and poor people, those who dressed well and those dressed in common clothes.

Mrs. Johnson and her two daughters stood near the coffin to meet many of the people who came. Mrs. Johnson wore a blue suit, and even though she was red-eyed, she smiled a lot as she greeted old friends and shook hands. In fact, she had a little courageous smile on her face throughout the long hours of greeting mourners. CBS News televised the event, and Walter Cronkite said Mrs. Johnson was magnificent in the receiving line. Dan Rather noted that the president once said, "If you think I'm tough, observe closely Lady Bird. She's the one who really has the courage." A constantly changing group of longtime Johnson acquaintances kept guard over the coffin. Among them were Walt Rostow, the national security adviser who spent so much time with Johnson during the Vietnam War; George Christian; Ed Clark, former ambassador to Australia; LBJ library director Harry Middleton; Austin mayor Roy Butler; and University of Texas football coach Darrell Royal.

I slipped away soon after the president's casket was situated in the Great Hall, assuring Mrs. Johnson I would be available by phone. I needed to coordinate plans with the White House and the Air Force for the trip to Washington the next day for the state funeral. President Nixon had agreed to send his presidential plane to fly Johnson's body to Washington. It was the same plane I had piloted on so many memorable Air Force One trips. When everything was set, I went home for some much-needed rest. I wanted to be as alert as possible for my last trip with the president in our old, familiar airplane.

The next morning, Mrs. Johnson surprised me again by taking my right arm as we left the LBJ Library to meet the limousine for the cross-town trip to Bergstrom, where we would board the presidential plane. The ride to Bergstrom couldn't have taken more than fifteen minutes, but I never got the chance to tell her she needed to take my left arm, not my right. When we climbed out of the limousine at Bergstrom, she still clung to my right arm. Before I could correct her, the military band started playing "Hail to the Chief" and "Ruffles and Flourishes." I could not render the military salute the songs demanded. Later, I found a quiet moment during the plane trip to Washington to inform Mrs. Johnson she should always be on my left.

My heart was heavy with despair for her and the girls. I knew the fast-moving events were nearly unbearable for them. It was heartbreaking for me, too, because the Johnsons had been like family to me for eleven-plus years. The military had trained me to be stoic and disciplined. Officers were expected to show little or no emotion in stressful situations like the one we faced on the tarmac at Bergstrom. But as six cannons saluted the president and the military honor guard lifted his body aboard the plane, my mind wandered back to the good times of the past. I thought of the many times I had piloted him and seen him bound aboard that majestic plane, exuberant and alive and always trusting in me to bring him safely home. This was the beginning of his last journey aboard that fantastic flying White House; perhaps mine, too. I know grown men aren't supposed to cry, but I simply couldn't hold back the tears. I thank God for Lynda Robb. She took my arm and squeezed it tightly as we stood with her mother on that cold, wind-swept ramp. Her thoughtful gesture gave me strength in that precious moment as memories of adventures with the president returned and flooded my soul.

Everywhere I turned that morning, emotions were on display. The president's grandson, six-year-old Lyn Nugent, raised his hand in a quick salute as the coffin was raised by hydraulic lift to the door of the plane. It was a scene reminiscent of November 1963, when three-year-old John F. Kennedy Jr. raised his tiny hand in a solemn salute to his assassinated father.

Some of the Johnsons' closest friends were on the presidential flight from Bergstrom to Washington, including Liz Carpenter, Mrs. Johnson's former press secretary; Dale Malechek, foreman of the LBJ Ranch, and his wife Jewell; former Supreme Court justice Abe Fortas; and Arthur Krim, chairman of the board of United Artists.

We touched down shortly before 1 P.M. at Andrews Air Force Base. A military honor guard placed the president's coffin in a hearse for the sixteen-mile drive into Washington. A thirty-car caravan that included the entire Texas congressional delegation accompanied the hearse, which crept along at twenty miles per hour. About an hour later, our procession reached Constitution Avenue alongside the Washington Monument. Just to the north, we could see the White House gleaming in the winter sunshine. The coffin was removed from the hearse by a military honor guard and lifted onto a four-wheel caisson pulled by six white horses.

The caisson moved slowly, almost as if in time with the muffled drums of the Marine Corps Band. Behind the caisson came Black Jack, the riderless horse carrying a saddle with boots facing backward to signify the death of a leader. The horse also had taken part in the funerals of Presidents Kennedy and Eisenhower. More than 1,800 servicemen from every branch of the military marched ahead of the caisson. The Joint Chiefs of Staff also marched in the procession. The streets were lined with thousands of people, some standing six or seven deep. They mostly were silent as the procession slowly passed.

I rode in a limousine with the Johnson family even though part of me wanted to be marching outside with the other generals. Our car was followed by one carrying President Nixon, which was just ahead of sedans carrying Vice President Agnew and other dignitaries. The East Plaza of the Capitol was crowded with thousands of people when our procession arrived at the steps of the Capitol and stopped. We got out of the car and waited for the soldiers to remove the coffin from the caisson and carry it up the Capitol steps and into the rotunda.

As we waited, President and Mrs. Nixon walked up and greeted Mrs. Johnson. Although the funeral plan called for me to stay with, and escort, Mrs. Johnson up the steps of the Capitol, President Nixon insisted on taking her arm. Both of us actually were moving toward Mrs. Johnson at the same time. President Nixon bumped into Chuck Robb in his haste to get to Mrs. Johnson. I figured it was best to step aside, and I gestured for him to go ahead. After all, he was president of the United States and I only a lowly retired Air Force brigadier general. Nixon and Mrs. Johnson slowly walked up the Capitol steps on that windblown day. I stayed over to Mrs. Johnson's right during the walk up the steps but didn't take her arm. Dan Rather noted on CBS that I gave way to President Nixon, and cited me as an example of the Southerners that President Johnson liked to have around him. I guess Rather was praising me as sort of a southern gentleman for deferring to Nixon.

I never did find out how Mrs. Johnson felt about Nixon's move. I certainly never asked, out of respect for this thoughtful and gracious woman. On the other hand, I suspect that Lyndon Baines Johnson himself might have been somewhat upset, had he been able to say so. I say this because I always had the impression the president was not a strong Nixon fan. In fact, just a few minutes earlier, when the procession passed the District of Columbia federal courthouse where one of the Watergate trials was going on, Walter Cronkite noted that President Johnson had been incensed by Watergate. "He hardly viewed it as a small political trick," Cronkite told millions of viewers. "He thought it was a serious infringement on the political process."

Inside the Capitol rotunda, Mrs. Johnson and the girls were strong and composed throughout the eulogies. The rotunda was packed with VIPs— Hubert Humphrey, Spiro Agnew, and dozens of senators, congressmen, and government movers and shakers. The television broadcast noted that Van Cliburn was there too, but I never saw him. It was crowded, and it was stuffy. A couple of military people fainted, as did Mrs. William Rogers, the wife of Nixon's secretary of state. The president would have been happy with the turnout. CBS newsman Roger Mudd noted that the scene was almost like a political meeting in the best sense of the word. Harry McPherson said that this was the first time that LBJ had come to Capitol Hill with no laundry list of legislation.

After several hymns and prayers, Congressman J. J. "Jake" Pickle of Austin delivered a eulogy that proclaimed the Johnson presidency had changed America forever for the good. I believed that too, with my whole heart and soul. Former Secretary of State Dean Rusk acknowledged criticism of the president's Vietnam policies but said, "In a simpler and more robust age, we might have known him as Lyndon the Liberator."

After the ceremony, hundreds of people, friends and strangers alike, wanted to express condolences to Mrs. Johnson and the girls. The press of so many well-wishers was crushing, and I was concerned the Johnson family would be injured. Texas Governor Dolph Briscoe and his wife, Janey, were desperately trying to reach Mrs. Johnson, but were being pushed away by the crowd. I had to literally shove people out of the way to clear a path for the Briscoes. After the dignitaries cleared out, the rotunda was opened to the public. About 40,000 people filed past the coffin that day and into the night.

I helped the Johnsons make their way out of the throng, and we headed for Blair House, where President Nixon had arranged for the funeral party to stay Wednesday night. Tom Johnson and I spent a good portion of the evening attempting to sort out problems and firm up plans for the trip back to Texas for the interment. The original plan called for the funeral party to accompany the president's body back to Texas aboard a DC-9 hospital plane, a two-engine jet small enough to land at the LBJ Ranch. But the weather forecast predicted rain and poor visibility, making it impossible for the plane to make the trip as planned. We had to ask the White House if we could change plans and transport the president's body more safely back to Texas aboard the presidential aircraft, which could land at Bergstrom.

And Mrs. Johnson wanted General William Westmoreland to be at the funeral. I talked to the general, who was in South Carolina, but he said he could not make it unless he had some military transportation to get there. I tried to get him a T-39 Sabreliner, which was a little six-seat, two-engine military jet. But H. R. Haldeman, who was Nixon's chief of staff, said, "No, absolutely not. Let him get himself a private plane." Haldeman also objected to the use of the presidential airplane to transport the president's body back to Texas. So we had a big fuss about that. It's entirely possible that President Nixon himself could have had a hand in the resistance we encountered in both instances.

Tom Johnson and I got together, and we called Haldeman. We told him, "Hey, we're going to the press if y'all hold out on this deal." It worked. We got a T-39 to bring Westmoreland to Texas, though Haldeman was royally pissed. And we got use of the presidential aircraft. I have since suspected that President Nixon probably became aware of this potentially embarrassing development and directed a more friendly solution.

We awakened the next day to a cold and dreary Washington winter morning, but by the time of the funeral service the weather had cleared and the sun was bright. Walter Cronkite noted that Mrs. Johnson was holding up well as the coffin was taken from the Capitol and transported in a procession to the National City Christian Church. Several thousand people were waiting at the church when our motorcade arrived. Mrs. Johnson was on my arm as we exited the limousine and walked up to the church. We were greeted by the pastor, Dr. George R. Davis. I helped Mrs.

Johnson get seated inside the church and then took a seat behind her and the Robbs and the Nugents.

I listened with a heavy heart as Marvin Watson, who had served as the president's chief of staff before becoming postmaster general, praised our former boss as the "man who taught me to live in this city that drives men insane and to early graves." Like always, the cloud of Vietnam hung over the president. Watson, his voice cracking, noted that he had watched the gray come into the president's hair as he struggled with the war.

Some of the emotional peaks of the ceremony came during two solos sung by Leontyne Price, the Metropolitan Opera soprano who had sung at Johnson's inauguration eight years earlier. Many people dabbed at their eyes as she sang "Precious Lord, Take My Hand" and "Onward Christian Soldiers." Walter Cronkite noted in his broadcast that "the gathering of so many old friends and such beautiful music from Leontyne Price combined to make it difficult to maintain a composure" that had been so apparent earlier. As I sat there behind Mrs. Johnson and her daughters, listening to the eulogies, I could barely hold my own emotions in check. The president could be petty at times, difficult to please, impossible on occasion. But he could be thoughtful, compassionate, considerate, and a captivating storyteller with a wonderful sense of humor. He was an uncommon common man who defied description. As I remembered all of our times together, it was nearly impossible to sit there and hold back the tears. On the other hand, I felt the family was depending on me to be strong and resolute, as the president had so often expected of me. So I was determined to steel my emotions until the end.

I was relieved when the singing and eulogies finally concluded with a prayer and it was time to escort Mrs. Johnson from the church. She whispered that she should say good-bye to the Nixons, so we moved across the aisle, where she thanked them for coming. Then we walked slowly out of the church and down the long set of stairs. As we watched the president's casket being taken from the church, I leaned over to whisper to Mrs. Johnson. Everyone watching on television probably wondered what sort of comforting or personal remark I was making. Actually, I was just making sure she knew our next move would be by motorcade to Andrews Air Force Base for the flight back to Texas. She was concerned about General Westmoreland and asked if he would be able to fly with us. At that point, she probably was not aware that Westmoreland wasn't in Washington but was at home in South Carolina. She knew nothing of the trouble we had gone through arranging his transportation to Texas, and I did not want to trouble her with that information.

The trip down to Texas in the presidential aircraft was uneventful. I made a few radio telephone calls to ascertain that plans were under way for the motorcade to the ranch and that General Westmoreland was en route in the plane we had arranged for him. No one really felt like talking too much. And I knew this would be the last time I ever flew in this big plane, so I took a private farewell tour and soaked up the memories.

The weather was terrible when we landed in Austin. We just stood there while the president's body was unloaded from the plane. Without thinking, I said something about "the body."

Mrs. Johnson was offended. "Jim," she said, "it's not 'the body,' it's the president."

And I thought, "Oh, Lord, why have I made such an insensitive comment to this gracious lady?" So I turned and busied myself with directing the motorcade into place and getting everyone into a car for that seventy-mile drive from Austin to the ranch. It was rainy, cold, and just plain miserable. I was supposed to ride with Mrs. Johnson, Lynda, and Luci in the first limousine behind the hearse. But in the confusion of the moment, Luci and her husband, Pat Nugent, ended up in the third car. By hustling around and trying to make sure everyone had a ride, I missed the car with Mrs. Johnson. I panicked for a quick second, but as the motorcade started to move I just snatched open the door of the nearest big Cadillac and jumped in. Inside were Luci, Pat Nugent, and Anita Bryant and her husband. I remembered that my wife and I had once been to a concert of some sort at the State Department, and Anita Bryant was the star. We had front-row seats, but we didn't particularly like her then.

I was up in the front seat with the driver, and the other four were in back. During the trip, the conversation was somewhat relaxed, compared to the stress of the preceding four days. The president's passing had begun to sink in, and the healing process was under way. As we got to the outskirts of Austin, those dark, mean-looking clouds finally broke, and there was the greatest, most beautiful sunshine you ever saw.

I was just trying to make light conversation, and I turned to the four of them and said, "Well, wouldn't you know it? Here we are on the way to the president's funeral, and the weather's been terrible. Wouldn't it be just like the president to order up some nice weather for his burial?"

I thought I was among friends and my remark was harmless; I realized only too late that I had said the wrong thing. Anita Bryant looked like she had bit down on a stinkbug, and she lit into me. "Only God is in control of the weather," she said. She hadn't liked my remark at all. But I think Pat and Luci agreed with me about the president. I'm a believer in God too, and I trust He will forgive me if I committed a mortal sin when making such an innocent remark.

Riding the seventy miles to the ranch had to be painful for Mrs. Johnson, particularly as we passed through Johnson City, then Hye, where the president, as a young boy, had mailed his first letter in the same country store and post office that was still there. The procession moved down Ranch Road 1, then crossed the bridge over the Pedernales River and passed the one-room country school young Lyndon attended. Then we were at the cemetery, 150 yards from the edge of the Pedernales River, where the president had taken me for the first time more than a decade earlier.

Several thousand mourners, many of them Hill Country residents who had known Johnson all their lives, stood outside the low cemetery wall. Because of wet grounds, mourners parked two miles away at Lyndon Baines Johnson State Park and took shuttle buses to the cemetery. Some of them stood out in the rain for nearly two hours.

The Fifth Army Band from Fort Sam Houston began the service by playing "Ruffles and Flourishes" and the national anthem. During the service, Johnson ally and former Texas Governor John Connally showed he understood how the president felt about the Hill Country. "Along this stream and under these trees he loved, he will now rest. He first saw light here. He last felt life here. May he now find peace here."

Pallbearers fought the wind to hold the American flag horizontally over the casket during the service. I thought it would blow away during Billy Graham's eulogy. Graham recalled that LBJ once had taken him to the cemetery and said, "Billy, one day you're going to be asked to preach my funeral." I realized I had not been the only friend to receive graveside instructions from the president. He had calculated everything in life, down to his last moment in the spotlight.

After Reverend Graham wrapped up his remarks, the Texas National Guard fired a twenty-one-gun salute with six 105mm howitzers in a pasture beyond the stone wall of the cemetery. Master Sergeant Patrick B. Mastroleo then played taps on his bugle, just as he had done a month earlier at President Truman's funeral. Anita Bryant, wearing a black coat with a big white collar fastened with two giant black buttons, then stepped up to the microphone. The cemetery was absolutely quiet when, without any introduction, she began singing an a capella version of "The Battle Hymn of the Republic." Her voice was so low and deep, almost otherworldly, that it sounded like grief personified. Mrs. Johnson was standing between Lynda and Luci, who was clutching her hand for emotional support. During the mournful song, Mrs. Johnson kept her sad eyes on the silver casket. For me, time stood still. All the old, familiar memories collided with the reality that my beloved friend was gone. I was numb.

Then it was over. I snapped back to reality just as the pallbearers were folding the flag that had been draped over the coffin. Now it was time for me to present the triangular bundle to Mrs. Johnson. The military had given me a little note card with a prepared message of condolence, sort of a boilerplate, fits-all message. Now, that was crap. Those were sterile, impersonal words. It would have been an insult to read them to Mrs. Johnson. So I took her hand, and said, simply, "I love your family and I loved him, and I am honored beyond measure to have the privilege of presenting you his flag today as we mourn his loss. Thank you for permitting me to be your friend." No one else could hear what was said. In fact, the *New York Times* and other media reported that I spoke the words on the preprinted card. Not true. It was strictly private between Mrs. Johnson and me. Mrs. Johnson kissed the flag. Then General Westmoreland placed a wreath at the foot of the casket, saluted, and walked away. As I escorted Mrs. Johnson to the limousine, I couldn't help looking one last time at the coffin. It was my last chance to say good-bye. I wiped away tears as I stood at the open door of the car, waiting for the rest of the family. I didn't care that a national television audience was watching.

After the service at the cemetery, the Johnsons invited some of the guests to the house for iced tea and visiting. Sometimes the ugly side of people comes out at times like this. Mrs. Johnson wanted the guests to come inside the house, but actor Hugh O'Brian took it upon himself to be a self-important doorman. He stood at the front door, bossing everybody except for Mrs. Johnson and the girls. He stopped guests and said things like "Now just hold up a minute. We're getting too many people in here at once." I'd seen him on TV playing Wyatt Earp, but I'd never known him to be a family friend. He was rude and, it appeared to me, he was taking advantage of a grieving family to grab the limelight. I wanted to give him a knuckle sandwich but managed to keep myself in check. I reminded him that he was just one of many guests and that I would take care of his worries in due time. That shut him up.

And Senator Mike Mansfield, who flew to the ranch on a private plane, became testy when he didn't think we were returning him to his plane quickly enough. He told me he had to leave, and I said, "Well, sir, we're doing the best we can. We'll get you there whenever we can." I was no longer in the Air Force. I didn't care what Mansfield or anybody else said. I was trying to do what I thought best for my friends, the Johnson family. And if he was upset, that was his problem.

A few days later, Mrs. Johnson, knowing I was running a small cattle ranch of my own, presented me with one of her husband's prized Hereford bulls. Like the entire Johnson herd, it was branded on its horns with the president's initials. My children promptly named him LBJ. That unexpected gift meant the world to me, and it kept the Johnson legacy alive on my ranch and in my own family.

TODAY, IN THE NEW MILENNIUM, AS I RECALL THOSE ELEVEN exciting and eventful years from late 1961 until the president's death in 1973, I am first reminded of Mr. Johnson's vast energy and determination to pull the nation from the depths of despair after the JFK assassination. From that beginning came the whirlwind campaign in 1964 to win his own term in the presidency. Thereafter he pushed forth and signed into law the greatest watershed body of social legislation in the history of the nation. Most regrettably, however, the Vietnam War had already begun taking a terrible toll on his energy, his health, and his resolve.

I am convinced Johnson's life was foreshortened by the pressures he faced in those trying last months of his presidency. He lived only four years and a few days after leaving office, and I witnessed him ill and tired, but also happy as he made a peaceful transition back to his lifelong love, the life of a gentleman rancher. Unlike some other former presidents, he never spoke out on the issues of the day, nor did he ever publicly criticize the incumbent president, Richard Nixon, although they were poles apart in matters of philosophy and governance.

To have been given the opportunity to build a relationship with this uncommon common man was the gift of a lifetime, one shared by few others. I remain humbled by the experience.

AFTER LYNDON JOHNSON RETIRED FROM THE WHITE HOUSE, he and Lady Bird often invited my wife, Marie, and me to their Hill Country ranch for dinner. Usually other members of the LBJ inner circle were there too, and we traded stories and memories about our historic days together. On one of those occasions, the former president turned to me and said, "Cross, you're probably going to want to write a book someday." I knew from his tone that he was more interested in giving me a warning than making an inquiry. It was clear that he didn't want his most private moments laid bare. I assured him that I had no intention of writing a book.

That dinner conversation occurred more than thirty-three years ago. With the passage of time, I realized that the unique adventures I shared with Lyndon Johnson would be lost to history if I did not write them down. I was a one-man army in service to LBJ and my country. Today, it might take as many as 100 people to perform the myriad White House jobs I held. I know Lyndon Johnson was proud of the efficiency we demonstrated. I think he would enjoy these stories, too. Many of the moments I write about were private conversations, but I respectfully share them in hopes that they show the indefatigable energy and fearless nature of a great man.

Military aviation was my chosen career path, so when I began to think about writing my story, I reached out to a respected newspaper reporter for help in shaping this book. Denise Gamino of the *Austin American-Statesman* wrote about me and my Air Force One experiences for a newspaper article in January 2001. It was a good experience, and later she agreed to work with me on a book. Denise has been a newspaper journalist for more than thirty years and has won numerous national and regional reporting awards for investigative journalism and feature writing. From 2001 to 2005, she taped nearly forty hours of interviews with me at my ranch near Gatesville, Texas. She also brought in one of her former *Statesman* colleagues to assist us in writing this book. Gary Rice had been one of Denise's editors at the *Statesman*. Gary was a veteran journalist who left the newspaper business to pursue a Ph.D. He received a doctorate degree in history from the University of Texas at Austin and now is an award-winning journalism professor at California State University–Fresno.

We relied on scores of historical documents for this book. At my ranch, I had a large collection of original daily diaries from my White House office, memos, photos, and other papers. We also dug deep into the twelve linear feet of documents that I donated some years ago to the Lyndon Baines Johnson Library and Museum in Austin. In addition, we pulled together many other documents at the LBJ Library, including the president's daily diaries, oral histories, telephone transcripts, trip logs, correspondence, newspaper articles, internal White House memos, and television footage. We are deeply grateful to the LBJ Library archivists and staff for their reference services and good cheer. We also used material from the following libraries: the LBJ Ranch, University of Texas, Austin History Center, Austin Public Library, *Austin American-Statesman*, St. Edwards University, San Antonio Public Library, Oklahoma City University, University of Central Oklahoma, and Martin Luther King Jr. Memorial Library, Washingtoniana Division, Washington, D.C.

All dialogue in the book comes from historical documents and accounts or from my personal memories.

Many written accounts of the Johnson years inspired and aided us in our research. The books include:

Albertazzie, Colonel Ralph, and J. F. terHorst. *The Flying White House: The Story of Air Force One.* Coward, McCann & Geoghegan, 1979.
Beschloss, Michael R. *Taking Charge: The Johnson White House Tapes, 1963–64.* Simon & Schuster, 1997.
———. *Reaching for Glory: Lyndon Johnson's Secret White House Tapes, 1964–65.* Simon & Schuster, 2001.
Carpenter, Liz. *Ruffles & Flourishes.* Texas A&M University Press, 1993.
Christian, George. *The President Steps Down: A Personal Memoir of the Transfer of Power.* The Macmillan Company, 1970.

Cortright, Edgar M. *Apollo Expeditions to the Moon*. National Aeronautics and Space Administration, 1975.

Cowger, Thomas W., and Sherwin Markman. *Lyndon Johnson Remembered: An Intimate Portrait of a Presidency*. Rowman & Littlefield, 2003.

Cray, Ed. *Chief Justice: A Biography of Earl Warren*. Simon & Schuster, 1997.

Glenn, John, with Nick Taylor. *John Glenn: A Memoir*. Bantam Books, 1999.

Goodwin, Doris Kearns. *Lyndon Johnson and the American Dream*. Harper & Row, 1976.

Gulley, Bill. *Breaking Cover*. Simon and Schuster, 1980.

Isaacs, Jeremy, and Taylor Downing. *Cold War: An Illustrated History, 1945–1991*. Little, Brown and Company, 1998.

Johnson, Lady Bird. *A White House Diary*. Holt, Rinehart and Winston, 1970.

Johnson, Lyndon Baines. *The Vantage Point: Perspectives of the Presidency, 1963–1969*. Holt, Rinehart and Winston, 1971.

Johnson, Sam Houston. *My Brother Lyndon*. Cowles Book Company, 1970.

Kraft, Chris. *My Life in Mission Control*. Dutton, 2001.

Lyndon B. Johnson National Historical Park. *Final General Management Plan—Environmental Impact Statement*, 1999.

McClendon, Sarah. *My Eight Presidents*. Wyden Books, 1978.

———. *Mr. President, Mr. President!: My Fifty Years of Covering the White House*. General Publishing Group, 1996.

Miller, Merle. *Lyndon: An Oral Biography*. G. P. Putnam's Sons, 1980.

Rothman, Hal K. *LBJ's Texas White House*. Texas A&M University Press, 2001.

Valenti, Jack. *A Very Human President*. W. W. Norton & Company, 1975.

Warren, Earl. *The Memoirs of Chief Justice Earl Warren*. Doubleday & Company, 1977.

Watson, W. Marvin, with Sherwin Markman. *Chief of Staff: Lyndon Johnson and His Presidency*. Thomas Dunne Books, 2004.

West, J. B., and Mary Lynn Kotz. *Upstairs at the White House*. Coward, McCann & Geoghegan, 1973.

White, G. Edward. *Earl Warren: A Public Life*. Oxford University Press, 1987.

In addition, we relied on numerous periodicals and various other materials, including: *Abilene Reporter-News*; *Air & Space/Smithsonian* magazine; *Austin American*; *Austin American-Statesman*; *Austin Statesman*; C. Brian Kelly, "All the Way with LBJ," historynet.com; CBS News; *Christian Century*;

Erie (Pennsylvania) *Daily Times*; Joseph L. Frasketi Jr., "The Grand Turk Island Connection with The Project Mercury/Glenn Flight," from http://www.spacecovers.com; Debi Goode, "My Little Feller: Profile of Paul L. Thornhill," unpublished paper, 1987; *Life*; *Los Angeles Times*; *Nation*; *Newsweek*; *New York Times*; *Overseas Press Club Bulletin*; *San Antonio Express-News*; *San Antonio Light*; *Time*; *U.S. News & World Report*; *Wall Street Journal*; *Washington Evening Star*; and *Washington Post*.

Page numbers in *italics* indicate photographs.

CPSIA information can be obtained at www.ICGtesting.com
Printed in the USA
LVOW06s0130080114

368434LV00001B/33/P